The Valley's Legends and Legacies

THE VALLEY'S
Legends
&
Legacies

By Catherine Morison Rehart

To Carole & Dave
Best wishes
Cathy Rehart
8/10/99

Word Dancer Press

Fresno, California

Published by
Quill Driver Books/Word Dancer Press, Inc.
8386 N. Madsen
Clovis, CA 93611
209-322-5917
800-497-4909

Word Dancer Press books may be purchased for educational, fund-raising, business or promotional use. Please contact Special Markets, Quill Driver Books/Word Dancer Press, Inc. at the above address.

ISBN 1-884995-12-8

Rehart, Catherine Morison, 1940-
     The valley's legends & legacies / by Catherine Morison Rehart.
              p.   cm.
     Scripts of the KMJ radio program, The valley's legends & legacies.
     ISBN 1-884995-12-8 (pbk.)
     1. Fresno County (Calif.)--History--Anecdotes.   2. Fresno County
     (Calif.)--Biography--Anecdotes. 3. San Joaquin Valley (Calif.)-
     -History--Anecdotes. 4. San Joaquin Valley (Calif.)--Biography-
     -Anecdotes.   I. Valley's legends and legacies (radio program)
     II. Title.
     F868.F8R44   1996
     979.4'82--dc21   96-36997
                              CIP

First printing November 1996
Second printing January 1997
Third Printing November 1997

Front Cover Photo: *Snow in Courthouse Park on January 1, 1910.*
Fresno Historical Society Archives, photographer Fred C. Ninnis
Back Cover Photos (clockwise from top): *See pages: 73, 292, 246, 31, 15, 67, 55.*

Foster
325 I. St.
NEXT TO HUGHES HOTEL
FRESNO, CAL.

To the memory of my beloved grandmother Eugenie Loverne Kinsley McKay—shown here in her high school graduation dress (Fresno High, 1896) with her grandmother Laura Amanda Stevens—and to my children Bill, Anne and Kate, the keepers of the legacy.

Contents

Contents

Contents

Contents

Contents

Contents

Contents

Contents

Foreword

This book is about the people and stories of the San Joaquin Valley. It will satisfy the curiosity of people who wonder about the people who first came to this Valley, the wonderful stories of those who followed in their footsteps, and the legends and legacies they left for us to pass on to future generations.

When I first came to the Valley in the late 1980s, I saw a growing area with many new people without a source of information about local history. I wondered when driving over the Grapevine how it got its name. Why was this city called Fresno? Why did they call it tule fog? If the walls could talk what stories would they tell? What tales did the men and women of this great Valley leave behind?

This led to a collaboration between KMJ program director John Broeske, Cathy Rehart, whom we met through the Fresno City and County Historical Society, and me. Together, we came up with the concept of the series, which we agreed would be broad in scope, necessitating a title that would give us as much leeway as possible for topic material. We chose "The Valley's Legends and Legacies."

Cathy volunteered to do the research and writing. I can't emphasize enough how this project would never have gotten off the ground without her effort. Since those first talks in the early months of 1990, she has researched and written over 400 features. When we first met we thought we might do a total of fifty. Then we went for a hundred. Now, Cathy promises to just keep going until we run out of ideas. I agreed to voice the features and have the KMJ production staff produce them.

I typically get three different kinds of reactions to the series from people I meet. One is from the group of people who are new to the Valley and appreciate learning something about the area.

Second is the reaction from people who have lived here and re-member the story. And the third is from those who have lived here but hadn't heard about it.

We have learned much about our city and valley since this project first began. I can't believe it has already been six years. And now we have the printed version that we can pick up and read at our leisure. I hope this will be just the first of several print-ings of collections from "The Valley's Legends and Legacies."

— Al Smith
General Manger, KMJ Radio

Preface

In 1873, two men left Michigan to travel to a small train stop in central California. Barely a year old, this bustling wild west town was known as Fresno Station. They bought two pieces of property from Charles Crocker of the Central Pacific Railway, one on L Street where they built flats (an apartment building) and a corner parcel on L and Fresno Streets. Here, they established their place of business, the Black Hawk Stables. These men were my great-great uncles. They convinced the rest of the family to move west, which they did, arriving during the next few years.

As the rest of the family came, they settled in the area today known as the Civic Center. My great-grandfather was the purchasing agent for the Central Pacific Railroad, operating out of a freight shed near the tracks while the present-day Southern Pacific Depot was built. From their home on O Street, my Grandmother watched the Water Tower being built. During her long life, she watched Fresno grow into a major city. But, she never forgot her pioneer roots.

Grandma lived with us. In those days before television took hold on our lives, I spent my evenings listening to her tell marvelous stories about her youth. She told tales about the time she and her mother were walking on Van Ness Avenue and had to duck into a doorway because the Sheriff's Posse was chasing Sontag and Evans through town on horseback; about her love and respect for Dr. Chester Rowell, who was her family's doctor; about the aspects of daily life...cooking, washing, cleaning; about "at home" afternoons and calling cards; about courtship; about Courthouse Park and all that it meant in the life of a young city; about school, especially Fresno High, and how she and her friend Maud Poole would sit on the front steps of her home and study Latin; and so many other things. The main thread that tied her stories together was her love for this community. Through her eyes, I could see how Fresno had been, how it had developed and how important it was to remember and to honor all those who had worked so hard to build our city. Just before she died in 1964, the city she knew so well was undergoing major changes. It hurt her that this was happening. One day, she said to me with real pain in her eyes, "I just hope no one tears down the Water Tower."

While I was still working at the Fresno Historical Society, John Broesky of KMJ called me. He said that KMJ wanted to begin a series of radio spots on Fresno history, entitled, "Legends of the Valley," that would promote all the positive aspects of our community and would make citizens aware of the special things about Fresno. Al Smith, the General Manager of KMJ Radio, would do the voice work, and John would handle the production part. He asked me if I would be interested in writing the scripts. I jumped at the chance. He asked me to write fifteen scripts, initially, and then KMJ would assess how well they were received. If their listeners liked them, then he would ask me to write more. They were well received, and the rest, as they say, is history. With almost 450 in production, it has been one of the most gratifying experiences of my life. For four years, most of my off-duty time—weekends, vacations—has been spent interviewing people, taking day trips to nearby historic sites, and writing either at my computer or with my yellow legal pad and pencil at a table on the patio of La Boulangerie at Fig Garden Village. This project has made me look at my city with new eyes. I have also realized that even though, at times, this city frustrates me, saddens me and infuriates me; I love this city with a fierce passion that surprises me. Grandma's legacy has borne fruit…her love for Fresno has been handed down to her granddaughter and, I hope, is apparent at the basis of this work.

The original title, "Legends of the Valley" was a good choice. I suggested that we add the word, legacy, which means a bequest, something that is handed down. These stories about the people and places of our county are part of the fabric of who and what we are. In their retelling, we hand them down to another generation. That is our legacy to the future.

As you read these stories, you may say about some of them, "but that did not happen that way, instead this happened." On the day each story was written it was as accurate as I could make it. But, a year later the building I had written about might have been torn down or a building that had seemed threatened with imminent demolition might have been rescued and is now being restored. Each day we make history.

I hope these legends and legacies have brought new insights about our community to you, the reader and listener. I am grateful for your calls and suggestions and for your support. My dearest wish is that these stories give you a sense of the uniqueness of our valley, its communities, its people, and its history.

— Cathy Rehart

Acknowledgments

A work such as this cannot be accomplished without the help of many people. My gratitude to the following cannot be overstated.

Special thanks to Archivists of the Fresno Historical Society, John Panter and Robert Ellis, for allowing me to peruse special collections, dairies, books, and for granting me unlimited access to the Ben Walker collection; Linda Sitterding, Fresno County History Librarian, for her assistance and suggestions; John Edward Powell, architectural historian, for sharing his knowledge and information from his files; Doug Hansen, *The Fresno Bee*, for our frequent chats sharing ideas and information; Joyce Hall, Fresno County Library California History Room, for providing her knowledge and assistance; and Marjorie Arnold, Nancy Ramirez and Mabel Wilson at the *Fresno Bee* Library for allowing me access to their files.

I wish to thank Mary Graham for reading many of the scripts prior to submission to KMJ. My late mother, Catherine L. Morison, also read many of the scripts and gave me the benefit of her sage advice, her insights, and memories of growing up in Fresno. My sincere gratitude to Bobbye Sisk Temple for editing this work and for her most helpful suggestions and unfailing friendship.

It has been a pleasure to meet so many people connected to local businesses and organizations. The information they have provided has been invaluable and I am most grateful. Their contributions are listed in the bibliography of this work.

Personal interviews are always rewarding. I wish to thank Charles Alstrom, Ray Appleton, Buddy Arkelian, State Park Ranger Jonathan M. Burgasser, Rose Caglia, Mary Carr, Donna Drith, Art Dyson, Iver Eriksen, Tom Folsom, the late Rabbi David L. Greenberg, Ken Hohmann, Sharon Huber, Don Kleim, B. Franklin Knapp, Lillie Lew, the late Dr.

Arthur Margosian, Alan Mar, Brigader General Edward E. Munger, Chuck Pansarosa, Esther Phipps, Karen Moore Reynolds, Jose Ruano, Richard Samuelian, Sheldon Solo, Roger Taylor, Bud Warner, Gordon M. Webster, Norman A. Webster, Althea Wheat, and for sharing their rich knowledge and stories.

I want to thank the staff at KMJ for conceiving the idea for this project, for making it happen, and for their unfailing kindness and support to me. Special thanks to General Manager of KMJ Radio, Al Smith, for making the scripts come alive; to John Broeske, Program Director, for his excellent ideas and production expertise; and to Rich Withers for his creative handling of the production elements in the studio.

Special thanks also to Robert Koligian, Jr., and Dr. John Zelezny, whose friendship and wise counsel is deeply appreciated.

On a personal level, I want to thank my cousin, Mary Helen McKay, who never failed to offer accurate information and marvelous story ideas; and my children, Bill, Anne, and Kate, who have endured the yellow legal pad during weekends and vacations, and, in spite of that, have been unfailing supporters of this project. Special thanks to Kate, my companion on trips to the cemetery at Academy, the Courthouse at Millerton and other historical sites. These outings had the added benefit of providing a time for us to share the beauty and history of our valley.

Most of all I am grateful to all the KMJ listeners. Your calls have meant a great deal to me. Al Smith forwarded your letters to me so that I would know what stories you would like to hear. I have tried to follow-up on your ideas whenever possible. I have saved all your letters and, if I have not yet written on the subjects that you requested, I may do so in the future.

—CMR

Introduction

The Fresno Historical Society's Archives is the cornerstone of the Society's collections. Photographs, newspapers, diaries, journals, tax records, court dockets, maps, essays, scrapbooks, letters, family histories, architectural drawings, books and more—a veritable treasure house of information—are all a part of the Archives. An important part of the Historical Society's mission is to preserve and hold in public trust these priceless records that document the history of Fresno County and the Central California region and to make this resource available to the community.

During the course of writing *Legends & Legacies*, the Archives was available to Cathy for her research. Having this resource at her disposal made it possible for her to unearth stories that had not been told. There were also occasions when she came across documents that provided new insights into events that were well-known and enabled her to write about them with a new perspective. Most importantly, through her writings, some of the Society's large storehouse of information was made available to KMJ Radio's vast listening audience and now to the reading public through the publication of this book. The Board of Trustees of the Fresno Historical Society is pleased that the Archives has provided much of the material for *Legends and Legacies*.

—John Moffat
President,
Board of Trustees

The Valley's Legends and Legacies

In 1805, a Spanish lieutenant led an expedition through the great interior valley of California. The officer came out of curiosity—he wondered what this area was like. The Spanish had established missions along coastal California, but preliminary explorations had given only hints of what existed in the interior.

This expedition traveled north and passed through what was to become Fresno County. On January 6, the feast day of the Holy Kings, this Spanish officer saw a great river that he named the Rio de los Santos Reyes, the River of the Holy Kings. Today, this river is called the Kings River. He considered the banks of this river an excellent site for a mission. On March 20, the feast day of Saint Joachim, the father of the Virgin Mary, he sighted another river which he named the San Joaquin.

A year later, in 1806, this same officer led a second expedition into the Valley. Leaving San Juan Bautista, he and his party reached the San Joaquin River near present-day Firebaugh. They traveled northeast across what is now Merced County. Here they saw swarms of yellow butterflies, called *mariposas* in Spanish. They named the vast area, which included most of the Central Valley, Mariposa County. The expedition traveled north, almost to the Sacramento River, and then went south down the eastern side of the Valley, visiting the future site of Millerton before ending the journey at Mission San Fernando.

Who was this handsome, eager, young officer who left a rich legacy of Spanish names in our valley?

Lieutenant Gabriel Moraga.

In 1827, twenty years after the explorations of the San Joaquin Valley by the Spanish, Jedediah Strong Smith became the first American to travel the vast expanse of Central California. Smith, an explorer, trapper, fur trader and mountain man, was one of the most interesting trailblazers of his time. A well-educated Christian man from a New England family, his background was different from most fur trappers in the West.

Seventeen years later another expedition set out to explore the Central Valley. This party left from Sutter's Fort in 1844 and traveled south. The month was April and its leader was enchanted with the San Joaquin Valley. As far as he could see were fields of blue lupine, golden poppies and green alfilaria dotted with pink blossoms. The air was cool and filled with the scent of the wildflowers. Wild antelope, elk and horses ran in herds or grazed lazily in the sun. As far as he could see was a world untouched by man, unspoiled and quiet. He was charmed by all he saw.

He and his party passed within sight of what is today Kearney Park, where a monument stands in his memory. Who was this man who kept a diary of his two expeditions to the area and whose guide was the famous Kit Carson? He was John C. Fremont, the Pathfinder.

The Indians of the Central Valley, with the exception of the Chowchilla tribe, were peaceful. They had a good life. They welcomed the strangers who visited their valley.

Then, in 1848, the discovery of gold suddenly filled their once tranquil foothills with the clank of shovels and picks as miners poured into the area in search of riches. The miners had little regard for the Indians' way of life. They settled where they wished and took what they wanted. Finally, the Indians could endure it no longer. On December 20, 1850, they raided and burned the trading post of Major James Savage on the Fresno River. They also killed Wiley Cassity at Cassity's Ferry on the San Joaquin River. No one considered what had provoked the Indians, only that atrocities had been committed.

The governor of California ordered the formation of the Mariposa Battalion under the command of Major Savage. An Indian Commission of three members was formed. Most of the reluctant Indian chiefs were rounded up (sixteen tribes were represented) and a peace conference to end what was called the Mariposa Indian War ensued. The date was April 17, 1851. The site was a flat area above the south bank of the San Joaquin River, later known as Camp Barbour. On April 29, a treaty was signed. The Camp Barbour Treaty established a huge reservation and provided for supplies and training for the Indians.

When the conference ended, the Indians dispersed, their spirit broken. What happened to the treaty? Congress never ratified it. It was soon forgotten.

The Colonel's New Clothes

Fort Miller Blockhouse, erected in 1851, is the oldest building in Fresno County. It was part of a complex of buildings that comprised Fort Miller, which was built at the close of the Mariposa Indian War to protect settlers from hostile Indians. The fort, the only military base in the San Joaquin Valley, was located on one of the widest portions of the San Joaquin River. (The Blockhouse was dismantled, moved to Roeding Park, and reassembled in 1944.)

In 1852 Rootville, which soon became known as Millerton, was founded one mile below the fort. Pro-Confederate feelings ran strong in Millerton, and, with the outbreak of the Civil War, Colonel James Olney was sent to Fort Miller with a company of soldiers. He had his troops on battle alert because he was certain that he would have to take Fort Miller by force. He was surprised to find that, instead, he and his men were welcomed to the community.

There was little for the soldiers to do in their off-duty hours, except to visit the saloons. Discipline was lax and officers might be found in the saloons as well. The colonel found he also had a great deal of time for off-duty carousing. After one memorable night on the town, he arose from bed, dressed, tried to eat breakfast, and eventually appeared on the parade ground. Struggling to keep his dignity intact, he proceeded to review his troops—it was inspection day. As he marched through the lines of men he noticed they had rather strange expressions on their faces. He wondered why. It wasn't until he looked down that he discovered he had forgotten to put on his pants.

View of the Fort Miller complex in 1914.
The Image Group from the Laval Historical Collection. Courtesy of William B. Secrest, Sr., Collection.

The town of Rootville, a mining camp later known as Millerton, was founded in 1852 a mile down the San Joaquin River from Fort Miller. When Fresno County was established in 1856, Millerton became the county seat. This was Millerton's golden era. Gambling dens and saloons did a flourishing business, reaping profits from the miners of the area. Stages brought colorful visitors to the town, as well as the news of the day.

Life in Millerton was rather devil-may-care. The Fresno County Court would adjourn so the jury could bet on the horse races. The Board of Supervisors would adjourn twenty times a day so that they could go to the nearest saloon to have a drink.

Up until this time there was no jail—prisoners were held in Mariposa. The supervisors decided it was necessary to build one. The bid went to Colonel Henry Burrough for $6,000. He hired one of the men who had bid against him, Alexander Wallace, to construct the jail. As later events proved, Wallace did a poor job.

On the day that the supervisors, accompanied by Colonel Burrough, were to inspect the new jail, a prisoner told the colonel that the construction was so poor he could break out in less than twenty minutes. The colonel begged him to delay his escape until after the supervisors accepted and approved the new jail or he would be ruined. The prisoner said he would and kept his word.

After the supervisors formally accepted the new jail, the prisoner set himself free with the aid of a tenpenny nail. The jail became a huge joke in the wild, wide-open town.

A Famous University,
A Railroad Boss & A New Town

In 1868, Moses Joshua Church, a blacksmith and canal builder, was summoned to Fresno by A. Y. Easterby, who had known Church in Napa County.

Easterby was experimenting with growing wheat in what is today known as the Sunnyside area. Water was scarce and the only way to bring it to his land was through canals from the Kings River. Easterby purchased ditches that had already been dug. He and Church formed the Fresno Canal & Irrigation Company. Under Church's watchful eye, the Fresno Canal System was expanded and completed. The Easterby Rancho produced four million pounds of wheat that year.

In November of 1871, Central Pacific Railroad officials were scouting the area for a route for a new railroad feeder line linking Stockton to the rest of the San Joaquin Valley. They also were looking for a location for a town site. When they saw the green wheat field of the Easterby Rancho in the middle of a desert, they decided to call on Easterby. They were impressed with Church's canals and the results of irrigating the land. They saw the vast potential for agriculture and how the railroad could profit from shipping crops as the area grew.

One of these officials decided that Fresno Station would be located ten miles south of the small community of Sycamore, at the place where Dry Creek drained into the plains. It seemed like a barren spot, but it was near Easterby's Rancho and close to sites for future farms.

The railroad came down the Valley, crossing the San Joaquin River on March 23, 1872. A month later, it reached the new town site and Fresno Station became a reality.

Who was the railroad official who had decided Fresno's location and who had the foresight to see its agricultural potential? Leland Stanford, the gentleman who endowed Stanford University.

A Green Bush & A New Town's Name

There is a river that comes out of the Sierra and flows into the great San Joaquin Valley. The Spanish named the river "Fresno," the Spanish word for ash, because of the low growing ash trees which lined its banks. During the 1850s, miners panned this river for gold at a place called "Coarse Gold Gulch." Six miles below this spot, Jim Savage, Dr. Lewis Leach, Samuel Bishop and Lorenzo Vinsonhaler founded their trading post on the river's banks. As the river descended to the valley floor, the ash trees, which at times grew in thickets, set the river apart from other valley water channels.

When the Central Pacific Railroad was being built through the Valley in 1872, C. M. Wooster was hired by the railroad to draw maps of the town sites and to write down the name of each town. When the railroad neared the newest town, Wooster wanted to call it after Stanford, Huntington, Crocker, or Hopkins, the owners of the railroad. The construction crews convinced him that he should not. He looked around and saw a green bush, the only sign of life on the sinks of Dry Creek, the site of the new town. He was told it was a Fresno or ash tree. He put that name on the map and claimed that was how Fresno was named. The green bush grew because of a spring that fed it water.

Almost one hundred years later, Mariposa Street was widened to accommodate the Mariposa Mall. Seventy-five feet had to be cut off the front of the stores facing the street. This uncovered the source of the spring under the basement of Sam's Luggage and Leather Goods.

Today the Green Bush Spring is fondly remembered for its role in the naming of Fresno. A plaque memorializing this lone sign of life on the desert plain of long ago can be found near the Fulton Mall.

From Muleskinner to Merchant —
The Big Gamble

Fresno Historical Society Archives
R.W. Riggs Collection

James Faber, muleskinner, ex-Union soldier and expert poker-player, a man who had survived the Sioux and Blackhawk battles in Montana, decided to take a real gamble in the new town to be established in the Sinks of Dry Creek.

In late April 1872, after purchasing a large supply of dry goods and a number of kegs of whiskey, he made a deal with a railroad conductor which would let him bypass the rules that forbade the delivery of freight south of Merced. His supplies were loaded on the train in Stockton and hidden under other items being shipped south. When the train neared the new town of Fresno Station, the conductor slowed the train and all the supplies were tossed out the window, spread over a half mile just north of present-day Belmont Avenue. From there they had to be retrieved and carted to the new town.

When the task was completed, Faber set up his business in a tent next to the railroad stop and became the first resident and merchant of Fresno Station.

Whiskey, Railroad Bosses and the Election of 1874

The new town of Fresno Station was established in the spring of 1872. By November of that year two stores, three saloons, four hotels and restaurants, three livery stables and two houses had been built in the new town.

By mid-1873, Fresno was a thriving place and some disgruntled residents of Fresno County began to wonder why the county seat was located in the rather bleak town of Millerton, where there was no sign of progress at all.

On March 23, 1874, an election was held to decide if the county seat should stay at Millerton or be moved to a new location. Fresno received the largest number of votes, 417, Centerville received 123 and Millerton 93. With this decision established, many residents of Millerton began to move to Fresno. Many dismantled their stores and homes, put the wood in wagons, and moved to the new city where they rebuilt their structures.

By July of 1874, Fresno had three hotels, two restaurants, four general stores, one drugstore, two doctors, one saddle shop, two butcher shops, three blacksmiths, two livery stables, one tinsmith, twenty-five homes, one newspaper, six saloons, but not even one church!

How did Fresno become the choice for county seat in the election of 1874? Tradition says that Fresno received the largest number of votes because the railroad bosses, who had much to gain by the relocation of the county seat, provided whiskey to those who voted for the new fast-growing town.

On the night of December 28, 1893, Chris Evans, the notorious outlaw, was preparing to eat dinner in the Fresno jail. A few minutes before six o'clock, Evans' wife, Molly, and Ed Morrell, Evans' friend and associate, arrived with a dinner tray. It was not unusual for Evans to have dinner guests. However, on this evening the dinner tray had two revolvers hidden inside. After a few minutes, Morrell called to jailer B. B. Scott to say that Evans had finished eating. When Scott went into the cell to get the dishes, Morrell yelled, "Up with your hands" and thrust a gun in Scott's face. Evans also had a pistol and Scott knew the two meant business.

Since Scott was the only officer on duty, escape was a simple matter. Holding Scott as a hostage, Evans and Morrell boldly walked out the front door of the jail and through Courthouse Park. When they reached M Street, they met ex-Mayor Stephen H. Cole who also was taken hostage. They fled toward O Street where a team of horses was waiting. At the corner of O and Mariposa streets they came upon the city marshal, who was on his way to a church dinner with a friend. The marshal caught Morrell, held his arm down and told his friend to get Morrell's gun. Morrell called to Evans to help him. Evans rushed forward, forgetting about his hostages, and said, "Let him go or I'll shoot you." The marshal turned Morrell around between himself and Evans. Evans shot the marshal in the side, and he and Morrell ran to the horses and fled.

Dr. J. L. Maupin, who lived across the street, took the marshal into his home and treated his wounds. After several days on the critical list, John D. Morgan, the last city marshal, one of the signers of the city charter in 1901, and the first chief of police of the City of Fresno, rallied—to live to the ripe old age of eighty-seven.

In 1874, a thirty-year-old doctor arrived in Fresno. A veteran of the Civil War, he had endured many hardships. As one of ten children from an Illinois farming family, he had had the values of honesty, discipline and hard work instilled in his personality.

From the moment of his arrival in Fresno, he embraced his new community with enthusiasm. He built a small home at Van Ness and Tulare streets and began his practice of medicine. No one who came to him for help was turned away. If they could not pay, he would accept an item in trade. He felt the practice of medicine was the highest calling a man could have and, not only did he work to heal his patients, he felt that this new, wild, wide-open town also needed his hand of moral influence to heal it.

He began the *Fresno Republican* newspaper in September 1876 to give a voice to Republican politics and to fight the immorality and poor conditions in Fresno. He fought hard for the incorporation of the city. He was elected to three terms as a state senator, he served as a member of the board of regents of the University of California and, in 1909, he was elected mayor of Fresno. When he died in 1912, his funeral was held in Courthouse Park, the only place large enough for the crowds who came.

A statue of this good man was erected in Courthouse Park—a seated figure with kindly eyes looking across the street to the site of his home. The inscription reads, "Good Physician, Good Friend, Good Citizen." Certainly, Fresno has never had a more beloved citizen than Dr. Chester Rowell.

Physician, publisher, state senator, mayor and regent of the University of California, Dr. Chester Rowell was a strong force in the development of Fresno from a small pioneer town to a thriving city.
Fresno Historical Society Archives

The election of 1905 ushered into office one of the most colorful and controversial mayors in Fresno history, W. Parker Lyon. The citizens who were pushing for reform were horrified at the election of a man who had the support of the saloons and the Tenderloin district. In spite of his reputation, he achieved some positive things for Fresno, including construction of the first City Hall.

He was not only a politician, but a businessman as well. The proprietor of a used furniture store on Broadway, Lyon had a thriving business due, in large part, to his collection of chamber pots. This utilitarian item had been his good luck charm ever since he had fallen out of bed as a child and lodged his head in a metal chamber pot, which had to be chiseled off by the local blacksmith. Since that time, he had confined his collecting instincts to the china variety.

When his store first opened, he placed an ad in the newspaper which read, "What is going to happen on Broadway Avenue on Friday at 9 A.M.? Big Surprise???"

At sunup on Friday, he stacked his chamber pots in a wagon and began placing pots two-and-a-half feet apart in a serpentine pattern, with arrows in between pointing to his store. When he finished, the snake-like procession of pots extended a block and a half down Broadway. By 9 A.M., hordes of people had followed the line of colorful china right into W. Parker Lyon's store. It was the biggest business day Fresno had ever seen.

W. Parker Lyon served as Mayor of Fresno from 1905 to 1908, a period when the head of city government had a lot of power and was considered a "strong" mayor. Lyon's base of power was the tenderloin district. He accomplished a great deal for Fresno, often in ways that by today's standards seem unconventional. He was forced from office by more traditional elements in the community. He left behind a city that seemed much less interesting without his colorful presence.

The Birth of a Great Newspaper

In 1876, Fresno was a bastion of Democratic politics. The only newspaper, the *Expositor*, was strong in its expression of the principles of the party of Thomas Jefferson. The majority of the citizens of Fresno supported those views.

However, there was a man who believed that another point of view should be heard. Dr. Chester Rowell, a Midwesterner whose brother had known many of Lincoln's associates, decided to launch another newspaper to give the community a voice for Republican politics. He put any capital he could spare into the enterprise and began rounding up subscribers. He found a small office on I Street (now Broadway) and hired an editor, who slept on a mattress in one room of the two-room shop. The hand-operated printing press occupied the other room.

Dr. Rowell was determined in the pursuit of his dream. An ardent and persuasive debater, he knew his editorials could inspire the people of Fresno to move the community forward. Many scoffed and said the newspaper would not make it to the streets of Fresno. Threats to burn down the office were made and were taken seriously.

When the paper was typeset and printing began, the staff sat up all night guarding the press. The next morning, September 23, 1876, the first issue of the *Fresno Republican* made its debut. Who could have known that from this humble beginning a great newspaper would emerge, one that would become a leader in breaking the monopoly of the Central Pacific Railroad and electing Hiram Johnson governor of California.

The Mayor's Gift to Los Angeles

Moocow Molly, Broadway's leading businesswoman, and others in her profession, were suffering because business was bad in Fresno. After the San Francisco earthquake of April 18, 1906, dozens of "ladies" from the Barbary Coast had fled the city by the Bay and sought refuge in Fresno. Because of the newcomers, prices had dropped and hostilities were about to break out.

A committee from the Broadway district sent a representative to talk to the mayor, who with the police chief, decided on a plan of action.

At nine o'clock the next morning twenty police officers and two matrons, with the mayor and police chief leading the way, began rounding up the San Francisco "ladies." They marched through Fresno to the Southern Pacific Depot. By the time they reached the station 186 women had joined the procession. However, the mayor discovered that some of the women who had joined the parade in the excitement of the moment were upstanding citizens of the community and had to be separated from the others. The president of the Ladies Aid Society, seven secretaries, a member of the Baptist choir, a woman suffragist, and one maiden lady were asked to leave the gathering.

With that accomplished, the unwilling passengers boarded a special train which proceeded to Los Angeles. One of the "ladies" was given a special card to present to the mayor of Los Angeles. It read: "Love from Mayor W. Parker Lyon. I heard you were short of entertainment and we've got too much, so here's some." The mayor of Los Angeles was not amused.

James Porteous was a prolific inventor. Over 200 patents are listed in his name at the U.S. Patent Office.

Fresno Historical Society Archives, R.W. Riggs Collection

The oldest continuous business in Fresno was founded in 1874 when a young Scotsman named James Porteous opened a shop at Mariposa and J streets. (J Street was renamed Fulton Street in honor of early-day businessman Fulton G. Berry. It is now known as Fulton Mall.) The purpose of the enterprise was to manufacture wagons and carriages. The business prospered because of the demand for heavy wagons to haul supplies to the Sierra lumber camps and communities.

Porteous later purchased a parcel of land at Tulare and L streets where he built a building that occupied the entire 2200 block of Tulare Street.

Porteous not only knew the blacksmithing and wagon-building trades, which he had learned from his father in Scotland, but he also was an inventor. The culmination of many experiments, his Fresno Scraper revolutionized the moving of large quantities of soil. Other inventions followed, and his business grew to become, with the exception of similar enterprises in Los Angeles and San Francisco, the largest agricultural implement business in California.

After Porteous' death in 1922, his son, William, continued his father's company. Later the business was sold. Tractors, irrigation pumps and farm hardware were added to the firm's inventory.

In 1952, the hardware part of the company was sold to John Rosetta. His brother, James, joined the firm and together they opened their present store at Gettysburg and Blackstone avenues. Once known as the Fresno Agricultural Works, this business is known today as Fresno Ag Hardware.

The Turkeys & The Army Worms

In the days before insecticides, infestations of bugs and worms were not uncommon in local vineyards. One such incident occurred in the vineyard of John Braly, an early-day farmer and banker.

One morning Braly's foreman came hurrying into the bank to say that army worms were threatening his vineyard. After telling the foreman to buy as many shovels as he could find, Braly hurried home. On his arrival, he was horrified to find army worms marching into his vineyard in a line a half-mile long. He ordered his workers to dig trenches around the vines and to fill them with water. The worms fell into the trenches and drowned, but there were so many of them that they filled the trenches and formed natural bridges over which other worms could march. Seeing that this was not going to work, Braly and his wife set off on horseback to visit every farm for miles around, to purchase every available turkey.

The next morning almost a thousand turkeys were delivered to Braly's farm. They were set free among the grape vines. Gobbling as they went, they ate every worm in their path. When they were full, they would stretch out on their stomachs, panting for breath until they could eat more. At the end of two weeks they had finished the job. The war of the worms had been won!

Braly made a nice profit on his investment by renting his turkeys to other farmers who had pests on their vines. And, when Thanksgiving came, the turkeys graced many local tables where they were lauded for their unusually juicy qualities.

Dirt Moving Made Easier

The farmers in the Fresno area were dependent on irrigation. To obtain water for their crops, canals had to be constructed. Digging canals by hand was a backbreaking proposition, so, in 1882, a local inventor began to develop a farm implement that would make it easier to move large quantities of dirt. It took him several years and many attempts, but he finally perfected his invention. The device, which was pulled by a horse, scraped along the ground collecting dirt. When full, it could be emptied by pushing a lever.

This new piece of equipment revolutionized the building of ditches, land leveling and road building. By 1891, this implement was being used in almost every part of the world, including Australia, Europe, the Orient, South Africa, South America and India. It was used by the United States Army on the European Front in World War I. It played an important role in building the Panama Canal. And, in 1941, it was attached to a Caterpillar tractor and was called a "bulldozer."

This incredible invention, which found its way into almost every part of the world, came to be known popularly as a "Fresno." Its proper name was the Fresno Scraper and it was the brainchild of James Porteous.

James Porteous' invention, the Fresno Scraper. This machine made road building, land leveling and ditch digging much faster. *Fresno Historical Society Archives, Hutchinson Collection*

One Man's Dream

In 1903, a carriage ride down Chateau Fresno Boulevard, re-named Kearney Boulevard the following year, prepared the visitor for the even lovelier vistas of Chateau Fresno Park. At the entrance to the park, today known as Kearney Park, stood a gardener's lodge. This three-storied round tower was copied from the watch tower at the Chateau de Chenonceaux in Tours, France. M. Theo Kearney had visited this French castle, which had been built for King Francis I and Queen Catherine de Medici. He hired architect Maurice Hebert to design and construct Chateau Fresno, based on the plan of Chenonceaux, deep within the park.

Other buildings were already in place. A superintendent's lodge, with adjoining servants' quarters, and a carriage house were de-signed in the French style. South of the lodge there was a com-pany town consisting of a blacksmith shop, ice house, stables, packing house, grocery store and bunkhouses for the farm work-ers who worked on Kearney's Fruit Vale Estate. Kearney minted the coins that he used to pay his workers, who then used them to make purchases in the company town.

Kearney's empire was in place, but the chateau was to be the culmination of his great dream. On a spring morning in May of 1906, as Kearney was leaving for Europe to meet with Hebert, he asked his chauffeur to stop the car at the site of the chateau so he could watch the workmen as they began to dig the foundation. As he left the park, his head filled with dreams, he could not know that in three weeks his death would bring an end to the construc-tion of the chateau. Today, the superintendent's lodge, known as Kearney Mansion, survives to tell the story of this fascinating man who left a rich legacy to Fresno County.

M. Theo Kearney, 1903
Fresno Historical Society Archieves,
Kearney Collection

An eleven-mile boulevard, stretching from Fresno Street to the city of Kerman, is one of the truly beautiful vistas in Fresno County. It is the result of careful planning by the world-renowned landscape architect, Rudolph Ulrich. Ulrich designed the landscaping for the World's Columbian Exposition in Chicago in 1893. M. Theo Kearney attended the exposition, was impressed with Ulrich's work, and hired him to design Kearney's private Chateau Fresno Boulevard and the 240-acre park which he wanted to develop on the northern part of his Fruit Vale Estate.

Ulrich's design for the park transformed a flat, barren expanse of land into a veritable garden of rolling hills surrounding a small lake, and winding, tree-lined roads. The boulevard was planted with eucalyptus trees, palm trees, pampas grass and oleanders. It was to serve as the impressive entrance to Kearney's Chateau Fresno Park.

Kearney donated the boulevard to Fresno County in the mid-1890s. In 1904, the Board of Supervisors passed a resolution re-naming the roadway Kearney Boulevard. In 1975, Kearney Park was placed in the National Register of Historic Places. Today, the park and the boulevard stand as a reminder of the man whose vision created something beautiful in the barren land of west Fresno County that would be enjoyed by many generations to come.

Catherine Morison Rehart

Mustang Ed &
The Methodist Episcopal Church

The year was 1876 and the new town of Fresno was four years old. Several of its citizens felt it was time to build a church. After all, with a saloon on every corner, wasn't a church needed to give some semblance of piety to this Wild West town?

Judge Gillum Baley thought so, so he and the other trustees of the Methodist Episcopal Church South began soliciting money. They went to local businesses for help, but, of course, everyone in the new city was struggling to get established and donations were not easy to obtain.

Members of the congregation had been holding church services in an upstairs room over Shannon and Hughes store and saloon. Gillum Baley often saw the most notorious gambler in town as he came down the stairs. They were not friends, but would exchange a nod of greeting. One day the gambler asked Baley, "How is the fund drive going for the new church?"

"Not well," Baley replied.

"I'll see what I can do about it," the gambler said. That night the gambler sat down at the poker table and had an incredible winning streak. He swept his winnings off the table. The next day he presented them to Gillum Baley. "Here," he said, "perhaps now you can build your church."

The Methodist Episcopal Church South was built on the northeast corner of Fresno and L streets and held its first service on March 3, 1876, with a congregation of twelve members. The name of the gambler who donated the money to make this possible is remembered only as Mustang Ed.

A Park for Fresno

In the 1860s, the German Syndicate, a group of San Franciscans of German extraction, purchased 80,000 acres of San Joaquin Valley land. It was from this group that the Central Pacific Railroad bosses bought land for the town site called Fresno Station. The rest of the holdings were divided among the members of the syndicate in proportion to their individual investments.

One of the investors, Frederick Christian Roeding, received 7,000 acres of land—eight parcels east of Fresno and three parcels northwest of the new town. In 1889, he retired as vice-president and cashier of the San Francisco German Savings and Loan Society to move to Fresno to devote his time to the development of his land holdings. One of Roeding's five children, George, became a nurseryman and established the Fancher Creek Nursery on his father's land at Belmont and Fowler avenues. He became one of the most respected men in his field.

By the late 1890s, Fresno needed open spaces for parks. After numerous editorials appeared in the *Fresno Republican* addressing the subject, Frederick Roeding offered the city 230 acres of land for a park, provided the city would spend $1,500 a year for planting and maintenance. The offer was rejected.

In 1903, Roeding made another offer of seventy-two acres. This time the land was accepted. The city of Fresno hired Johannes Reimers, a landscape architect, to design the layout of the park. Roeding then donated another forty-seven acres of land to the project. George Roeding, in his role of park commissioner, guided the planting of the new park and donated many trees and shrubs from his nursery. Due to the generosity and vision of Frederick and George Roeding, Roeding Park has become a horticultural paradise enjoyed by many generations of Fresnans.

By 1885, Fresno had more than three thousand permanent residents but no municipal government. Serious fires and floods and the wild, wide-open nature of the community made Fresno a difficult, albeit colorful, place to live.

The idea of forming a city government had been spoken of since 1874, but it was hard to fight the general apathy of the citizens, many of whom feared incorporation would mean taxes. In fact, incorporation proposals had been defeated in the elections of December 1883 and May 1884. The May election was held just after a disastrous flood. Fresnans were still trying to clean up their buildings and streets, but even with this proof of the need for city services, the proposal was defeated.

Finally, in May of 1885, the members of the fire commission took the lead in fighting for incorporation. The board of supervisors authorized the commission to take a census of Fresno to determine how many citizens were qualified to vote and ordered that an election be held on September 29.

Public debate on the issue was lively and a mass meeting was held the night before the election. The next day incorporation won by a vote of 277 to 185. Five trustees, W. L. Graves, J. M. Braly, A. Tombs, Thomas Hughes, and William Faymonville, were elected to govern the city.

The first meeting of the board of trustees was held on October 27, 1885, in the real estate office of Thomas Hughes. Faymonville was elected president of the board, thus becoming Fresno's first mayor.

The town was still primitive in many respects. Just a month after these important events, a band of fifteen hundred sheep was driven through town. However, an important step had been taken. The little town of Fresno Station had become a city.

In 1905, a building to house Fresno's city government had become a necessity. Since 1889, the city trustees had met in the firemen's dormitory room on the second floor of the city fire department. Because of the meeting site, the city fathers had passed an ordinance making it mandatory for the firemen to remain clothed during city meetings.

Mayor W. Parker Lyon urged the city to commission Eugene Mathewson, an architect who had designed a number of notable buildings in Fresno, to design the new city hall. This edifice was to stand at Broadway and Merced Street across from the Hotel Fresno. Hiring an architect solved one problem, but there was still the matter of raising the $75,000 necessary to build the structure. A bond issue would have to be approved by the trustees. Mayor Lyon knew this could be a problem, but he had a plan of action in mind.

Immediately beneath the meeting room was a large area where horses were stabled. Lyon poured ammonia on the floor of the horse stalls and near the air shafts that supplied ventilation for the upstairs room. The trustees gathered for their meeting. The summer night was hot. Tempers were short. The debate grew heated. The bond issue was in jeopardy. Then, the smell of ammonia, mingling with the scents of the horse stalls, began to waft upward through the vents. The intense summer heat caused the odor to increase its pungent quality. Suddenly, the debate ceased. The trustees quickly approved the bond issue for the new city hall and then fled into the summer night, gasping for breath and crying profusely.

The Boy with the Leaking Boot

Ever since 1874, when Fresno became the county seat, Courthouse Park had been not only the center of government, but a social center for the city as well. Its many varieties of trees and spacious walks were enjoyed by everyone in the community.

However, the park did not have a drinking fountain. Fresno's hot summer days would be more bearable, it was argued, if a free drink of water could be provided for the populace. The idea caught on and in 1891 Sergeant Nichols of the Salvation Army, the group that had conceived the idea for the project, led the fund-raising efforts. School children donated their pennies, and older citizens contributed larger amounts. In 1895, the board of supervisors added $500 to the fund and approved the design of the fountain called *The Boy With the Leaking Boot*. An order was placed with the Mott Company Foundry in New York for the central figure.

The statue arrived in late July and was dedicated on August 21, 1895. *The Boy With the Leaking Boot* and its pool stood at the Mariposa Street entrance to the park. Tin cups, hanging from eight faucets surrounding the fountain, invited passersby to stop for a cool drink. Each day the pipes leading to the taps were cooled by cakes of ice.

After some twenty-six years, the *Boy* was moved to a location near the L Street entrance to the park to make way for the Anna Woodward Memorial Fountain. The cups were replaced by bubblers.

Three times during the next fourteen years, vandals damaged the *Boy*'s arm. It was determined that it would cost $1,000 to have the *Boy* repaired and recast in bronze. Until funds could be raised, he was placed in storage. Eventually the schoolchildren of Fresno donated half the funds necessary to have the *Boy* restored and the statue returned to the park.

In 1995, again because of vandalism, the *Boy* was placed in storage. Happily, however, it has now been restored by Tim Willems, grandson of Goff Nutwell of Wilkerson and Nutwell, the company that recast the statue in bronze in 1947. It's new home is at the Fresno County Plaza on Tulare Street. It is felt it will be safer here. Whatever the location, the *Boy* still holds a special place in the history and hearts of the people of Fresno County.

Snow in Courthouse
Park on January 1, 1910.
*Fresno Historical Society
Archives, photographer:
Fred C. Ninnis*

In 1880, the southeast corner of N and Fresno streets became the site of the Champion Flour Mill. Moses Church built the mill and an open ditch that ran down the middle of Fresno Street. The ditch carried water from Fancher Creek to provide power to operate the mill. Church's wheat processing techniques produced such an excellent product that within three years he had to enlarge his mill. In 1886, the mill was sold to the Fresno Milling Company. A fire six years later destroyed the frame building, which was replaced by an attractive brick structure. A year later the mill was sold to the Sperry Flour Company, which continued to expand and improve the operation.

But, what about the mill ditch? Its location, running down the main street of town, was unsightly. The wooden slats that partially covered it at intervals of every three feet or so and the wooden foot bridges that were placed at the end of each block did not enhance the appearance of the neighborhood. The bridges were narrow and hard for horses and buggies to use.

Occasionally, the ditch was used for baptisms. It was used by dissatisfied customers of the Fresno Water Works. But, it was also used to dump refuse and in the hot summers when it dried up it had a "certain air about it" which caused a public outcry.

The local citizenry demanded that the ditch be filled in. The situation was publicly protested before the city trustees in March of 1886. In June of 1890, the trustees ordered it to be filled in, but the Sperry Flour Company protested and legal battles followed.

Finally, a group of citizens took matters into their own hands. Using Fresno Scrapers, they came in the dark of night and filled in the offending mill ditch.

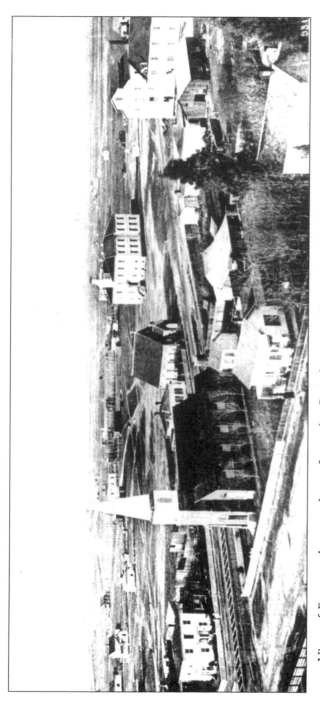

View of Fresno taken northeast from the Courthouse on December 25, 1886, the year after the city was incorporated. The open canal down Fresno Street can be seen. St. John's Catholic Church stands at the corner of M and Fresno Streets. The Champion Mill is in background to the right with the White School across Fresno Street.

Courtesy of William B. Secrest, Sr., Collection.

New City, New Mayor & New Laws

The evening of October 27, 1885, found five serious minded gentlemen clustered around a flat-topped desk in the Mariposa Street real estate office of Thomas Hughes. One was a physician, another was a harness-maker and the other three were in the real estate business. These men comprised Fresno's first board of trustees. The occasion was the first meeting of the new city government formed by the vote to incorporate Fresno. Their first item of business was to elect one of their number, William Faymonville, the first president of the board, making him, in effect, the first mayor of Fresno.

The second item of business was to begin work on ordinances designed to help govern the new city. They made it illegal to deposit ashes in a wooden vessel or on the floor of any building, obviously an effort to help alleviate the problem of fires. It also became illegal for anyone, except peace officers and travelers, to carry a concealed weapon. Fresnans could neither ride nor drive their animals on the sidewalk. Cows, horses, mules and goats could not be tethered or be allowed to graze on public streets.

Most of the new ordinances made sense for the rather primitive living conditions of the new city. However, one law was rather perplexing. If a Fresnan wanted to discharge a firearm within the city limits, he had to obtain a permit from the city clerk two hours before the time of firing. Old-timers felt it was rather sporting, but highly impractical, to give a man you intended to shoot two hours notice. It was argued that in two hours you might forget why you were mad at him in the first place!

Fresno's Horse Car Lines

By the time Fresno became a city in 1885, the need for some form of public transportation was apparent. As streets were added and distances became greater, it was clear that something had to be done.

In 1887, the city gave a franchise to George Bradley and his partners for a rail line that would run from H Street along Mariposa Street, south on K Street (now Van Ness Avenue) and then east on Tulare Street to U Street, the eastern boundary of the city. Known as the Fresno Street Railroad Company, it opened for business on January 25, 1889. The streetcars were drawn by horses and mules. Other lines were added and were eventually absorbed by the Fresno Street Railroad Company.

The first streetcars were used ones purchased from San Francisco, and the destination signs were rather startling. They read "To the Ferries" and "To the Cliff House" and were a little confusing until they were painted over several months later. The colorful horse cars transported Fresnans all over the city until 1903, when the first electric streetcar system opened for operation.

The success of the new system pointed the way to a new age when animals would not be needed for transportation. The entrance of the automobile was not far off. Soon Fresnans would be traveling faster through town. A leisurely, more relaxed pace of life was beginning to change as the horse cars made their departure from the streets of Fresno.

The year 1903 saw Fresnans preparing to celebrate Christmas in the Victorian tradition with all the hustle and bustle we experience still today. Kutner, Goldstein and Company's store had a banner reminding shoppers that "Today, Tomorrow, Thursday—Then Christmas." The store was featuring men's silk ties for fifty cents each, ladies' feather boas for ten dollars, and fancy candy at nine cents a pound. Radin & Kamp's store posed the question, "Are You Ready for Santa Claus?" Late hours were the rule for most department stores on Christmas Eve.

The post office was open on Christmas Day and guaranteed deliveries of each gift sent through its office. According to the postmaster, John Short, cluster raisins and Calimyrna figs were favorite presents and could be mailed for one cent an ounce.

Acts of charity were a part of the celebration, too. M. Theo Kearney donated money to finance a Christmas festival at Madison School. Mrs. C. J. Craycroft and her friends collected toys for the children at the Fresno County Orphanage. Fulton G. Berry was among those helping the Salvation Army gather donations from merchants.

Local churches featured special Christmas programs and distributed gifts to the children of their congregations. Community spirit was evident everywhere.

Chester H. Rowell, editor of the *Republican* newspaper, closed his Christmas Day editorial with the following words, "Blessed is the home, on this day, that has children in it. The day belongs to them. It is in commemoration of the birth of a Child. It is also a welcome to the returning sunshine, but children are the sunshine of life. There is no joy like their joy, and no memory in all of life like that of the Christmas days of the few brief years of childhood. Let nothing cloud the brightness of a single one of these rarest of golden days, in the life of any child."

Winter Amid the Tules

Newcomers to Fresno are well aware of the Valley's reputation for hot summers, but when the leaves of autumn are on the ground, they are not always prepared for Fresno's own brand of winter madness known as "tule fog." It is a phenomenon which can appear suddenly, enveloping people, cars and buildings. It is only human to ask what is this stuff, where does it come from, and how did it get its unusual name?

To answer this question, you must travel back in time to the days when Yokut Indians were the only inhabitants of the San Joaquin Valley. Three groups of Yokuts, the Tachi, the Chunut, and the Wowol, lived in the area around Tulare Lake. The Tachis' settlement was primarily on the western bank of the lake, and they often came into contact with Spanish soldiers and padres from the missions on the coast. The other groups lived on the east shore and in the Kaweah delta.

The bulrushes that grew along the streams which emptied into Tulare Lake produced a reed which the Spaniards called a *tule*. The Spaniards called these three Indian groups *Tularenos* or "those who dwell among the tules."

When winter comes to the Valley and the air becomes cold, the moisture which rises from the marshlands near the tules hits the cold air and forms a dense fog which has been called "tule fog." The density of the fog varies from area to area according to the amount of moisture that is in the ground. It is not an uncommon winter experience when driving at night to see a clear sky with stars and a moon, and then, suddenly, to drive into a curtain of fog so dense that even the road disappears.

The next time the tule fog descends, remember the Indians who wove the tule reeds into rafts to cross Tulare Lake. In wintertime, they endured the fog, too. Isn't it a comfort to know that some things do not change?

Wilbur Chandler's Field

When the airplane was introduced to Fresno in 1910, no official airfields existed, nor were they needed. Planes were so small they could land on any Valley field. Often a pilot would check the wind direction by looking at a cow's tail, knowing full well that cows eat facing upwind. As air traffic began to increase, it was finally decided that an airfield was a necessity.

In December 1918, the Fresno County Chamber of Commerce obtained land from J. C. Forkner west of Van Ness Boulevard and north of Dakota Avenue. It became known as Forkner Field. The land was level, but very dusty. The field was abandoned after about a year.

State Senator Wilbur Chandler owned agricultural land at Kearney Boulevard and Tehama Avenue. After his crops were harvested, he allowed aviators to use his field until he was ready to plant the next year's crops. Other local airfields were called Crematory, Billy Brown's, and Maddox Field.

Finally, as the airplane was beginning to show how it could be a great benefit for commercial use, such as transporting merchandise for local businesses, Senator Chandler and his wife deeded a portion of their farm land to the city. At last, a real airport could be built. The year was 1929. Today, Fresno's Chandler Municipal Airport continues to serve the needs of Fresno aviators.

Although one of the most exciting attractions of the annual Raisin Day Festival had been automobile races, in 1927 it was decided that the races would be replaced with a track and field event, which organizers hoped would bring together the best athletes on the Pacific Coast. It was called the West Coast Relays.

The crowd for the first relays on April 30, 1927, was small, but enthusiastic. More than three hundred athletes from forty institutions competed on the clay track at Ratcliffe Stadium.

The 1928 relays saw the setting of two new world records, one by John Kuck for his shot put toss of 51 feet ° inch, and the other by Lee Barnes for clearing 14 feet 1° inches in the pole vault.

By 1929, the event was drawing large crowds as more records were challenged and broken. Soon the event had grown so much it had to be held on two days rather than one.

As the years went by, thirty-six world records and many collegiate, interscholastic and national records were set during the West Coast Relays. By 1970, the event had grown so large that the participants had to be limited to 2,300 athletes. Problems began to develop. The old clay track was outdated and dusty when the wind blew, as it often did.

In 1982, the final West Coast Relays was held. It was hard to believe that this nationally recognized sporting event was over. A few years later, funds were raised to modernize Ratcliffe Stadium and to create an all-weather track. In April 1991, the old stadium came to life again as athletes from all over the West Coast journeyed to Fresno to compete in track and field events in the Fresno Relays. Once again, spirits soared as athletes pushed to achieve their greatest potential.

The first Fresno County Hospital began as a private establishment in Millerton in the 1850s. It was purchased by the county of Fresno in 1870 for three hundred and fifty dollars. Four years later, after the county seat had been moved to Fresno Station, a temporary hospital was set up in a building on Fresno Street between I (now Broadway) and J (now Fulton Mall) streets. The rent was twenty dollars a month.

Moving patients from Millerton to Fresno was not an easy task. Stagecoaches were the only mode of transportation available; but, under the supervision of the hospital superintendent, the operation went smoothly. This able administrator had an interesting background.

He was born in Susquehanna County, New York, in 1823. As a young man, he came west across the plains to California. Gold fever was rampant; however, money was to be made in areas other than mining. After establishing himself at Millerton, he and James Savage opened a trading post on the Fresno River six miles south of Coarse Gold Gulch. The year was 1851. The business supplied equipment and necessities to the men who mined the Fresno and Chowchilla rivers. Savage was killed a year later. The young man continued the business until gold fever subsided. He closed the trading post and moved to Millerton in 1861. There he began to practice medicine.

After moving to Fresno in 1874, he organized the town's first water company and served as its president. He played an important role in organizing Fresno's first gas company. He served as president of three early banks. He was also the first president of the Fresno Fairground Association. In 1888, a new county hospital was built on Ventura Avenue near the fairground. The head physician operated this facility, as he had the earlier one, at little profit to himself.

This man of many talents was Dr. Lewis Leach, Fresno County's first physician.

Dr. Lewis Leach came to California in 1850. He
served as a member of the Mariposa Battalion. He was
a trading post partner with Major Savage. In 1855, he
practiced medicine at the Fresno River Indian Farm and
at the town of Millerton. Later, he became the second
doctor in the community of Fresno.
Courtesy of William B. Secrest, Sr., Collection.

In 1898. Dr. Chester Rowell's newspaper, the *Fresno Morning Republican*, was the major newspaper for the Fresno area. The citizens of the community were so eager for news that Dr. Rowell and his associates had to purchase the latest equipment and a wire service to keep up with the demand for information.

The doctor asked his nephew to join the staff as editor. The new editor had no journalistic experience, but he had enthusiasm and intelligence. Within a short time he began to attack the problems of the community. He began by writing editorials and articles exposing the problems brought on by a weak city government, namely the police department, which allowed saloons, gamblers, brothels, and race track proprietors to operate freely.

The new editor led the fight for a new city charter which would lay the groundwork for a more responsible city government. The charter became a reality in 1899.

Not content with local problems alone, he began a statewide reform effort which culminated in breaking the control of state government by the Southern Pacific Railroad. He gathered the support of influential Californians and helped to create the Lincoln-Roosevelt League, which elected reformer Hiram Johnson governor of California in 1910. The *Fresno Morning Republican* had become the most influential daily newspaper in California, due to its crusading editor, Chester Harvey Rowell.

A Subway for Fresno Street

As you drive through the streets of Fresno, one of the major headaches is sitting at a railway crossing while a slow train makes its interminable way through town.

In the early years of this century there was another problem as well. The main crossing for the Southern Pacific Railroad at Fresno and I (now Broadway) streets contained twenty tracks. People had to walk over all of these. Terrible accidents occurred, and Mayor W. Parker Lyon decided to use his unique brand of influence to solve the problem.

He called the railroad's Fresno director and asked him to build a subway under the street. He pointed to the money the railroad would save with fewer lawsuits. The answer was no. "No" was not in Lyon's vocabulary, so he rolled up his sleeves and went to work. Using his own money, he hired two lawyers to run some checks on the railroad's legal matters. He never publicly revealed what he found out; however, when he told the railroad bosses his information, they decided they could build the subway with the stipulation that Fresno pay one-third of the estimated cost of $150,000. A friend of Lyon's, who was president of the street railway system, gave him a check for $50,000. He gave the check to the railroad and the project began. Lyon had neglected to mention to the railroad that the water level in that part of Fresno was only eight feet. In digging an eighteen-foot hole, the workers found they were battling torrents of water, and the project ended up costing the railroad $500,000.

The finished subway was cast in one solid piece of concrete. It was beautiful to behold and a joy to use. When the first heavy rain came, however, it also turned into a magnificent concrete ship as it floated to the surface of Fresno Street with twenty railroad tracks draped over it. It cost the railroad another $100,000 to anchor it, but, as Lyon pointed out, the railroad owned the subway and would not suffer any damage suits. The railroad bosses somehow found it hard to see any humor in the situation.

Fresno was built on a plain, with little change in elevation. The sewer pipes that had been laid in town had a fall of only four feet in the three miles they traveled out to "The Farm." There was fear of a terrible epidemic, but the townspeople did not want to pay for a new sewer system. Passing the needed bond issue in 1907 seemed almost impossible.

Once again, when the odds seemed to say no, Mayor W. Parker Lyon stepped forward with another innovative scheme. He began his campaign with a round of speeches focusing on the welfare of the children of Fresno, the possibility of an epidemic, and the likelihood of many deaths. Next, he enlisted the aid of an evangelist who was coming to town. Lyon told him his dilemma and his fears about the children. For twenty-five dollars the preacher promised him a sermon and, for an extra ten dollars, a four-minute prayer as well.

The tent meeting opened on one of those hot summer nights that Fresnans know so well. The subject was sin. On the second night the subject was plumbing. The temperature had reached 114 degrees in the shade that day, and the tent had become a Turkish bath. The preacher talked about the glory of childhood and the innocence of the little children. Tears began to flow. The preacher's starched collar began to melt in the heat. He loosened his tie and began to tackle his subject in earnest. He described the horrors of typhoid fever and threw in smallpox and cholera for good measure. By this time, the tears of his listeners were flowing like a river. The preacher fell to his knees and began to pray. After four minutes, Lyon handed him another ten dollars. The preacher opened one eye, looked at the bill, and prayed harder and louder then ever.

The tent meeting ended. The sewer bonds passed by an overwhelming vote. It was Lyon's grandest hour.

An Elephant Named Nosey

In 1949, a group of community-minded citizens and zoo enthusiasts launched a drive to raise money to buy a baby elephant for the zoo at Roeding Park.

School children of the Central Valley had long dreamed of a baby elephant and they went to work virtually taking over the fund-raising effort. Rummage sales were held, lemonade stands were set up—all sorts of business enterprises were undertaken to see that the goal was met. Children took their nickels, dimes and quarters to school where collection boxes were circulated. Finally, the goal of $3,750 was reached.

A contest to name the animal followed. Roselene Swensen of Orosi submitted the winning name of "Nosey."

Eventually, the long-awaited day arrived. On the morning of September 12, a parade through downtown Fresno officially opened the Fresno Police '49 Days Rodeo. Amid the long procession of mounted police, a baby elephant could be seen. After a brief moment of stage fright, when she turned around halfway down the block between Kern and Tulare streets, she got back on course with the help of her keeper's calming words.

The parade route was lined with thousands of laughing and applauding children. Nosey reared her head back and trumpeted loudly, as though to return their joy. As her keeper, E. M. Blocker, walked her to Roeding Park, she was followed by hundreds of adults and youngsters who did not want to lose sight of her.

Today, those children are adults and they still feel a special closeness to the elephant they brought to Fresno over forty-five years ago. During the intervening years, they brought their children and grandchildren to the zoo, now named the Chaffee Zoological Gardens, and they, too, fell under the spell of Nosey's special charm.

On July 17, 1993, her last birthday was celebrated with a public party which was attended by 3,926 people. Nosey died on November 14 of that same year, leaving a community that mourned her passing. In its history, Fresno has had many special residents, but few more beloved than Nosey.

Firebug on the Loose

On July 10, 1953, one of the most devastating days in the history of Fresno, thirteen fire alarms were answered in the space of four hours by the men of the Fresno Fire Department. The terrifying sequence of events began when a three alarm fire was reported at 1:45 P.M. at the Hughes Hotel. Nine minutes later an alarm went off signaling that the Adams and Golden hotels were burning. Eleven minutes later a fire was reported in the rest room of Gottschalk's department store at Kern and Fulton streets.

At this point it became obvious to Fire Chief Gayle Coger that these fires were not coincidental. A firebug was on the loose and where he would strike next was the question uppermost in the chief's mind. The answer came thirty minutes later when the Sequoia Hotel, the Brix Apartments and the Hotel Californian began to burn. Fires were next reported one minute apart at the Alta Apartments and the First Christian Church.

By now, theaters began to empty as people heard what was happening. First aid stations and food lines were set up in front of Courthouse Park to help the weary fire fighters as they continued to do battle with a faceless enemy. Two more hotels, the Fine Arts Gallery, and the J. C. Penney Company reported fires in the next hour. The last fire was reported at Hammer Field at 5:57 P.M., just four hours after the first fire had been set.

By eight o'clock that evening, the two largest fires, at the Hughes Hotel and the Brix Apartments, were under control. Twenty-six firemen had been treated for heat exhaustion, smoke inhalation or minor injuries. Seventy pieces of fire-fighting equipment had been called into service. Damage estimates ran as high as $430,000. And what about the firebug? He was never caught.

A Sad Departure

In Mayor W. Parker Lyon's three years in office he had done all he could to make Fresno a better city in which to live. His accomplishments included Fresno's first city hall, a new sewer system, and a railroad underpass. He may have used unusual methods to achieve his goals, but no one could deny that the city had benefited from his leadership.

However, Lyon had been elected with the heavy support of the saloon interests. Always a source of great debate, the saloons could be found on almost every corner. They brought much-needed revenue to the city's coffers, but they did not always enhance the city's quality of life.

In July 1907, Lyon and four of the city's trustees approved a new saloon in the 900 block of J Street (now Fulton Mall), in spite of heavy opposition from the businessmen in the area. It was a move that stirred the wrath of one of the most powerful anti-saloon exponents in Fresno, the Reverend Doctor Thomas Boyd of the First Presbyterian Church.

On the following Sunday, Lyon was the subject of Doctor Boyd's sermon. It was of the hell fire and brimstone variety, with Boyd putting Lyon in a league with the powers of darkness. The sermon hurt Lyon. He wrote an emotional letter to both Fresno newspapers, the *Fresno Morning Republican* and the *Fresno Democrat*, trying to answer the minister's charges. Other anti-saloon sermons in other churches followed—all covered in the newspapers.

On March 10, 1908, 1,500 Fresnans attended a meeting where many people spoke against the vice interests in Fresno. The next day's papers lashed out at the city's fifty-seven saloons and their bad influence on the community.

Lyon could take no more. He resigned as mayor and left town, heading for Arcadia in Southern California. With his departure, Fresno lost one of its most colorful and delightful characters.

Seventeen miles northeast of Fresno, at a spot where the Valley rises into the foothills, a school was established in 1872. It was called the "Academy" and, as Fresno County's first secondary school, it gained a reputation for scholastic excellence. Graduates of the Academy who had achieved a good academic record were qualified to teach school or to enter college; no other Fresno County school at that time could offer a student these possibilities.

The money to build the Academy, $3,170, was raised through local citizens who formed a private corporation.

James Darwin Collins and his wife, Ann, were the first teachers. Later, Collins served as the sheriff of Fresno County.

By 1877, the school had fifty regular pupils, a diverse curriculum and an excellent library. Frank W. Blackmar was hired to teach the elementary-level subjects. In that same year, unfortunately, the secondary curriculum was dropped. It was a sad development for the school which never again was able to play the important role that it had in the educational life of Fresno County.

However, the schoolhouse, which had been built in a grove of trees on the south bank of Dog Creek near the Millerton-Visalia stage route, made another kind of contribution to the history of Fresno County. It gave its name to the village that grew up around it, the town of Academy.

The Red Brick Church

At the corner of Ventura and M streets stands Holy Trinity Armenian Apostolic Church, which was at the center of "Armenian Town" from the time of its construction in 1914 until the mid-1960s, when redevelopment projects and the building of the new convention center complex changed this neighborhood dramatically.

Indeed, the building was much more than just the geographical center of the Armenian community. It was and is its religious and cultural center. It has served as a refuge for those who fled the Turkish massacres and for those who suffered from discrimination in Fresno. It continues to provide a sense of cultural identity for Fresno's large Armenian community.

Designed by Fresno's first Armenian architect, L. K. Condrajian, its very construction made history in a twofold manner. It was the first church in the United States to be designed in the traditional Armenian-Orthodox style, and the first Armenian church designed by an Armenian architect.

When you enter the church, you notice a beautiful crystal chandelier which hangs from the center dome. At the top of the chandelier is an inscription which tells the story of two brothers who escaped from the Turkish massacres and made their way to Cairo. In a cafe they overheard two soldiers bragging about killing an Armenian family. They realized the soldiers were talking about their family. The brothers killed the soldiers. One brother was caught and executed. The other brother made his way to Fresno, where he donated the chandelier to the church as a memorial to his family.

Many such stories form the history of this building. William Saroyan affectionately called it the Red Brick Church and referred to it as the place where children came to learn to read and to sing classical Armenian.

Now listed in the National Register of Historic Places, this church today stands as a proud symbol of a group of people who have made great contributions to Fresno.

**Gillum Baley
was elected county
treasurer in 1884**
*Courtesy of Willetta
Pokorny and
Charles W. Baley.*

Traveling across country in 1858 was difficult at best, but for brothers Gillum and Right Baley, Joel Hedgepeth, their wives and seventeen children, it was downright dangerous. Leaving Missouri, they traveled in a train of five oxen wagons and 200 head of purebred Durham cattle. En route they joined another group, the Rose party, bringing their number to sixty. As they neared the Colorado River, they were attacked by 300 hostile Mojave Indians. The battle ended after three hours of fighting when Gillum killed the chief of the tribe. None of the Baley family was killed, but their cattle and supplies were gone. They walked for fourteen days to reach Albuquerque, New Mexico.

Nine months later, they felt ready to resume their journey to California. By the end of 1859, they reached Visalia, where Right Baley decided to settle.

In January 1860, Gillum Baley and his family arrived at Millerton. Gillum had studied law, but had never practiced law. Soon after settling at Millerton, he was named justice of the peace. In 1867, he was elected a county judge. When the county seat was moved to Fresno in 1874, he moved his family to the new community and continued to serve as judge. Having been ordained a Methodist minister as a young man, he organized the first church in Fresno, the Methodist Episcopal Church South, in 1876.

Rebecca Baley, daughter of Gillum and Permelia Baley, was the first schoolteacher in Fresno County. Her class of 12 students met in the hospital at Fort Miller in 1860. She later married Jefferson Shannon.
Courtesy of Willetta Pokorny and Charles W. Baley.

William Krug and his wife, Amelia Catherine Baley Krug, a daughter of Gillum and Permelia Baley. They married during the journey to Millerton.
Courtesy of Willetta Pokorny and Charles W. Baley.

Maher's Symbol for Fresno

By 1887, the classic water tank at Fresno and O streets was no longer adequate to serve the needs of the community. The Fresno Water Works dug two new 150-foot wells at Fresno and O streets. The new wells had black holding tanks which were considered unattractive by the citizens of Fresno. Not only were they unsightly, but there was a feeling that bare tanks made Fresno seem like a small town.

As the 1890s approached, Fresnans were becoming more concerned with architectural aesthetics and wanted a symbol of civic pride. Chicago architect George W. Maher was commissioned to design a $20,000 water tower at Fresno and O streets to replace the existing black tanks. Fresno's water tower would stand 100 feet high and would hold a 250,000-gallon water tank.

The Chicago Avenue Water Tower, which served as Maher's inspiration, was one of the few buildings to survive the Chicago Fire of 1872. Like Chicago's water tower, Maher chose a Romanesque design for Fresno's structure. Looking a great deal like a medieval watchtower with ornately detailed windows and doors, a wrought iron railing and a turret, the new tower also had elements of Victorian design in its weather vane and balcony.

In the arid climate of Fresno, water was a symbol of prosperity. The new Water Tower added grandeur to Fresno and increased civic pride. In the 1890s and again in the 1920s, when Fresno joined the national City Beautiful Movement, the Water Tower inspired Fresnans to become more interested in city beautification and architectural harmony.

The Water Tower continued to be an integral part of Fresno's water system until 1963. Today, listed in the National Register of Historic Places, Fresno's best-known landmark proudly stands as a reminder that it was water that provided the source of life in an untamed desert. It was water that allowed Fresno to exist.

Shown here in a drawing by Fresno artist Robert Nidy, Fresno's most-famous landmark was in use until 1963. *Courtesy Robert Nidy*

Telephones, Operators & a Parrot

The telephone found its way to Fresno six years after its invention by Alexander Graham Bell. The year was 1882 and the man responsible for establishing the first local telephone exchange was S. A. Miller, the owner-publisher of the *Fresno Morning Republican* newspaper. Phone service was offered by the Fresno Telephone Company for four dollars a month, plus a twenty-five-dollar installation fee. The first telephone directory, published in 1883, had twenty subscribers.

The telephone exchange was in the office of the *Fresno Morning Republican*. Calls were received by Mrs. S. A. Miller, who had to share the office with a parrot. Callers usually would hear the parrot squawk "Hello" several times when their call came into the exchange, often followed by a colorful shout of "Go to hell!," also courtesy of the parrot.

The Eggers ranch, located where the Fresno Air Terminal is today, received the first long distance telephone line. Herman and George Eggers bought out Miller's interests in 1886. In May of 1887 they obtained a franchise from the Bell Telephone Company.

Telephone service began expanding as telephone poles, made from eucalyptus trees, were erected throughout the town. The switchboard was moved to Smith's Drug Store on Fulton Street and was open until 11 P.M. Callers using the system after that time had to use a special alarm system to wake the operator.

By the turn of the century, one thousand Fresnans had telephones. The first dial system was installed in 1927. No longer was a central operator needed to direct a local call. And no longer was there the chance of hearing a parrot's voice screeching "Hello." Placing a call had become a bit more impersonal than in the early days of telephone service in Fresno.

The Modern Dexter Stables

In the days before the automobile ruled the roadways, Fresnans depended on horses for transportation. One of the oldest businesses in Fresno was the Dexter Stables.

In 1891, a young Scotsman from Nova Scotia, John Robert Cameron McKay, who had worked for James Porteous since his arrival in Fresno, purchased a blacksmith shop. Two years later, he began operating a livery business in the old Dexter building at I (now Broadway) and Inyo streets. The business did well and within a year he had acquired a partner, H. W. Wilbur, and a coach dog named Sally.

In 1896, McKay and Wilbur built a new establishment on I Street near the Hughes Hotel. The new Dexter Stables was the most modern facility of its kind in Fresno. Built of brick with a corrugated iron roof, it was totally fireproof. A huge open space allowed free movement of carriages without danger of having them scratched. Stalls that would comfortably accommodate seventy horses lined the perimeter—all were well lighted, provided good ventilation and contained chutes for hay which were automatically filled from an upstairs loft.

With such excellent accommodations, the Dexter became the favorite place for prominent families to board their horses. A quick call on the local phone exchange, the Dexter's number was 9, would assure a speedy delivery of one's horse and carriage which would be driven through town, with Sally running under the wheels, to one's front door. Such service was a byword for McKay. With typical Scots pride and ingenuity, he built his business into a model for the young community.

One feature of the new Dexter Stables did not go unnoticed by the female population of Fresno, who were not accustomed to being extended special courtesies in establishments of this kind. Just inside the door and next to the office was a finely appointed Ladies' Waiting Room. Tastefully furnished and carpeted, it also contained a powder room, with every modern convenience. For 1896 Fresno, with its unpaved, dusty streets and frontier flavor, this was indeed a step toward the twentieth century.

James Faber's name will live in the history of Fresno because, in setting up his tent next to the new railroad stop called Fresno Station, he became Fresno's first resident and merchant. Who was this man who braved the vast desert surrounding the sinks of Dry Creek, inhabited only by wild elk and deer?

Faber was born in Oxford, Ohio. He ran off to join the Union Army in 1862, was severely wounded in action and sent home to die. However, he recovered and rejoined the army. After the Civil War ended, he headed west. In Montana Territory, he found himself in a battle with Sioux and Blackfoot Indians. During this engagement, he was gored by a crazed ox and almost died. However, once again he recovered and continued west.

After reaching Sacramento, he traveled to San Francisco by steamer. Here he bought horses, wagons and farm supplies and settled in what is today Madera County. The weather proved to be uncooperative for farming and, after suffering through two dry years, he turned to hauling freight. Using his wagons, he transported goods from Stockton to points south, including Borden, Jones Ferry and Millerton.

About this time, he learned that the Central Pacific Railroad was building a line through the Valley, which would compete with his operation. Fearing he would be put out of business, he stocked up on dry goods and plotted his arrival in Fresno Station, the next railroad stop to be established. As told in a previous "Legends & Legacies," his appearance in the new town was unusual to say the least.

Faber's ingenuity and courage were legendary, but Fresno has never recognized his enterprise. Fresno's first citizen has never been honored by having a street or school named in his memory. For most Fresnans, the name James Faber carries no special meaning. Perhaps one day a fitting way to remember his contribution to Fresno's earliest beginnings will be found.

The Call to Battle

When the United States entered World War I on April 5, 1917, Fresnans responded valiantly. Young men flocked to recruiting stations to volunteer their service. Others, heeding the call to register for the draft turned out in such numbers that by July 11, 263 men in Fresno County had signed their draft forms. This figure exceeded the county's Army enlistment quota.

In September, the first group of draftees formed a parade that marched through downtown Fresno on the way to the Santa Fe Depot. The streets were lined with patriotic crowds cheering them on. As the young men boarded the train, many tearful farewells were observed.

Eager to show their support, Fresnans found many ways to help the war effort. Many became involved by volunteering for the Red Cross and relief projects. A call for used shoes to aid French and Belgian refugees resulted in a mountainous pile of footwear in Courthouse Park. Fresno Normal School coeds planted and tended a "victory" garden on their Maroa and University avenues campus. Newspapers, lead and tin foil were collected for salvage programs.

In every way imaginable Fresnans supported the young men who risked their lives for the cause of freedom. By the time the war was over, 165 Fresno County servicemen had given their lives in service to their country.

Fireworks & Jubilation

Fresnans had given their all to the war-relief efforts of World War I. They had sent their sons off to battle, supported them by volunteering their time and talents for war-related causes, and had watched the daily newspapers for the latest news from the front. Having been so wholeheartedly involved in the daily aspect of the wartime situation, the reaction to the war's end was heartfelt also.

The news of the Armistice reached Mayor William F. Toomey at two o'clock the morning of November 11, 1918. He immediately began a celebration. The sounds of horns and whistles roused Fresnans from their sleep. Thousands of excited people—as many as twenty-seven thousand, it was said—formed an impromptu parade that made its way through downtown, bound for Courthouse Park. Factory whistles blew, church bells rang, and railroad locomotives sounded their whistles as well, an accompaniment to the marching throng. Fireworks filled the night sky over Chinatown with red, white, and blue explosions of color.

As the sun came up over Fresno, some two thousand of the celebrants gathered at the steps to the Courthouse to offer prayers of thanksgiving for the war's end. The wild excitement of the crowd turned to hushed silence as Mayor Toomey began the service. A delegation of ministers from Fresno churches joined him in leading prayers and singing hymns.

It wasn't until a year later that the troops were officially welcomed home in another Courthouse Park ceremony. This celebration was marred, however, by a Spanish flu epidemic. Most of the participants wore face masks out of fear of catching the terrible disease that was killing people all over the world. One kind of war had ended, but another battle was being waged on another front.

Timber & the Toll House Grade

The Pine Ridge area, due east of Auberry, drew lumbermen as early as 1852. In that year, the first sawmill was built in Corlew Meadows. James Hulz, the builder, lost it in a poker game. However, other operations rapidly followed his. Stands of sugar pine, fir and yellow pine filled the area, which, because of the precipitous mountain cliffs, was almost inaccessible.

As the county began to grow, these forests were seen as an important source of building materials. The problem of getting the logs out of the mountains began to pose a far greater problem than cutting down trees and sawing them up. Charles Converse, operating in an area on the north side of what is now known as Converse Basin, had put his logs into the Kings River, planning to retrieve them on the valley floor. They were never seen again.

By 1866, brothers J. N. and J. H. Woods were cutting timber into shakes. Because there was no road, they forged a primitive trail from their camp to Sarvers Peak. From there it was a thousand-foot drop to the Valley. It was steep and treacherous. The Woods brothers hired Indians to carry the shakes down the mountain.

In the fall of 1866, the Fresno County Board of Supervisors gave the Woods brothers permission to construct a toll road up Sarvers Mountain. They were aided by John Humphrey, a Mariposa lumberman, and Chinese laborers from Millerton. When completed, it was called the Toll House Grade. Toll rates were set at $1.50 for a wagon and one span of horses, mules or oxen; each additional span, 50 cents; $1.00 for a horse and buggy; 50 cents for a horseman; 25 cents for a pack animal; 10 cents for loose mules, horses or cattle; and 2 cents each for hogs or sheep. During the next few years, others improved the road, which was sold to Fresno County in 1878. It would be another twenty years before an easier way to bring lumber out of the mountains would be found.

Sawmills, Swift & Shaver

In the late 1880s, the focus of lumber operations began to shift northward from the Pine Ridge area. The Fresno Flume & Irrigation Company, headed by Frank Bullard, purchased 12,000 acres of timberland in the vicinity of Stevenson Creek and Meadow. The company also acquired a steam-powered mill already in operation. By 1890 the company had plans to construct a flume down the mountain to present-day Clovis. Two years later, the company built a dam across Stevenson Creek, but warm rains, followed by a flash flood, washed most of it away.

The many difficulties the company was experiencing led the directors to allow two of the partners, Lewis P. Swift and Charles Shaver, Michigan lumbermen recently arrived in California, to take control of the company. Shortly afterward, these two men bought out their partners and divided the responsibilities. Swift's job was to administer construction and operation. Shaver dealt with sales and handled the management duties.

Swift began his tenure by overseeing the building of a rock dam sixty feet high across Stevenson Creek. A reservoir, formed behind the dam, was named Shaver Lake. The lake was to provide a millpond for the storage of cut logs.

An impressive mill was built on the northeast side of the lake. With its up-to-date methods, the mill could produce 155,000 board feet every twenty-four hours. The best quality lumber was brought down Toll House Grade in horse-drawn wagons. The rest of the lumber was sent down a forty-two-mile flume which dropped 4,900 feet into the Valley. When the wood reached the end of the flume in Clovis it arrived at a company mill located next to the railroad tracks that developer Marcus Pollasky had built in the early 1890s. The railroad provided transport for the lumber to Fresno. By 1914, when the mill ceased operation, it had logged 15,000 acres and cut 450 million board feet of lumber. The site of the former mill is at Clovis Avenue and Fifth Street.

A Fluming We Will Go

The building of the forty-two-mile flume from the Shaver Lake mill to Clovis was not an easy task. The flume began where Shaver Dam is today, at 5,275 feet above sea level. When finished, it had to descend 4,900 feet into the Valley below. The flume was designed as a V-shaped trough which had to be watertight and strong enough to withstand the jostling of the loose timber that would travel along its course. As the construction teams approached Tollhouse, they were faced with a sheer granite cliff. Workmen had to be suspended on ropes to blast for flume footings. Twenty-eight trestles also had to be built across canyons, one eighty-four feet high. The flume dropped 27° feet per mile. This engineering feat was accomplished, and the flume was completed in 1894.

The purpose of the flume was to carry lumber to the company's mill in Clovis. However, it served another purpose as well. A boat was constructed to fit the V-shaped, four-foot high trough of the flume. The stern of the boat was left open so that the water running down the flume could enter it and keep the boat on a steady course. Slats were nailed across the boat, with one long slat placed lengthwise. Here passengers could sit, balancing themselves as they traveled.

The trip to Fresno on the flume boat was a harrowing one as, at terrific speeds, the passengers raced through pine forests, across canyons and down sheer granite cliffs, looking down 1,000 feet or more as they continued the exciting journey until they reached the Clovis mill. The Shavers, Swifts and other Fresno Flume & Irrigation Company officials found the dangerous ride much more fun and, certainly, quicker than spending hours in a horse-drawn wagon making the long journey to Fresno.

The Gateway to the Sierra

In the beginning, the area that we now think of as Clovis was primarily a wheat field farmed by Clovis Cole. When Pollasky's railroad traversed the east side of the Valley, one of its three stations was established on land donated by Cole. It stood at what is now Fourth Street and Clovis Avenue.

In the same year, 1891, Ingvart Teilman surveyed the land for a town site. He was hired by property owners near the Fresno Flume & Irrigation Company's mill. The new town was named Clovis to honor Clovis Cole. Developers who owned large parcels of land began to subdivide and sell small lots to private investors. Clovis began to grow, mostly north and west of the depot, upwind from the rather odoriferous plant burners of the mill.

In February of 1893, a post office was established in Turner's Livery Stable, and by the mid-1890s, a variety of businesses, as well as two hotels, were doing well. The town also had a constable, a justice of the peace, one saloon and one church.

By 1894, the mill was in full operation and employed between three hundred and five hundred people. The mill plant also contained a box factory, planing mill, warehouse, drying kiln, housing for employees and five acres of pasture for the company horses. Many who came to Clovis to work in the mill decided to go into farming instead.

The main street of the town was called Fulton, after Fulton G. Berry, a director of Pollasky's railroad that had established Clovis Station. Later it was called Front Street; today it is Clovis Avenue. The town continued to grow, and on February 27, 1912, the citizens voted to incorporate their city.

Clovis is continuing its pattern of growth as the city spreads to the north and east. Growth tends to bring change, but, just as a century ago lumber wagons made their way down Toll House Grade and through Academy to Clovis, so Valley residents of today travel through Clovis as they head for the mountain lakes or skiing. Clovis is still affectionately known as the "Gateway to the Sierra."

Wheat
farming using
mule teams in
the Clovis area
c. 1880s.
Courtesy of
William B. Secrest,
Sr., Collection.

A Courthouse for Millerton

On June 11, 1866, the board of supervisors considered three bids from contractors who wanted to build Fresno County's first Courthouse. Charles Porter Converse, who submitted the lowest bid, was chosen for the job. The supervisors were not pleased to hire Converse, whom they regarded as "difficult," so they appointed Fresno County District Attorney Cladius Gordon Sayle to oversee the project.

The Courthouse was an ambitious project. The foundation was made of granite from a quarry a quarter of a mile below Millerton. The blocks, some weighing over a ton, were hauled to the site by oxen. The two-story building contained a jail and offices for the sheriff, assessor, treasurer, and clerk. The courtroom occupied most of the second floor. The building was completed in mid-1867.

With the decline of Millerton, after the county seat was moved to Fresno in 1874, the Courthouse was used for a schoolhouse and for social events. Finally, it was left vacant. By 1940, it was the only building left where the town of Millerton once stood.

With the completion of Friant Dam in 1944, the Courthouse was destined to be at the bottom of the lake that would form behind the dam. The Native Sons and Daughters of the Golden West began a fund drive and raised enough money to dismantle the Courthouse. The granite blocks, all carefully marked, were stored above the town of Friant.

In 1956, the Fresno County Centennial Millerton Memorial Committee, led by Willis Ball of Friant, raised $13,000 toward reconstruction of the building. In 1965, the Courthouse was reconstructed on high ground, with additional funds from the California Legislature.

Today, the Millerton Courthouse stands on Mariner's Point. It contains a museum of early county history, a proud symbol of Fresno County's beginnings, and a reminder of a colorful era when the West was a land of dreams and opportunity for those willing to endure hardships to make their dreams a reality.

Fresno County's first courthouse. The building stands deserted after most of the citizens of Millerton moved to Fresno Station in 1874 and the years following. The courthouse was dismanteled and rebuilt years later, using a combination of original and new materials, on Mariner's Point overlooking Millerton Lake.

Courtesy of William B. Secrest, Sr., Collection.

The Fresno Sanitarium

For a small pioneer community, early-day Fresno had several fine doctors. Dr. H. C. Coley, Dr. Lewis Leach and Dr. Chester Rowell served the community well and were highly regarded. In 1891, two new doctors, a husband and wife, arrived in Fresno after receiving degrees from Michigan State University and taking postgraduate work at Harvard. In July of that year they opened a private sanitarium at N and Mariposa streets, where the police department is now situated.

A year later they moved their hospital, by then called the Fresno Sanitarium, to the northwest corner of K (now Van Ness Avenue) and Stanislaus streets. The new structure was of Eastlake Victorian design with chimneys and finials on the roof. It was in this building that the doctors opened Fresno's first surgical operating room.

In 1895, they began the community's first accredited training school for nurses. Using homemade equipment, they took the first X-rays west of the Mississippi and for the next three years ran the only X-ray equipment in the Western United States. For many years, Doctors George and Jessie Hare provided excellent medical care for the citizens of Fresno and broke new ground in the diagnosis and treatment of illness. Dr. George Hare held top offices in local, state, and national medical societies.

In 1914, they built a home on McKinley Avenue near Wishon Avenue. This two-story California craftsman bungalow-style building became their home and the location for their private medical practice.

The site of the Fresno Sanitarium is now occupied by the offices and parking lot of the Fresno Metropolitan Museum.

Big Dry Creek & Its Church

In 1852, John Greenup Simpson, William Harshfield, and William Lewis Lovely Witt settled in an area northeast of present-day Clovis called Big Dry Creek. Witt and Harshfield were grain and hay farmers. Simpson began raising cattle, increasing his land holdings by buying property from homesteaders who left the area after they became disheartened in their attempts to farm their land. Simpson later became the first Fresno County tax collector.

Other settlers arrived in 1868, including Major Thomas Nelson, David Cowan Sample, and William Shipp, who came from Solano County, bringing their flocks of sheep with them. They were followed by Jesse Blasingame and Lewis P. Clark.

A small community had begun to form which would eventually take its name from the Academy, a school built nearby. Henry Neal, a circuit rider and preacher, came to this community on a regular basis. By the mid-1860s, a Methodist Episcopal Church South congregation had been formed, led by the Reverend Joel Hedgpeth. John Simpson donated land for a church, and money was raised to erect the building.

Today, although the community of Academy consists of only a few buildings, this church, believed to be the oldest in Fresno County, still stands, a stark white building easily visible from Highway 168. At least four times a year services are held here. Most of the people in attendance at these times have surnames which are stirring reminders of a past era. The Simpson, Sample and Blasingame families, among others, have chosen to remain in this beautiful section of Fresno County, handing down to each succeeding generation a legacy rich in history and respect for the land that their ancestors settled so many years ago.

The twelfth of February, 1966, was a busy day. The new Fresno County Courthouse was completed and, on this day, the files from the county clerk's office were being moved into the new building.

On March 7, two thousand items from the old building were up for auction. Standing among the crowds of people hoping to successfully bid for a piece of Fresno County history was William Saroyan. Sadly, he shook his head and said that none of this made any sense. He had been part of the group that tried to save the building.

On March 15, the cupola was separated from the dome and lowered to a flatbed truck. Five days later, the statues of the two Goddesses of Justice, each weighing four hundred pounds, and Liberty were brought down from the parapet. They had watched over Fresno from the roof of the Courthouse for ninety-two years.

On March 23, demolition began. First the north part of the building would be leveled, then the south, and finally the central core, the oldest part.

On April 7, crowds gathered—the dome was going to be toppled. In spite of the experts' warnings that even a slight earthquake would bring the building down, an operation that was thought would take two hours turned into a mighty struggle. The stately old building was not going down without a fight. It took nine hours of difficult work before the dome finally came crashing down.

For ninety-two years, the old Courthouse had stood at the center of community life. On great occasions, such as the funeral of Dr. Chester Rowell or the end of World War I, the citizens of Fresno had flocked to its steps to find comfort or to give thanks. Couples had courted in its park, and band concerts were enjoyed there every Sunday afternoon. The grand old building had borne witness to the pageant of life in a young pioneer town as it grew and developed into a great city.

Ninety-two years earlier, at the laying of the cornerstone, District Attorney Claudius Golon Sayle had said the building would "stand the storms of winter and the heat of summer for a period

The dome of the historic Fresno County Courthouse
comes crashing down on April 7, 1966.
Carl Crawford photo. Courtesy of the Fresno Bee Library.

of a thousand years or more." The building was not destined to
fulfill his prophecy, but the memory of that great building will
live on in the hearts of Fresnans for as long as Fresno endures.

Catherine Morison Rehart

73

One of the sad components of progress is that change often means the loss of something cherished by some, but viewed by others as standing in the way of new development.

In the spring of 1962, the residents of Fresno were faced with a sad dilemma—the members of the board of supervisors were considering tearing down the Fresno County Courthouse and building a new structure rather than spending the money necessary to rehabilitate the old building.

There was a tremendous public outcry. The board of directors of the Fresno City and County Historical Society issued a resolution stating that "No more beautiful, stately, and historic building exists in the county. It represents the very heart and personality of Fresno and represents a tie with Fresno pioneer days. It is more significant and cherished than any museum or gallery could be." The *Fresno Bee*, the San Joaquin Chapter of the American Institute of Architects, the Fresno County Bar Association and others joined in the appeal to save the old building.

On July 24, 1963, Fresno County received a $1,949,300 federal grant for a new courthouse building with the provision that the work begin within 120 days.

The battle now began in earnest. A citizens group was formed to fight demolition. Led by Edward Vagim, this group fought hard, successfully gathering sufficient signatures on petitions to place the issue before the voters. After the issue was placed on the ballot, the Fifth District Court of Appeal ruled that the supervisors had the right to make the decision. An election was not necessary. In spite of attempts by Vagim's group to stem the tide, the site work on the new Courthouse began.

In November of 1964, Vagim was defeated in a bid for election to the board of supervisors. The cause was lost and the way was paved for the demolition of Fresno's historic Courthouse.

The Cemetery at Academy

Traveling east from Clovis the land rises gracefully into the foothills. After leaving the citrus groves and orchards behind, Toll House Road takes the traveler into a land that seems untouched by time. In spring, fields of goldenrod spread like an orange carpet, covering the hills. Huge oak trees dot the landscape above tall, green grass.

A left turn on Mendocino Avenue at the community of Academy brings the traveler onto a country road which dead-ends at a pair of iron gates. Stone pillars with the words "Academy Cemetery" anchor these gates and bid the traveler to enter on foot. The visitor is struck by a sense of peace. The only sounds are birds singing, the gentle rustling of leaves, and water running through Dog Creek at the cemetery's north boundary.

Standing in this place is to experience what it must have been like for those who settled this land. Walking past the graves, the visitor realizes that he is in the presence of those whose sacrifices and dedication helped to build Fresno County.

The land for the cemetery was donated by Sarah Simpson on March 2, 1890. Until 1913, this was a family cemetery, used as a resting place for the pioneers of the foothill area. Gillum Baley, James D. Collins, the Reverend Joel Hedgpeth, and John G. Simpson are buried in their family plots. The names Armstrong, Sample, Blasingame, Musick, and Clark are reminders of the beginning of Fresno County history.

In the north portion of the cemetery there are newer headstones. Here, the Simpson family has planted an English garden with foxgloves, lilacs, pansies, and day lilies, expressing in this simple way a loving tribute to their family and to the land they settled over 140 years ago.

Rather than a sad reminder of the past, a visit to this corner of Fresno County gives one a strong sense of continuity and strength. In today's fast-paced world, this is, indeed, a welcome experience.

A Tuneful Treasure

Thrilling experiences are not usually the stuff of everyday life, but on those special, rare occasions when they happen, the spirit soars. Such experiences were offered to those who attended live stage performances or silent films at Fresno's Pantages Theater, for accompanying those shows was a rather incredible theater pipe organ. The last of its kind to be built by the Morton Organ Company of Van Nuys, this organ, with fourteen ranks and 1,035 pipes, contained 720 keys, pedals and combination pistons. Installed when the theater was built in 1928, it contained all types of sound effects: percussion, wind and string instruments, bells, sirens, bird calls, and other sounds necessary to accompany films and vaudeville acts.

Instead of mounting the organ pipes to the left and right of the stage, Alexander Pantages decided to install the pipes under the stage so the sound emanated from the orchestra pit and more closely re-created the illusion of an entire orchestra. The placement of the pipes, along with the magnificent acoustics of the theater, produced an unforgettable sound. The organ was mounted on an elevator at basement level and could be raised to the house level. At one time, Fresnan Arthur Mantor played concerts on the organ which were broadcast over KMJ Radio.

Today, the Pantages is called Warnors Theater, but its Morton organ is still in place, having undergone a complete restoration. It is the only organ of its kind in Fresno still in its original setting and is a showpiece for special events, benefits and concerts. On these occasions, the house lights dim, a hush falls over the audience, and the organist begins to play as the organ slowly rises to the orchestra pit. A single spotlight bathes the organ in light. The theater fills with music, with incredible sounds that surround the listeners; exciting, soaring sounds that enchant and delight. The listener would not be at all surprised if the great performers of vaudeville magically reappeared. At such thrilling moments anything is truly possible.

During the United States Bicentennial celebration in 1976, communities across the country initiated special projects to commemorate the event. One of Fresno's projects involved an 1880s residence in a downtown neighborhood.

The gentleman who built this home for his family was born in Tennessee. He graduated from the University of Pennsylvania Medical School in 1860 when he was twenty-two years old. A year later, he enlisted in the Confederate Army and took part in the battles of Shiloh and Atlanta. After serving for four years, he was discharged from the Army as an assistant surgeon with the rank of captain.

In December of 1887, he moved to Fresno with his wife and three children. Three months later, he selected a site for the home he wanted to build in a new development just east of Courthouse Park. The home was a mix of architectural styles, which was a common practice at that time. This eclectic mix gave the home towers, ornate cornices, scrolls, fans and stained glass windows— all kinds of elaborate details. It was completed in 1889. In the same year the owner established his medical practice in Fresno. He was elected president of the Fresno County Medical Society in 1896. He continued his career as a doctor until his death in 1929. His family continued to live in the house until the death of his only surviving daughter in 1970.

Today, the home that Dr. Thomas Meux built proudly stands at the corner of R and Tulare streets. Listed in the National Register of Historic Places, it is the last remaining home of its kind in a neighborhood which was one of Fresno's finest. Operated as a museum, it allows Fresnans and visitors alike an opportunity to experience what life was like in the Fresno of 1890. The home is significant because the Meux family lived in it for eighty-one continuous years, a record for a Fresno residence. But, it is significant for another reason as well. The restoration of the Meux Home involved individuals and businesses working together in a preservation project aimed at saving an important part of Fresno's past.

A Cathedral for Saint John

The first Catholic Mass celebrated in Fresno County was at Millerton in the spring of 1863. Father Daniel Dade made regular trips from his parish in Visalia to tend to the religious needs of the people of Millerton. His visits continued until September of 1872 when many residents of Millerton were moving to Fresno.

In the beginning Fresno was a mission of the Visalia parish, but by 1878 local Catholics began a drive to raise money to build a church in Fresno. The new building would be at the southeast corner of M and Fresno streets on two lots donated by the Central Pacific Railroad. After reciting Mass at Magnolia Hall, Bishop Mora of the Monterey-Los Angeles Diocese promised to buy three more lots adjacent to the site. Fund-raising efforts were launched and on May 21, 1882, the brick church, named after Saint John the Baptist, was dedicated by Bishop Mora. Father Aguilera, the new pastor, had tremendous faith in Fresno's future. The site at M and Fresno was far from the commercial district of Fresno, but he knew the city would grow.

In 1898, a residence and two lots were purchased at Mariposa and R streets. Here a school was built and a convent was established for the Sisters of the Holy Cross, who taught in the school. Saint John's new pastor, Father McCarthy, was directed by his bishop to build a new and larger church, farther from town. The bishop wanted the new church to be located near the school. Many opposed the idea—Mariposa and R streets was at the edge of town—but Bishop Montgomery believed that one day Fresno would grow to be the leading city in the Central Valley.

The new church was built. Romanesque and Gothic in design, it was dedicated on June 7, 1903. Today, Saint John's Cathedral is the oldest church building in Fresno. In 1903 it stood on the outskirts of a young town. Today, it stands at the center of Fresno, a beautiful and proud symbol of a faith in Fresno's future.

St. John's Cathedral, as it looked in 1922. It still graces the corner of Mariposa and R Streets today.
Fresno Historical Society Archives

In 1940, war was raging in Europe. Most Fresnans echoed the sentiments of the rest of the country, hoping to stay out of the conflict. A local minister, at a Peace Rally, urged parents to refuse to send their sons to war unless the nation's borders were crossed.

However, Fresnans took steps to be prepared in case the unthinkable happened. A Home Guard was organized to fill the shoes of the National Guard if the men of that organization had to enter federal service. By October 16, six draft boards had been set up to register eligible young men to serve for one year. Many volunteered, thinking they would complete their service quickly.

Congressman Bud Gearhart revealed that the War Department had chosen Chandler Field as a major bomber base. By early 1941, it was decided that the space at Chandler was not sufficient and plans were drawn for a new site bounded by Clovis, Shields, Winery and McKinley avenues. Fresno bought the site and leased it to the Army Air Corps.

Construction of runways, hangars, barracks, and office buildings was begun. By April 22, 1941, the new facility was ready to receive the first of seventy-five bombers that were to be based there. In honor of Lieutenant Earl M. Hammer, the first member of the Army Air Corps killed in World War I, the new base was called Hammer Field.

By late summer, Fresno made another major concession to the war effort. All the streetcar tracks were torn up to be re-smelted and used in the weapons industry. Motorized buses became the new method of mass transit.

On December 7, 1941, the Japanese bombed Pearl Harbor. Shortly word was received that twenty-one-year-old Sammy Gantner had been killed in action, the first Fresno County man to lose his life in World War II combat. Two years later a destroyer, the *USS Gantner*, was named for him. But, on a bleak December day in 1941, Fresno County mourned his death. The war had reached home.

Courtship, Carts & Horses

Courtship at the turn of the century usually followed a specified pattern. After being formally introduced, the young man could send flowers, make formal calls at the young lady's home, escort her to a social event, or take her for a walk in Courthouse Park.

However, one Fresno couple found another way to spend time together. The young lady, Loverne Kinsley, lived two houses north of Fresno Street on O Street, just catty-corner from the Water Tower. Loverne was a tall, slender, beautiful young woman who always wore white dresses with long sleeves and high necklines. Her suitor, Henry McKay, owned the Fashion Shoeing Shop on I Street (now Broadway), a blacksmithing establishment. His brother, J. R. McKay, owned the very modern Dexter Stables next door. Between them they had the largest businesses of their kind between Los Angeles and San Francisco.

One of J. R.'s customers, M. Theo Kearney, spent a lot of time at the Dexter Stables discussing horses. From time to time wild horses were brought into town by train. Kearney would always be at the Southern Pacific Depot to watch them unload, and, perhaps, would choose a fine horse for himself which later would be brought to the Fruit Vale Estate by J. R.

It was Henry's job to break the wild horses. After hitching a horse to a breaking cart, he would head north on I Street, turning right on unpaved Fresno Street. Loverne, hearing thundering hooves approaching and seeing the cloud of dust coming toward her home, would call to her mother that she was going out and would run down the steps in front of her house to wait. After turning onto O Street, Henry would sometimes have to go around the block several times until he could slow the horse enough so that Loverne could jump onto the cart. And jump on she would, even in her lovely white dress, and off they would go until the horse was broken.

And, that was how the author's grandfather, Mr. Henry McKay, courted her grandmother, Miss Loverne Kinsley, in the Fresno of 1900.

The tremendous growth of Fresno during the boom period of the 1880s brought about many changes. One of the most important was the establishing of the city's first high school in 1889. It was named Fresno High because it would serve all high school-age young people in Fresno.

The initial student body totaled fifty students with three teachers and three grade levels, ninth, junior and middle. The senior class was formed a year later by those who passed the third level. At that time, it became a four-year school.

The first classes were held on September 16, 1889, on the second floor of the K Street School, located at Santa Clara and K (now Van Ness Avenue) streets. T. L. Heaton was the principal. The curriculum was classical—four years of Latin as well as English, history, science and math. In June of 1891, the first commencement exercises were held at the Barton Opera House. There were seven graduates.

The new school rapidly outgrew the available space and had to be moved to the White School, where the Memorial Auditorium is located today. Plans for a new high school building were underway. In September of 1896, the school year began in the new building on O Street between Stanislaus and Tuolumne streets. The new brick structure, with its stately clock tower, had the latest and most modern facilities, including a library, a chemistry lab, a gymnasium and a theater-style lecture hall. There were those who felt it was too far from town and that the land, which cost $7,500, was too expensive. In 1922, the school moved to its present site on Echo Avenue.

Over a hundred years after its founding, Fresno High continues to serve the students of this community. Although the curriculum has been broadened to meet the needs of today, the administrators of the school are well aware of the commitment to traditional learning that was made by those who formed the school. Today, the opportunity to pursue a classical education, including the study of Latin, still is available to the students of Fresno High School.

Fresno's first high school, Fresno High, was built in 1896. Located on O Street, it featured a theater-style lecture hall, a gymnasium, a library and a chemistry laboratory.
Fresno Historical Society Archives; photographer: A. W. Peters

Fresno's Favorite Native Son

Fresno residents in the late 1960s and 1970s often noticed an older man wearing a fedora hat and with a rather incredible walrus mustache pedaling his bicycle through the city's streets. The Gillis Branch Library on Dakota Avenue was a favorite stopping place for this gentleman. Always in a hurry, he would come flying through the library's front door and head straight for the newspapers. There he would settle himself in a comfortable chair and talk to the library patrons. He took a childlike delight in being recognized and for those who approached him he had many stories to tell. The normal silence of the library was broken by his booming voice, but no one seemed to mind.

This gentleman had been born on a hot August night in 1908 in an area of Fresno where many Armenian families lived. When he was three his father died. He and his brother and sisters spent the next five years in an Oakland orphanage, finally returning to Fresno to live with their mother. His jobs as a newspaper boy and a telegraph messenger allowed him to experience the drama of life that played itself out on the streets of Fresno.

He was determined to become a writer. He left his hometown in 1926 and lived in San Francisco, New York, Malibu and Paris, occasionally making brief visits to Fresno. He became a famous writer and the foremost exponent of the Armenian experience. But Fresno had shaped him and the need to touch base with his home increased as the years went by. In 1963, after purchasing an apartment in Paris, he bought two side-by-side homes in Fresno. For the rest of his life, he divided his time between the two cities.

For the people of his hometown, this great writer, this winner of a Pulitzer Prize and an Oscar, was a figure to be cherished. He put into words the unique things about Fresno that those who lived here felt, but could not always adequately express. The special scents of the harvest season, the abundant yields of the vineyards and orchards, the memories of a city growing up, and the joy and sadness of the Armenian experience all mingled to produce works that spoke to Fresnans in a singular way. For many Fresnans, William Saroyan was more than a great writer, he was one who was able to convey the essence of life in Fresno in a way that touched their souls.

Fresno-born, author William Saroyan was awarded the Pulitzer Prize and the Critics Circle Award for his play "The Time of Your Life." During his career, he lived in San Francisco, Paris and Hollywood, but for the last decade of his life he returned to his birthplace where he lived in a modest home on West Griffith Way in the northwest part of the city.

Cheney's Vision for Fresno

On June 1, 1918, Charles Henry Cheney submitted a general report to the Fresno City Planning Commission titled "Progress of a City Plan For Fresno." For Cheney, a French-trained architect and consultant in city planning, this report was the result of a two-year study. The report addressed alignment of railroad lines, streets and parks, but perhaps the most interesting aspect of the study was his design for Fresno's Civic Center.

Cheney saw Mariposa Street as "the grand central axis of the city." He considered the architecture of the old Courthouse to be of the highest quality and felt the view from the Southern Pacific Depot down Mariposa Street to that building was as inspiring as was to be found anywhere in America. He also noted that Courthouse Park was one of the finest public squares in California.

Cheney's plan called for creating an open square on Mariposa Street running from the Courthouse to P Street. A rectangular pool, flanked by topiary trees, would run down the center of Mariposa from M Street to O Street. Facing the pool would be public buildings in the classic revival tradition of the Courthouse. The mall would end on a concave curve with an auditorium and an open-air theater where the State and Federal buildings stand today.

Like other visionary plans for Fresno, this one was promptly forgotten. Today, the classic revival Courthouse no longer stands. Mariposa Street, however, has become a tree-lined mall with public buildings dotting its length. A new City Hall stands at the end of Mariposa facing the contemporary Fresno County Courthouse four blocks away, completing the Civic Center. The new City Hall is gracefully U-shaped. The curve of the building reaches out to embrace the mall the way that Cheney conceived in his plan. Cheney surely would be gratified.

Warehouse Row

One of the most distinctive of Fresno's National Register sites is Warehouse Row. Rather than a single building, the row is made up of three structures side by side. Located on P Street just adjacent to the Santa Fe Railway tracks, the row reflects a time when it was important for commercial development to be located close to transportation outlets.

The Wormser Warehouse was built in 1903 for the Wormser Furniture Company. In 1910, the Swift Company meat packing plant was built directly to the south. Like the Wormser Warehouse, it was constructed of brick. In 1919 it was expanded. Loading docks were added in the mid-1930s. In 1951, a tunnel was built under P Street to provide a direct connection to the eviscerating plant across the street. The Swift Company also built a hatchery across P Street. Having become exclusively involved with turkey production, the plant now could buy eggs, hatch them and sell the turkey chicks to farmers who would raise them to maturity. Then the farmers would bring them back for processing.

The Fresno Consumers Ice Company next door was built in 1903. Fresno summers made ice an important commodity. In these pre-air-conditioning days, a block of ice in the kitchen washtub with a fan placed strategically next to it provided the only available cool air.

It was the first ice company locally to make home deliveries. The delivery trucks were horse drawn and when the company decided to make the transition to trucks in 1924, it caused a near revolt among the drivers. The horses knew the routes so well that, while the ice man made his delivery at one house, his horse would pull the truck to the next home on the route and wait. The driver did not have to remember the patrons on his route! In 1946, the company moved from ice production to cold storage. At the same time the Swift Company next door leased the building and used it to store fresh-frozen turkeys.

Warehouse Row stands as a symbol of Fresno's early commercial development. A restaurant, architectural firm, design business and offices fit amicably into these buildings.

Of all the legends that live on in our Valley, none is more controversial than that of a young man from the Pueblo de Murrieta in Sonora, Mexico. Like many others, he was drawn to the mining camps of California when gold was discovered in 1849. His first mining claim was in Calaveras County. While he was there, a group of unruly men beat him, jumped his claim and assaulted his wife. He and his wife then moved to Angels Camp, where another tragedy befell them. His brother was accused of stealing a mule that he had purchased. The brother was lynched and the young man, Joaquin Murrieta, was horsewhipped.

Because he had been honest in his dealings, but had been treated so shamefully, these experiences turned him against the law. Out of a need to avenge these acts, he sought those who had wronged him to see that they were punished. When he found the miners who had abused his wife, he roped them and dragged them behind his horse until they were dead. Knowing a price was on his head, he sent his wife into hiding.

By 1852, his anger took another turn. He recruited a number of men to help him with his criminal operations, mainly horse stealing. Several gangs were formed. Among the gang members was Manuel Duarte, better known as "Three-fingered Jack." The Arroyo de Cantua, near Coalinga, was the headquarters and main hideout for the gangs. From there, they began stealing horses until one of the members shot and killed General Joshua Bean in Southern California. Then their activities moved north into the gold country where they went on a rampage of robberies and murders. Posses were formed, but the gang always eluded capture. Rewards were posted for the capture of the leader of the gang, but they went unclaimed.

Finally, the state legislature raised a company of men, led by Captain Harry Love, to bring the outlaws to justice. This company, called the California Rangers, forced the desperados to move their operations to the west side of the San Joaquin Valley.

On July 25, 1853, Captain Love happened on Murrieta's camp on the banks of Cantua Creek. A battle ensued during which Murrieta, on horseback, jumped off a twelve-foot cliff, falling from his horse. He was severely wounded, but tried to run toward the hills. He was shot again, this time fatally. "Three-fingered Jack" also was killed. The era of the Murrieta gang was over.

Today, the legend of Joaquin Murrieta lives on in the rocks and caves of the Valley that were his fabled hideouts. Each year on July 25 a trail ride is held at Cantua Creek to commemorate the end of his exploits.

The life of Fulton G. Berry was one of joyous fun and practical jokes. He also was a staunch supporter of Fresno and an important businessman, as owner of the Grand Central Hotel at the corner of J and Mariposa streets. As his life was lived with humor and wit, he decided that his funeral must reflect this important side of his personality and he planned it with great thoroughness.

The night after his daughter, actress Maude Lillian Berri, played in *The Rich Mr. Hoggenheimer* at the Barton Opera House, Fulton G. Berry died suddenly. Three days later, Fresnans crowded the large room at the Elks Lodge, which was decorated in the way it had been for the Berrys' golden anniversary party two and a half years before. Palm fronds and magnolia blossoms adorned the walls, evoking spring rather than a funeral. As the family entered, Mendelssohn's "Spring Song" was played, followed by "Home Sweet Home" and other songs that had been favorites of Mr. Berry. In the absence of a clergyman, M. F. Tarpey delivered the eulogy, which expressed the joy of knowing this man who had such a "contagious good nature." As the crowds filed past the casket, Theodore Rietz's orchestra played "La Paloma."

When the coffin was carried from the Elks Lodge to the sidewalk, a brass band was waiting. The funeral cortege, with the band leading the way, proceeded down Tulare Street to J Street playing such tunes as "There'll be a Hot Time in the Old Town Tonight." As the procession reached the Grand Central Hotel, the band began to play "Auld Lang Syne." Suddenly, a beer wagon appeared, dispensing draughts to the mourners. The marchers proceeded to the cemetery gates where the band launched into "Stars and Stripes Forever."

On this memorable day in Fresno history, the prankster played his ultimate practical joke, much to the enjoyment of all present. He also left an important legacy to the city he loved and supported so faithfully—a reminder that life is to be enjoyed and savored. In return, a grateful citizenry changed the name of J Street to Fulton Street in his memory.

The Physicians Building

The Physician's Building located at Fresno and P Streets. *Courtesy of Fresno County Free Library*

In 1926, six physicians formed an association to construct a medical building to house their offices. Their affiliation was not a group practice, each doctor had his own office and patients; but by pooling their resources they were able to build an architecturally significant structure with a shared waiting room for their patients.

They hired local architect Charles E. Butner to design the building which would contain twenty-eight rooms grouped into separate office units, each opening onto a central interior court. The court featured an octagonal fountain, a fish pond and a deeply coffered skylight which covered the ceiling area, allowing natural light to filter into the room. The exterior of the structure, at the northeast corner of Fresno and P streets, had white stucco walls and a red tile roof.

At the time of construction, this building was on the edge of town near residential areas, convenient to those who lived nearby. In the late 1960s, the building was modernized and many of its unique architectural details were lost or covered up.

However, in the 1970s, it was purchased by the Klein Group, and an extensive restoration project began which culminated in the structure being placed in the National Register of Historic Places. Today, the Physicians Building, the first of its kind in Central California, stands as a reminder of the grace of Spanish revival architecture which was unique to California in the 1920s.

In the early days of our city, before the new city charter of 1900, which designated a mayor-council form of government, was adopted, Fresno was governed by five trustees. They were elected in partisan contests from geographically defined wards.

West Fresno, which had the largest concentration of gambling dens, brothels and saloons in the city, wielded a great deal of power at City Hall. So great was this influence that the trustee from the Fifth Ward of West Fresno became the political boss of the city. Conditions were ripe for the entrance of the most corrupt politician in Fresno's history, up to that time.

At first glance Joe Spinney, a short, balding man with an enormous handlebar mustache, did not look like a man of influence; but, although he called himself an independent Republican, he had no party loyalty, was totally corrupt and represented mostly the vice interests of his district. Because two trustees were Democrats and two were Republicans, Spinney held the swing vote. He used that vote to push through political appointments, to secure building contracts, and to influence the hiring of police officers and firemen. A building contractor himself, he made a great deal of money erecting many downtown structures using the cheapest available labor.

At the first meeting of the board of trustees after Spinney's election in 1893, he was made chairman, thus holding the position of mayor of Fresno. He seized the moment to push through a number of political appointments and then resigned, nominating C. J. Craycroft to take his place. Spinney, who was illiterate and signed official documents with an X, preferred to remain behind the scenes where he could play power broker.

Even though he was Fresno's mayor for only a few minutes, his picture hangs at City Hall with the other mayors of Fresno, a symbol of the fact that he ran the city during the decade of the 1890s.

Joseph Spinney, whose headquarters was the Europa Hotel on G Street, was boss of the Fresno's tenderloin district in the 1890s.
Fresno Historical Society Archives

Thomas C. Hughes, the man who was to become known as the "Father of Fresno," was born in North Carolina on June 6, 1830. In 1853, Hughes traveled to California with his wife, Mary, and other members of his family. The women rode in a wagon pulled by four cows. The men drove a herd of cattle as they made their way across the country. After they crossed the California state line, the party was met by the eldest brother in the family who brought them new teams of horses and supplies. They settled in Murphy's Camp.

Two years later Mary and Thomas returned to the South, only to find that California beckoned. On the long journey back, Mary died, leaving her husband with three sons to raise. He settled in Stockton and engaged in farming and cattle raising. In 1866, he remarried and began a second family.

When he moved to San Francisco in 1874, Hughes met Dr. E. B. Perrin, a land speculator who was selling real estate in Fresno County. Perrin contracted with Hughes and his sons to take care of his seven thousand sheep. Perrin would furnish the range land. One half of the wool and lambs would belong to Hughes, who let his boys handle the sheep business while he became involved in real estate.

The Central Pacific Railroad made Hughes its agent. He began buying and selling land. Large profits were to be made, and wealthy men were brought to Fresno on special excursion trains to entice them to buy land in Fresno County.

Hughes began to dabble in other business ventures. In 1881, he helped to establish the Fresno County Bank. Later that year he incorporated the Fresno Fruit Packing Company. In 1888, he built the finest hotel in Fresno at I (now Broadway) and Tulare streets. By 1893, he was probably the best known man in Central California. However, that year witnessed a collapse of the land boom. Hughes was forced into bankruptcy and moved his family to Mexico.

When he died in 1919, flags flew at half-mast from all the public buildings in Fresno. It was an appropriate gesture for Thomas C. Hughes, the "Father of Fresno," the man for whom Hughes Avenue is named.

Seropians, Raisins & Boureg

One of the benefits of life in the Central Valley of California is the vast mosaic of cultures that exists peacefully together, enriching life and providing an expanded awareness for all who live here. One of these groups of people came here quite by chance.

Hagop Seropian left his native Armenia and settled in Worcester, Massachusetts. He soon developed a respiratory illness in the cold, moist New England climate. He needed to move to an area where many months of the year were warm and dry. The terrain and climate of the central San Joaquin Valley reminded him of his native Armenia. So, in 1881, he and his younger brother settled in Fresno. Two other brothers soon followed. They went into business, establishing packing houses where raisins and figs were boxed and shipped to markets outside of Fresno.

The Southern Pacific Railroad raised freight rates so high at one time, that the Seropian brothers refused to pay. Instead, they packed their produce on mule-drawn wagons and sent it over the Pacheco Pass to San Francisco. This dramatic display was reported in newspapers all over the Valley and gave impetus to the building of a second railroad now known as the Santa Fe.

More Armenian families came to Fresno, eager to become involved in farming. One of the major contributions they made was the development of the packing industry, which provided a connection between the grower and consumer.

As events in Armenia caused hundreds of thousands to flee, many came to Fresno where an Armenian community was already established. By the 1930s, Armenian young people were leaving agriculture and training to become professionals in other fields.

Today, four churches and a school provide a focal point for the Armenian community in Fresno. However, Armenian traditions are available to all Fresnans each August when the festival of the Blessing of the Grapes takes place. The religious celebration of the harvest is followed by food and dancing.

Next time you take a succulent bite of shish-kebab or taste a delicious cheese boureg, remember the Seropian brothers who paved the way for you to enjoy this mouth-watering experience.

The Temperance Movement in the latter half of the nineteenth century was supported by individuals who wanted to restrict the drinking of alcoholic beverages. Two national organizations, the Women's Christian Temperance Union and the Anti-Saloon League, exercised a great deal of political power. They influenced the passage of liquor laws which eventually led to the adoption of the Eighteenth Amendment to the Constitution, which prohibited the sale of alcoholic beverages.

Moses Church, the creator of the canal system in Fresno County, was a Seventh-day Adventist who devoutly opposed alcohol consumption. In 1877, he founded the Temperance Colony, also called the Church Temperance Colony, in an area of Fresno today known as Sunnyside. Church subdivided the land into twenty-acre lots which adjoined canals for easy access to irrigation. He sold his parcels only to purchasers who would pledge to refrain from smoking, to keep the air pure. They also could not make or sell intoxicating liquors and could not belong to any secret organization. Church was quite insistent that buyers of his land be people of the highest moral character.

In spite of these restrictions, the colony, containing thirty-two twenty-acre parcels, was sold out by March of 1878. Today, Temperance Avenue and Temperance-Kutner Elementary School are reminders of that long ago tract of land.

A Name Is a Name?

The names of cities in the Central Valley were often decided by the officials of the railroad that gave them birth. Some had Spanish or Indian names; others were named for prominent pioneers. Some present-day cities were renamed after their founding.

Scottsburg, located in Moody's Slough on the Kings River, was named for Fresno County's second sheriff. Its inhabitants were called Scottsburgers. After two devastating floods, the town was moved to higher ground and then moved again to its present location on the Kings Canyon Highway 180. In 1868, it was renamed Centerville. It was Fresno County's second largest community.

The town of Friant began its existence as Jones' Store. Then it was called Hamptonville and, later, Pollasky.

Herndon was originally called Sycamore.

The origin of the name of one Fresno County city remained a mystery for many years. Sanger was established in April 1887 when the Southern Pacific Railroad was completed from Fresno to Porterville. For many years local residents wondered how their town was named. Finally, someone asked the Post Office in Washington D.C., and the mystery was solved. A woman named Alice B. Sanger, who, in 1889, had been the first woman clerk in the White House, had just retired from the Washington Post Office after working there for forty years. After contacting Miss Sanger, it was discovered that her father, Joseph Sanger, had worked for the Southern Pacific Railroad. Officials of that company had named the new town in his honor.

As one travels through the great Central Valley, there are stories to be uncovered at every turn. Not the least of these are to be found in the origins of city names.

Fresno's Castle

As you travel east on Olive Avenue toward Blackstone Avenue, in the neighborhood where Zapp's Park used to be, a fascinating structure comes into view. At first glance, you might think you are seeing things, rub your eyes and look again. For there, silhouetted against the sky, is a castle in all its Norman glory. "In Fresno?" you ask. Well, yes indeed, and why not? After all, this section of Fresno, better known as the Tower District, contains the richest variety of architectural styles in the city. A castle, therefore, is most appropriate.

The castle was completed in November of 1928 and represents the major work of its original owner, Paul Kindler. Kindler, a German immigrant, was a master mason who worked with architect Richard Felchlin, designer of many of the major buildings in downtown Fresno. Kindler did all the stone and terra cotta work on the castle, which was designed by Felchlin. Shortly before he built his castle, he did the masonry work for the Security Bank Building at Fulton and Mariposa streets. Some of the terra cotta stonework that was not needed for that building was installed in the castle. The castle turret contains a carved terra cotta cornice over the front door, a fine example of Kindler's work.

When the news of the stock market crash of 1929 came over the radio, Paul Kindler and his wife, Meta, were seated in front of the living room fireplace. All of Kindler's money was invested in the market. He gathered up his worthless stock certificates and threw them in the fire. Broke and unhappy, he sold his home to Alfonso Borrelli, the founder of the Perfection Macaroni Company.

Today, Paul Kindler's castle is in the National Register of Historic Places and stands as a memorial to the talents of the master mason whose work adorns many of Fresno's finest buildings.

A Brick Church on U Street

At the corner of Mariposa and U streets stands a brick church of French Gothic design, with modified flying buttresses. The congregation that owns this distinctive building has a long history in Fresno.

Over a hundred years ago, in 1882, a band of people met in a home on F Street. Their pastor, the Reverend Aaron Walton, led the meeting. The result of this gathering was the establishment of the Bethel African Methodist Episcopal Church, one of the first churches in California organized by African-American residents and the first such church in Fresno. After meeting in several different locations, even a blacksmith shop, the congregation finally was able to build its first church in 1891. It was at Tuolumne and G streets.

By 1922, the congregation had outgrown its building, and it was decided that a new church should be built. This new building was the dream of the congregation's pastor, the Reverend C. C. Carter. Carter died unexpectedly, so when the new church was dedicated it was renamed Carter Memorial African Methodist Episcopal Church in his memory. On the day the congregation moved to the new building at San Joaquin and E streets, the members and many Fresno residents, led by the Reverend Hughes, marched from the old church structure to the new singing "Marching to Zion."

In the early 1960s, redevelopment projects forced the church to look for a new location. The vacant church at U and Mariposa filled the bill and with its move to this location, Carter Memorial Church became the first African-American congregation in downtown Fresno.

In 1969, the church became the first in Fresno to sponsor local federal housing programs. The Kearney-Cooley Plaza development serves as a symbol of the dedication of the Carter Memorial Church.

From its humble beginnings at that small meeting on F Street in 1882, the Carter Memorial Church has grown into a major congregation with great influence in the Fresno community.

A Sign for Van Ness

Kate Rehart Byerly photograph

A welcoming sign at the south end of Van Ness Avenue.

In the days before freeways cut their giant swaths across the landscape, the main road through the Central Valley detoured travelers into all the major towns. It made journeys by car rather long and tedious, but it gave travelers an opportunity to become acquainted with each city.

In 1917, a group of downtown Fresno merchants decided that it would help business if they made certain that travelers would follow a route through town that would bring them past their commercial establishments. They built a stucco and terra cotta arch over the southernmost end of Van Ness Avenue that officially welcomed visitors to Fresno.

Cars traveling north on Highway 99 turned onto Railroad Avenue, drove under the arch and continued along Van Ness Avenue through downtown Fresno. After a fire destroyed the arch, it was replaced with two Ionic columns and an arched truss that held a metal sign reading, "Fresno, Van Ness Avenue Entrance."

In the 1950s, the new Highway 99 bypassed the old entrance to Fresno. The arch became a victim of neglect. In 1980, the sign was repaired and illuminated with blue and rose-colored neon.

Now, Fresno's official arch has another addition, a slogan added by owner Frank Caglia. Just below the word "Fresno" he added, "The Best Little City in the U.S.A." Once again, the Fresno sign shines with a sense of community pride.

KMJ—Fresno's First Radio Station

Before World War I, newspapers and the telegraph were the only ways that news events could be communicated to the public. During the war, merchant ships and battleships began sending radio communication using Morse code. One ship, the *S. S. Matoa*, was assigned the call letters "KMJ."

In 1922, the San Joaquin Light and Power Company began an experimental radio station that was assigned the Matoa's old call letters "KMJ." The new station's broadcasts were infrequent and did not attract regular listeners.

Three years later a new owner, the *Fresno Bee*, promised at least two hours of broadcasts each night. At precisely 7:15 P.M. on June 12, 1925, Fresno's first radio station went on the air. The program that evening featured music by John C. Edwards and his Hotel Californian Orchestra, Spike Hennessey and his Rainbow Ballroom Band, the Crockett Mountaineers of Fowler, and a song called "Radio Love" written by two Fresno women. At 9:15 on October 28 a regular Monday through Saturday newscast debuted, using wire service material and stories gathered by *Fresno Bee* reporters. In 1929, KMJ became affiliated with the small Don Lee Network. Access to more programing allowed expanded listening hours. Six months later, the Don Lee Network became associated with the Columbia Broadcasting System and the first coast-to-coast programs were available in Fresno.

By 1940, the station had increased its power to 5,000 watts and changed to its present-day 580 frequency. In this year, KMJ left the Don Lee Network and became affiliated with the National Broadcasting Company. This allowed Valley listeners to hear Jack Benny, Fibber McGee and Molly, Lowell Thomas, Burns and Allen, Fanny Brice, and Will Rogers at 580 on their radio dial. Such regional programs as the Nation's Christmas Tree Ceremony and "The Forum for Better Understanding" were developed and broadcast nationally.

In the years since it went on the air, KMJ has developed into a station devoted to news and talk shows with an eye to heightening listener awareness of local issues while maintaining the highest standards of broadcasting.

Ralph
Giordano, profes-
sionally known as
Young Corbett III,
became Welter-
weight Champion
of the World in
1933. In the photo
above, Fresno
Mayor Z. S. Leymel
places a crown on
Corbett.
*Fresno Historical So-
ciety Archives*

Fresno's Finest Fighter

Boxing was a respected sport in turn-of-the-century Fresno. The old YMCA building on Broadway was the training spot for the fighters of that era.

In 1904, after the death of a boxer following a match, the board of supervisors outlawed professional boxing in Fresno County. However, boxing continued to be a popular neighborhood sport. By the time professional boxing was legalized in 1924, a number of fine young fighters were training in Fresno. One stood out from all the rest.

Ralph Giordano was born in Italy in 1905 and came to Fresno with his family four years later. He made his first boxing appearance by fighting Freddie Hall in a four-round draw—he was fourteen years old and weighed ninety pounds. Giordano had a unique left punch that, even at that young age, set him apart from other boxers. Those who watched him knew they were looking at a future champion. Time proved them correct as he went on to win the lightweight, welterweight and middleweight championships of California. But the best was yet to come. On February 23, 1933, this young Fresnan won the title of Welterweight Champion of the World.

On his return home three days later, he was accorded a hero's welcome. Driving south on Highway 99, his motorcade, with a police escort, approached Belmont Avenue where a thousand people awaited him at Roeding Park. He left his motorcade and walked through the crunch of adoring fans to greet his family. After posing for numerous photos, he got into another automobile, and as sirens, bells and whistles sounded throughout the city, the returning hero journeyed to Courthouse Park. Here, Ralph Giordano, better known as Young Corbett III, was honored at a reception and one of the most enthusiastic homecomings ever accorded a local hero.

Today, a statue of Young Corbett III stands outside Selland Arena. Frozen in bronze, the mighty left punch is there for future generations of Fresnans to look upon and to remember with pride.

Catherine Morison Rehart

103

In the decade of the 1950s, Fresno was still a small town. Downtown was a vital, pulsing area—filled with beautiful stores, lovely historic buildings, hotels with excellent restaurants and sidewalks bustling with people. Fresno State College sat nestled amid trees and lovely old buildings at Maroa and University avenues. There were only three high schools and the rivalry between two of them, Fresno High and Roosevelt, was the stuff of which legends are made. With the exception of Old Fig Garden, the city's northern boundary was Shields Avenue. Shaw Avenue was a two-lane road, urban sprawl was an unknown term, and the Sierra could be seen almost every day because the air was clear. It was the best of times to live in this beautiful Valley town.

The favorite pastime for teen-agers was "dragging the main." As the sun went down, in those days before the Mall, Fulton Street filled with cars filled with young people. After cruising up and down Fulton, the cars headed for the northwest corner of Broadway and Sacramento Street to Stan's Drive-In.

Besides offering the best burgers, fries and milk shakes in town, Stan's was the social hub of Fresno's teen-age community. The jukebox played all the favorites, including Chuck Berry and a new teen idol named Elvis Presley. At 11:00 each night, all car radios were playing KMJ. A program called "Stan's Private Line," which originated at the drive-in, played musical requests for two hours.

As the decade of the 1950s faded into the 1960s, the lovely small Valley town changed dramatically. Rapid growth brought with it new terminology—urban renewal, redevelopment, shopping malls, tract homes and, most frightening in its consequences, demolition. The face of the city changed irretrievably as buildings as diverse as Stan's and the Fresno County Courthouse faced the wrecking ball. Now the corner of Broadway and Sacramento is still. The songs of Elvis can no longer be heard. The downtown streets are quieter than before. When the heart of a city is torn apart, it takes a long time to heal.

Stan's Drive-Inn was located at the southeast corner of Sacramento and Broadway Avenues. It was one of the major social hubs for Fresno teenagers in the 1950s.
Courtesy of the Fresno Bee Library

In 1894, a railroad strike hit California. Rail service came to a halt for three weeks. Not only was passenger service into and out of the Valley nonexistent, but mail delivery ceased as well.

The postal delivery problem lasted only a short time due to the ingenuity of Arthur C. Banta, owner of the Victor Cyclery. He printed and issued a special stamp which read, "A.R.U. Strike, 1894, Fresno-San Francisco Bicycle Mail Service, 25 cents." This green stamp bore the picture of a cyclist crossing the Valley with mountains in the background and sagebrush in the foreground.

Banta then organized a group of cyclists to carry the mail. They rode in relays. From Fresno, the first rider's route went out Kearney Boulevard, over White's Bridge Road to White's Bridge, and into Firebaugh. The next rider took the mail on to Los Banos. A third rider rode over Pacheco Pass to Gilroy, a fourth rode the mail to San Jose and the fifth took it on to San Francisco. Each rider waited at his destination for the south-bound mail, and carried it back to his original starting place, thus making a round trip each day.

The service began on July 7, 1894. The Valley run was made through the hot, unirrigated sands of the west side. Creeks had to be waded, with bicycles and mail held over the cyclist's head. It was a race against time as each rider turned his packet over to the one who would carry it on. As hard as it was, the mail got through. Mail that was picked up in Fresno early in the morning was delivered in San Francisco eighteen hours later. A rather incredible fete for such an arduous trip.

On July 18, the rail strike ended and the bicycle mail passed into history. Today, the bicycle mail stamp lives on in the collections of stamp enthusiasts.

The Nation's Christmas Tree

In 1924, many years after the General Grant Tree in Kings Canyon National Park was dedicated to the memory of that great Civil War hero, Charles Lee of the Sanger Chamber of Commerce was visiting the Grant Grove area. As he stood at the base of the huge tree, a small girl approached. Looking up at the tree in awe, she stood for a moment in silence. Then she said quietly, "What a lovely Christmas tree that would be!" She turned and raced off. Lee stood silently watching her leave.

He returned to Sanger, but could not forget her words. He was so moved that he wrote to President Calvin Coolidge telling him about his experience. On April 28, 1926, President Coolidge officially designated the General Grant Tree as the Nation's Christmas Tree.

In 1925, the people of Sanger sponsored a religious service at the base of the General Grant Tree. As the years progressed, hundreds made the trip to the "Nation's Christmas Tree." The service held there on the second Sunday of each December is broadcast throughout the country.

The tree took on added significance in 1956 when it was dedicated as a permanent shrine to those who have died in our nation's wars.

As one stands before this giant sequoia, remembering that it was alive when Christ was born and that it is the oldest and largest growing thing on earth, one feels a sense of eternity and an overwhelming awe at this most precious legacy that has been given to us to treasure not only at Christmas, but forever.

A Memorial for General Grant

As you travel east on Highway 180, the road passes through the vineyards of the east side of the Valley, through Centerville and, finally takes you to the Sierra Nevada Mountains and the Big Trees area of Kings Canyon National Park. This extraordinary corner of Fresno County draws visitors from all over the world who walk awestruck beneath the magnificent splendor of these huge giant sequoias. The feeling of peace which envelops those who visit this spot is never to be forgotten.

Over a hundred years ago, in 1885, this area of the Sierra was not yet a national park. Only a few hardy pioneers lived nearby. In the summer of that year an event of great significance occurred. Ex-president Ulysses S. Grant, who, as general of the United States Army had led his Union troops to victory in the Civil War, passed away. The women who lived in the tiny Sierra community of Comstock Mill decided that a fitting memorial to the deceased president would be to dedicate the largest and oldest of the giant sequoias to his memory. Using dress material, they made a black silk rosette wreath with flowing streamers and planned a proper ceremony.

On the following Sunday, all of the residents of Comstock Mill set out on their journey. Babies and their mothers traveled in a light horse-drawn wagon. Everyone else walked or rode horseback up the steep hills to the grove of big trees. Along the way they gathered flowers, mostly purple penny royal, yellow wild iris, tiger lilies, and laurel. When they reached the tree, the little group placed the wreath high on the tree's large bulge and scattered the bouquets of wild flowers about the base. They sang a hymn, Arley Pursell gave a short prayer, and this small band of people stood in silence and paid their most sincere tribute to President Grant.

Today, visitors come from all over the world to stand at the base of the General Grant tree, which has stood for an estimated 2,000 years and stands 267 feet tall. As they gaze in wonder at this eternal monarch of the forest, time and eternity in this corner of California seem to stand still.

Soon after Fresno Station was established in 1872, residential areas began to develop east of the H Street commercial district. Because the area was hilly, the new streets had to be leveled. Teams of horses pulling scraping devices were used to accomplish this feat. When the process was completed, the streets were at one level with steps leading up to higher ground where homes were soon built.

K Street, which was to become Fresno's longest and most prestigious avenue, began its existence as a dirt road with a very undistinguished name. Nonetheless, prominent citizens such as Dr. Chester Rowell, Louis Einstein, Ed Schwarz and Frank Short built their homes along this street. The western boundary of Courthouse Park skirted it also. As the years went by, the city grew north and, with its development, K Street was extended.

On March 1, 1915, the name of K Street was changed to Van Ness Street, in honor of Van Ness Avenue in San Francisco, a wide boulevard lined with homes owned by prominent families. When Divisadero Street was crossed, Van Ness became an avenue, continued north to University Avenue and curved to Weldon Avenue, where median islands still give a certain prestige to this street in the two blocks that it takes to reach the curve onto Van Ness Boulevard. At this point Van Ness truly becomes a focal point for prestigious addresses in Fresno. As the boulevard continues through Old Fig Garden and curves toward Shaw Avenue, it is interesting to note that originally Shaw Avenue was named Van Ness and continued west until it made the grand sweep north to the San Joaquin River. Soon Fresnans began to call this stretch Van Ness "Extension."

Looking back to the beginning of K Street from the vantage point of 1996, it is interesting to note that a K Street or Van Ness address has always signified social or economic prestige. Like its counterpart in San Francisco, which was named for 1855 Mayor James Van Ness, to live on this street has always meant that one has truly "arrived."

Excitement filled the Fresno air on the night of Saturday, January 29, 1904, for, on that evening, one of the most famous English actresses of the turn of the century was appearing at the Barton Opera House. The vehicle for her performance was a play titled *Mrs. Dearing's Divorce*. Theater goers that night were not as interested in witnessing a classical performance as they were in seeing one of the most beautiful and acknowledged women of the time. The fact that this actress was also a particular friend of King Edward VII of England only added to her glamour and appeal.

On the following morning, the *Fresno Morning Republican*'s society column reported that the most fashionable audience ever to grace the Barton was in attendance that evening. The English actress was praised for her fine performance. Her beauty was acknowledged, but the reporter felt a scene in which she disrobed behind a screen exhibited her charms unnecessarily. Nevertheless, the applause from the gallery during the aforementioned scene showed that there were those in the audience who felt differently.

A fashionable after-theater supper, held in the rooms of Mr. and Mrs. Fulton G. Berry at the Grand Central Hotel, followed her performance. Those in attendance were entertained by the witty repartee between Mr. Berry and his beautiful guest, the actress Lillie Langtry, the legendary "Jersey Lily."

For many years a grand old home has proudly graced T Street. Built in 1910 by Henry Gundelfinger, this structure had been a part of a prestigious neighborhood which built up around Saint John's Cathedral.

By the later 1960s, the area had greatly changed and the Gundelfinger home was purchased by Bill and Esther Phipps, sight unseen, and was slated for demolition. Bill told Esther that she was not to go into the house and get any ideas about keeping it because the site was to become a parking lot for their mortuary business next door. As Bill left the next day to attend a week-long conference, his parting words were, "Stay out of that house!" Esther tried to, but the key on the dresser beckoned her to go next door.

As she walked through the house, her imagination soared. It was love at first sight. As she walked from room to room, she knew that this home, which had fallen into disrepair, could be beautiful once again.

Seizing her opportunity, she got busy scraping wood and painting. When Bill returned, the solarium was finished. When she told him what she had done, he was not pleased, but agreed to sit in that room and have a cup of tea. By the time the tea was consumed, he had agreed to let her work on the master bedroom, but with no guarantees that he would spare the home. When he saw the finished bedroom, however, he caught her enthusiasm and said he would lend his support.

For months Esther worked eight hours a day at her restoration task. All the activity piqued the curiosity of passersby who noticed debris being tossed out of upstairs windows as she worked at her feverish pace. Finally, all the work was finished. Esther had transformed the neglect of many years into a beautiful home once again. Today, the Gundelfinger Home is listed on the Local Register of Historic Resources. A preservation success story, it stands as a tribute to the imagination, determination and hard work of Esther Phipps, a lady who was not about to let an important Fresno legacy be destroyed.

The earliest recorded visit of an Episcopal minister to the Millerton area occurred in October of 1855. It happened in this manner.

Major E. A. Townsend of the Benicia Arsenal received orders to inspect Fort Tejon and Fort Miller and report his findings to Washington. He gathered a group of people to make the trip with him, including the Right Reverend W. Ingraham Kip, Episcopal Bishop of California.

They boarded the steamer *Republic* and sailed from San Francisco to Point San Pedro. At San Pedro, the party boarded a wagon which was pulled by four wild mustangs. The horses, when released, leaped forward and continued at a dead run until their destination of Los Angeles was reached. The exciting ride was made even more unforgettable by the driver, who kept asking his passengers which side they wished to fall on when the wagon turned over. The party visited the San Gabriel Mission and then traveled in a four-mule wagon to Fort Tejon. The trip took four adventure-filled days.

Bishop Kip conducted services at the fort. Then the party began another harrowing trip into the San Joaquin Valley. As the wagon traveled along the old stage road skirting the foothills, many groups of Indians were spotted.

On the morning of October 20, 1855, the party reached Millerton and continued on to Fort Miller. On Sunday evening, October 21, Bishop Kip conducted services in a large room in the officers' quarters. All of the officers and many of the soldiers attended. Young Mary Carroll, the first child born in Millerton, was baptized that evening.

Sixty-four years later on October 20, 1929, the Right Reverend William Ford Nichols, Bishop of California, and the Right Reverend Louis Sanford, Bishop of San Joaquin, along with other Episcopal clergy, celebrated this event by conducting services at Fort Miller. Today, the site of the fort is at the bottom of Lake Millerton, but the events of that historic day live on in the legends of the Valley.

A House of Learning

The campus at Fresno City College is the site of a Romanesque-style brick building which houses the library. It was constructed in 1933 at a cost of $260,000 and was designed to harmonize with the Administration Building which had been built earlier. There are more than 100,000 bricks on the outer walls, ranging in color from buff to purple. Eight terra cotta columns grace the front entrance.

As you climb the steps and enter the building through large oak doors, your eye goes to the large brass chandelier in the lobby. You also notice a graceful stairway which climbs to the second floor, its railing, with a grape design, providing a reminder of Valley agriculture.

As you approach the main reading room, today called the reference room, an inscription over the door catches your eye. It is taken from *The Souls of Books* by Edward Lytton and reminds students that "There is no past so long as books shall live." The reading room is the heart of the building. Long oak tables, their oak chairs filled with students, fill the room. The walls are lined with books. Light filters in from high windows on the north side of the room, supplemented by bronze lamps which hang from the ceiling.

But it is the ceiling that takes one's breath away. A mural portraying the evolution of civilization and Western culture through history covers the ceiling. Featuring portraits of John Amos Comenius, Jean Jacques Rousseau, Johann Heinrich Pestalozzi, Johann Friedrich Herbart, Friedrich Froebel, Horace Mann, Herbert Spenser, and John Dewey—the eight men who have had the greatest influence on modern education—it is a feast for the eyes. Designed and executed by Anthony Heinsbergen of Los Angeles, it alone is worth a visit to this building that is on Fresno's List of Historic Resources.

Steamboats on the San Joaquin

In the 1840s, before Fresno County was carved out of Mariposa, Merced, and Tulare counties, supplies for the few inhabitants of this area had to be hauled overland from Stockton. The going rate for this service was twelve to fifteen cents a pound. This system worked well when the weather was fine, but when the rains came, the roads became flooded and impassable. However, when the winter rains were extremely heavy, the streams and rivers filled and provided an opportunity for boats to take on the role of transporter of goods.

As the 1840s turned into the 1850s, Sacramento and Stockton, with their immediate access to waterways, developed shipyards. Most of the boats were light, needing only two feet of water in which to navigate the shallow and winding river channels. One of the little steamboats which was produced, named *Georgiana*, wended its way up the San Joaquin River as far as Tuolumne City.

After the Indian War of 1851, United States troops were posted at Camp Barbour, which was soon renamed Fort Miller. As more buildings were erected at the fort, the need for materials and supplies increased. As the Sierra snows melted in early summer, the San Joaquin River swelled in size, making it possible for the first steamboat to reach Sycamore Point near present-day Herndon. Government wagons met the boat and transported its cargo up the hill to Fort Miller. This was the beginning of an important business.

During the ensuing years, river traffic grew during the river's flood periods. Boats also carried freight to settlements on the Kings River. As the Central Valley developed into an agricultural region and canals rerouted the water to irrigate crops, the volume of the rivers decreased, and the romantic steamboats and barges faded into history.

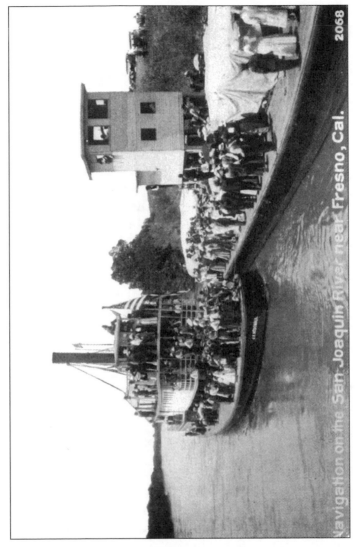

Navigation on the San Joaquin River near Fresno, Cal.

2068

The steamboat was a popular form of transport on the San Joaquin River during the 1860s and 1870s. This particular one, the J. R. McDonald, is shown taking on passengers.
Fresno Historical Society Archives

The Blockhouse at Fort Miller

The rush of miners to the San Joaquin River caused out breaks of violence among the Indians of the area whose way of life was being threatened by these newcomers. The ongoing violence became known as the Mariposa Indian War. The resulting peace conference and the drafting of the Camp Barbour Treaty, which was never ratified by Congress, created a huge reservation for the Indians, but left their spirits broken.

It was quickly decided that a military post should be established to maintain the peace. The site for this facility was to be one of the most beautiful spots along the river. This sweeping, flat land was covered with large oak trees and surrounded by hills. It had one problem, however; it was also the site of an Indian village. Lieutenant Tredwell Moore, the commanding officer sent to establish the military post, ordered the village burned to the ground. His soldiers then began to fell trees and build a fort, assisted by Indian labor.

The first building to be completed was the blockhouse. Built entirely of logs, which were punctuated at intervals with slots for rifles, the blockhouse consisted of two separate rooms connected by an open corridor. It was completed in 1851. Other buildings were soon finished: officers' quarters, a kitchen, a mess hall and a hospital. The complex was named Fort Miller by Lieutenant Moore, to honor Major Albert S. Miller, commander at the Army base at Benicia, a man whom Moore admired tremendously.

As soon as the soldiers moved in, the area became quiet. The town of Millerton, one mile down the river, became an important element in the social life of the rather bored men. The saloons reaped much of their profit from soldiers on passes from the fort. In 1856, the fort was deactivated. Many of the newcomers to the Millerton area found housing in the empty buildings. On March 19, 1860, the first school session in Fresno County was held in the hospital.

In 1863, at the height of the Civil War, the fort was activated once more. Colonel James N. Olney and his troops were sent to Millerton to keep the peace between the Southern sympathizers and those loyal to the Union. With arms drawn, they entered the town, but, to their surprise, they were greeted warmly. They occupied the fort until the following year when it was decommissioned.

The old blockhouse (as it looked at the turn of the centruy) stood on its original site until 1943 when the water behind newly built Friant Dam began to create Lake Millerton. The blockhouse was dismantled and relocated in Roeding Park. Today it is a museum administered by the Fresno City and County Historical Society. More important, as the oldest building in the county, it is a reminder of the time when the Indian population was threatened by westward expansion and of the new civilization that resulted.
The Image Group from the Laval Historical Collection. Courtesy of William B. Secrest, Sr. Collection

Dr. Buntaro Okonogi at the Okonogi Hospital, 708 E Street c. 1920. *Fresno County Free Library Photo Archive Japanese American Project. Collected by Yoshino Hasegawa and Keith Boettcher 1980.*

A white frame home tucked away on tree-lined A Street in West Fresno holds the story of one of the most beloved members of Fresno's Japanese community. Dr. Buntaro Okonogi was born in Fukushima, Japan, in 1872, the ninth son of a doctor.

After obtaining his medical education in Tokyo, New York and at Stanford University Medical School, he came to Fresno in 1901 to minister to the medical needs of Fresno's Japanese population. A year later he married Kiko Akiyama of Menlo Park. They had two children, a son and a daughter.

In 1901, Dr. Okonogi started his first hospital in a building at 736 E Street. Twenty-five years later he built a thirty-eight room brick hospital at the corner of E and Mono streets, where the Danish Creamery plant is now located. This full service hospital operated at this site until the beginning of World War II, when it was moved, in its entirety, to the Pinedale Assembly Center to tend to the needs of the Japanese people who were housed there. Both his son, Dr. Hugo Okonogi, and his daughter, Ena, joined him there; his wife had died in 1936. Dr. Hugo Okonogi was soon sent to the Merced Assembly Center where medical help was sorely needed.

Hugo enlisted in the 442nd Infantry, a combat unit comprised of native Americans of Japanese descent, and served in Europe throughout the remainder of the war. After the war, he remained in the Army as a career officer.

Dr. Buntaro Okonogi and Ena were sent to the internment camp at Poston, Arizona, where he was camp physician. When the war ended Dr. Okonogi returned to Fresno, where he practiced medicine once again.

In the years before World War II, Dr. Okonogi had served as president of the Japanese Association of Fresno and had established the Industrial Bank of Fresno. The bank gave Japanese Americans an opportunity to acquire property by offering loans during the years when it was difficult for Americans of Asian descent to make such purchases.

In 1950 Dr. Okonogi died. His great humanitarian spirit was reflected in his will, which provided that all of his patients' debts be canceled. The frame house on A Street remains unchanged. So, too, does the memory of the great man who once resided there and who dedicated his life to the needs of his people. The spirit of Dr. Okonogi will long be felt in the Japanese community of Fresno.

Right Out of Hollywood

Old Hollywood Western movies never seem to lose their popularity. They also carry a picture of life in America all over the world which is not altogether accurate. However, the early days of the western United States are reflected in the old movies.

There is one scene that all of these pictures seem to have in common—where the "bad man" comes into the bar and a shoot-out follows with everyone ducking for cover. It might surprise Fresnans to know that in the early days of our county, when the seat of government was in that wild town of Millerton, this scene was sometimes played out. In fact, Millerton's first murder was the result of whiskey and cards in Ira Stroud's Saloon.

The players of what began as a sociable game of poker were a man named Howard, a lawyer; a "bad man" from Texas named "Screwdriver Smith"; Dan Woods; Harris, a gambler from San Francisco; and David Bice James, a former soldier who came to the area with Colonel Barbour and John C. Fremont and stayed on to mine for gold. The card game was proceeding when an argument began between Howard and Smith. When Howard failed to locate his shotgun behind the bar, he fled. The game continued and Smith lost everything. He asked Woods if he could borrow ten dollars, but Woods refused. By this time the whiskey had overtaken any reasonable thoughts in Smith's mind and he threatened to kill Woods. Woods left the saloon and so did Smith.

By the next day, rumors were circulating that Woods planned to ambush Smith. And so he did. As Smith entered the doors of the saloon, everyone ran for cover. Having hidden outside, Woods entered the saloon and shot Smith in the back, killing him. Smith, who had a Texas five-shooter in his holster, never had a chance to draw his gun.

At the trial, Woods was easily found not guilty because the jury was prejudiced against bad men. Thus ended another chapter in the tales of the Valley, one not unlike those that have appeared on movie screens all over the world.

The area of Fresno which today is called "Old Fig Garden" was the result of the dreams and planning efforts of Wylie M. Giffen and J. C. Forkner. Advertised as the "Garden Home Tract" in 1919, this new development came with a guarantee to buyers which included the promise that the subdivision would ultimately be the finest residential area in Central California. Also, buyers were assured plenty of free water and that the trees and shrubberies on the avenues within the neighborhood would be planted and maintained free of charge for three years.

Along with these guarantees came a number of other "extras," such as electric lights and telephone service. Of particular interest to the modern homemaker was the assurance of free delivery of groceries, laundry, milk, ice and other essentials. After all, for a family moving so far north of downtown, this was an important plus. However, the Fresno Traction Lines ran nearby, thus creating the advantage to purchasers that downtown was only ten minutes away by streetcar.

The Garden Home lots were advertised as equal to ten city lots. The developers envisioned each lot containing a home set amid fifty Kadota fig trees. These trees, when producing, would give homeowners additional income from their property. It was from these trees that the area became known as "The Fig Gardens." Each parcel sold for from $1,250 to $1,500 with no interest or taxes for the first three years. Many years have gone by since the first lot was sold, but true to the promise of Mr. Giffen and Mr. Forkner, their subdivision became one of the finest residential neighborhoods in Central California.

Early Fresnans were fortunate in that there were several retail stores offering shoppers an excellent choice of wares. One of the earliest of these establishments was Kutner, Goldstein & Company, the "Universal Providers," which opened its doors in 1874. The store's humble beginnings were evident by the fact it was housed in a 25- by 60-foot room on H Street.

As the business grew, the owners purchased adjacent properties, adding to the size of their building. By the early 1880s, customers could visit three different departments. The hardware department offered all kinds of tools and nails as well as a varied selection of the most stylish Henry buggies, surreys, carts and wagons. The grocery department prided itself on its size, which was the equal of any similar establishment in San Francisco. Its shelves were filled with a full line of staple groceries and, for those who loved to entertain, a line of fancy foods. All of these items could be selected at the store and then delivered in a handsome horse-drawn wagon emblazoned with the Kutner, Goldstein name. Quite a boon for the housewife who had to walk some distance from home to make her purchases!

The third department, which stocked dry goods, was in a second building on I Street (now Broadway). A complete line of men's clothing, including domestic and imported suitings, awaited the fashionable gentlemen. For the lady who wanted that special gown for her "at home" afternoons when friends dropped in for tea, parlor gowns from Paris were available in a variety of fabrics and colors. Furnishings for the home, including parlor sets, sideboards, bookcases, carpets, curtains and wallpaper were displayed.

By 1889, branch stores had been opened in four Valley cities and in San Francisco. By this time Kutner, Goldstein & Company had become one of the largest businesses of its kind in the San Joaquin Valley. It flourished until 1929 when the Fresno and Selma stores were closed. Only the grain, seed and feed departments, which were the largest in the Valley, were kept in operation.

Kutner, Goldstein &
Company building.
Every imaginable item
could be purchased
within its walls.
*Fresno Historical Society
Archives*

A home on South Peach Avenue and a baseball park near Ratcliffe Stadium are tangible reminders of a very special Fresnan, John Milford Euless, affectionately known during his lifetime as "Mr. Baseball." As a young man growing up in Bellbuckle, Tennessee, Euless played on a sandlot baseball team, filling the positions of first baseman and, on occasion, pitcher. His passion for the sport continued after he came to Fresno in 1906.

In the late 1920s, he sponsored the Euless Realty team which was a part of Fresno's Twilight Leagues. One of the stars of the team was Monte Pearson, who later, as a right-handed pitcher for the New York Yankees, pitched victories in four World Series in a row during the 1930s. In 1941, "Mr. Baseball" became president of the Fresno Cardinals baseball team. A part of the California League, the Cardinals won pennants in 1941 and in 1948. Euless led a subscription drive to build a home for the Cardinals. The resulting ballpark was completed in 1941 and was named John Euless Baseball Park in his honor.

In addition to his contributions to baseball, John Euless conducted a successful real estate and insurance business. In 1913, he built a home for his family on South Peach Avenue that included such special features as sleeping porches, a deep porch, and a cement basement. Beautifully restored, the home is a proud part of its neighborhood.

The Euless home and ballpark are only a part of the legacy left by the man who was primarily responsible for bringing professional baseball to Fresno. Those who knew John Euless personally shared another legacy as well—memories of a tall, dignified Southern gentleman standing beside his roll-top desk in his Rowell Building office overlooking Courthouse Park. They remember a stately man whose warmth made him a friend to everyone—a man whose quiet sense of humor and charm went hand in hand with his professionalism and honesty in business. A truly legendary figure in local history was John Milford Euless, Fresno's "Mr. Baseball."

A Heroic Deed

As the modern woman asserts her right to equality and joins the work force in jobs that before were held only by men, it is interesting to look back to the women who lived a hundred years ago. The tales of the Valley hold the stories of a number of incredible women whose strength and courage led them to heroic deeds in a time when equality was never discussed.

One Fresno woman's story begins with her birth in Culpepper County, Virginia, in 1830. She was named Mary Brannan. Her first husband was Joseph W. Roberts, who enlisted in the Union Army during the Civil War and was killed in the Battle of Bull Run. Nurses to tend the wounded and dying were desperately needed, so Mary Roberts joined the hospital corps. The hospital where she was serving was captured by Confederate soldiers. In spite of their presence, she ran the Stars and Stripes up the flagpole to prevent the Union Army from shelling the building. The Union soldiers retook the hospital without harming those inside. Her quick thinking and courageous act saved many lives. At the close of the war, Mary Roberts moved to Bloomington, Illinois, where she managed an orphanage.

She married W. H. Donleavy in 1872. They came to California in 1880 and settled in Fresno. In 1892, Mr. Donleavy died. A widow once more, Mary Donleavy became involved in the plight of Fresno orphans who, because there was no local facility, were sent to a state-run orphanage in Vallejo. Appalled, she appeared before the board of supervisors to discuss the matter. The result was the establishment of the Fresno County Orphanage, which she managed as superintendent for three years. She adopted a boy, naming him for her late husband. Mary Donleavy's contributions to the orphaned children of Fresno County will long be remembered.

A footnote to this tale is that the Union flag which Mary courageously flew over the field hospital stayed with her throughout her life. Old and tattered, it comforted her in old age and was placed in her coffin when she died in 1927.

The Tower Theatre is located on the northwest corner of Wishon and Olive Avenues. This landmark building gave it's name to the neighborhood around it.
Courtesy of the Fresno Bee Library

In the 1930s, a small group of neighborhood shops began to develop around a five-block area two miles north of downtown Fresno. They served the new residential areas near Fresno State College and Fresno High School, which also began to grow during this time. And, they offered plenty of free parking to shoppers.

On the corner of Olive and Wishon avenues where, until recently, the Wishon Playground had been enjoyed by people in the neighborhood, a new structure was being built. By the time it was completed in late 1939, the Tower Theatre, with its "fluted concrete tower with linear ribbons of colored light capped by a flashing, starlike, neon-pronged orb," as described by architectural historian John Powell, had become such a landmark that it gave its name to the neighborhood.

On opening night, December 14, 1939, a private showing of the film *Balalaika* was followed by a party hosted by A. Emory Wishon, owner and developer of the theater, and Charles P. Skouras, president of Fox West Coast Theaters. The next day the public was allowed in to see *Dancing Coed* and *Henry Goes Arizona*.

As the years passed the Tower Theatre served the public well. Fresnans came to the Tower to view first-run feature films and enjoy free on-site parking. In those days before television, children stood in line on Saturday mornings, clutching their quarters, waiting to watch a morning's worth of cartoons. As the decade of the 1980s progressed, a repertory film program and, later, foreign films were shown.

Time, television and new theaters in the sprawling new neighborhoods all around the city dealt a blow—the theater had to close. The Tower's owner, Dottie Abbate, however, decided to save this historic landmark and threw all her energies into a plan for rehabilitating the structure. With the architectural firm of Kennedy Lutz Seng & Boudreau, interior designer Gary Steinert, and Venueteck Management Group of Napa heading the project, the plan to rehab the building into a theater for the performing arts was underway.

By 1990, the project was completed and the theater reopened. Since then it has received awards from the California Preservation Foundation, the San Joaquin Chapter, American Institute of Architects, and, in 1992, it won the highest restoration award from the League of Historic American Theaters, Washington, D.C.

On September 24, 1992, the Tower Theater was placed in the National Register of Historic Places, thus assuring Fresnans that this unique building will play an important role in our community for many years to come.

In a professional preservation project, the behind-the-scenes work involved in bringing a building back to life is often as fascinating as the history of the building itself. This is especially true in the case of the restoration of the Tower Theatre.

For instance, the exotic hardwood veneers in the theater's foyer had been damaged beyond repair. In 1939, zebrawood and golden nara were popular and readily available. However, in the late 1980s, these veneers were hard to locate and finding sources for these products involved a great deal of detective work.

The carpet contained a burgundy background with a stylized acanthus leaf design in shades of taupe, cerulean blue and black. Not a pattern one could walk into a store and purchase. The design had to be carefully coordinated to replicate the carpet. It was then made in Great Britain.

One of the theater auditorium's most unusual features is ultraviolet or black light. The sources for the light were hidden in hammered tin sconces, shaped like palm fronds, that were spaced along the walls. When turned on, the black light illuminated fluorescent wall and ceiling murals that glowed in the dark. At the time it was built, the Tower was only the second theater in the nation to boast this unusual device. Restoring the murals proved interesting. The man responsible, along with his assistants, for meticulously cleaning them, was Anthony Heinsbergen of Los Angeles, the son of the man who had painted these murals, also named Anthony Heinsbergen.

Let your mind take you back to 1939 when the murals were created. The work had to be done after dark. When the theater was darkened, the black light was turned on. The artist, perched on a scaffold, began to paint. Those watching could see only the strokes of fluorescent paint moving eerily across the walls. The artist was invisible—only his handiwork seemed to live. Indeed, it seemed to have a life of its own.

As a result of the professionalism and expertise of the team of architects, designers and artists who gave countless hours to this restoration project, the Tower Theatre is, once more, an important part of the cultural life of our community. The next time you attend a performance there, take time to look closely at the beautiful woods that enhance the foyer, the replica carpet milled in Great Britain, and the bas-relief etched-glass panel of "The Huntsman." Then, as the house lights dim and the black light comes on, sit back and enjoy the beauty of the murals that grace the walls and ceiling. And, then—let the show begin!

The Ewing Home

On tree-lined T Street, adjacent to the downtown commercial district of Fresno, stands a stately brick home. Designed by architect Eugene Mathewson in 1916 for attorney D. S. Ewing, the two-story home features a wide front porch. The deep overhang of the roof line, as well as the covered porch, provides shade for the windows and protection from the hot summer sun. The interior rooms feature mahogany moldings and wainscoting. A coved ceiling in the living room gives it a sense of space. The home has been continually used as a residence since it was built. The only major exterior change is that the original shingle roof was replaced by one of barrel tile.

In 1929, the home was purchased by Dr. J. H. Pettis. In 1939, the Pettises sold the house. In their haste to finish up the moving process something happened that was so horrifying it would strike fear into the hearts of housewives everywhere. Just before escrow was to close, Mrs. Pettis decided to place quite a pile of trash in the fireplace and light it. The resulting conflagration burned off most of the roof.

The month was May, the weather was lovely, and the contractor took his time removing what was left of the roof. In July, the upstairs of the home was still open to the sky. Mother Nature, in one of her cruel practical jokes, decided that Fresno should be blessed with a heavy July rainstorm. As vast amounts of water collected in the second floor rooms, the staircase turned into a waterfall of tremendous force and volume. Workmen were quickly called. Pushing wheelbarrows full of dirt, they forced their way through the torrent and built dikes in the living and dining rooms to direct the water out the front door.

Through it all, the house never trembled. The owners survived. The house survived. Which just proves that a well-built historic home can withstand almost anything, except, perhaps, an uncaring citizenry and the ever-present threat of the wrecker's ball.

Whenever the urge to read a new book strikes, Fresnans can run to the nearest branch of the Fresno County Free Library, select a book, present their library card, hurry home and begin to read. Nothing is more luxurious on a lazy spring day than curling up with a glass of iced tea and something wonderful to read. How easy it is to take this for granted! Such joys were not available to Fresnans in the earliest years of our city. Indeed, for the first twenty years of Fresno's existence, there was no library.

In November of 1891, Fresno's Board of Trustees appointed a Library Board of Trustees to raise money and find a place to house a public library. Their fund-raising efforts grossed the grand sum of ninety-two dollars plus the rent for rooms at Fresno and I (now Broadway) streets for ten months. On February 1, 1892, the Fresno Public Library opened for business. With Mrs. E. J. Latimer serving as librarian and her son as the staff, Fresnans were welcomed into the new facility. However, if you wished to use the library, you had to pay a subscription fee of five dollars per month. A year later, the board voted to change this policy. If you lived within a six-mile radius of the library, the fee was three dollars per month per family.

By 1896, the fee was waived if the patron paid county taxes and passed a rigid character test. Evidently many Fresnans were able to pass the test, because two years later the library could boast 1,500 patrons and 900 volumes. No longer depending on donations of books from private citizens or the local congressman, a book budget was now the order of the day. Indeed, the rooms at Fresno and I streets were now too small, and the library moved to the Risley Building on the corner of Van Ness Avenue and Mariposa Street. Fresno's library was coming of age.

Carnegie's Library

The Fresno County Free Library, established on February 1, 1892, was so popular and was expanding so rapidly that before it was ten years old it had outgrown two locations. The need for a new building was timely; Andrew Carnegie, the steel baron, was donating large sums to communities that wished to build libraries.

In 1901, Chester Harvey Rowell, who was serving as president of the Library Board of Trustees, met with Carnegie in Washington, D.C. He soon received a letter from Carnegie stating that he would donate $30,000 for a library building if the city of Fresno would tax itself $3,000 a year to support the library and would agree to provide a suitable site for the building. The city fathers and the library board agreed to Carnegie's stipulations.

A site at 1330 Broadway was donated, and plans drawn by the architectural firm of Copeland and Dale of New York were accepted. On December 8, 1902, the cornerstone was laid. Construction began. The new building would contain 4,400 square feet of service area and would hold 3,000 books. The building was officially completed on April 2, 1904. However, need for this new library was so great that many of the books were moved to the new facility in January, and the public was allowed access to the building at that time.

The exterior of the new structure was all that a library should be. The long, imposing facade featured six classic Ionic columns supporting a portico over the main entrance. The librarian's counter was just inside the main door. As you passed it and entered the reading room, the feeling was one of openness. Spiral iron steps ascended to the stacks which were housed on floors with open balconies with iron grills that provided safety for the partons. The two floors of stacks seemed to contain endless rows of books—a treasure trove of knowledge and endless hours of enjoyment.

For some fifty-plus years, until a more modern building was erected in 1959 to meet the demand for more space, the Carnegie Library served the needs of Fresnans well.

The Carnegie Library located at 1340 Broadway. Built in 1902, it was torn down in the early 1960s.
Courtesy of Fresno County Free Library

Pacific Southwest Building

Today, a clock tower at the juncture of the Mariposa and Fulton malls is a landmark for Fresnans. It stands at a spot that has been a crossroads of our downtown for over 120 years.

If you can close your eyes and imagine a time when the streets were simple dirt paths, when sidewalks were wooden planks and when horses ruled the roadways, you would see a different downtown Fresno. In 1881, a small wooden shack was erected at the southeast corner of Mariposa and Fulton streets. It housed a photography gallery owned by K. W. Jones. As years went by the wooden shack was replaced by other buildings, in turn a carpenter shop, an ice cream parlor and a milliner.

Then it became the site of a series of banks, the last being the Pacific Southwest Trust and Savings Bank. This bank purchased the property in 1922 and immediately hired the R. F. Felchlin Company to build a fifteen-story structure the bank had had designed. As construction got underway, the skyline of Fresno began to change dramatically. By the time it was completed in 1925, it was the tallest building between San Francisco and Los Angeles. It remained so until the Del Webb Building was erected in the 1960s.

The first floor of the new building was devoted to banking operations; the other floors offered office space for lawyers, dentists and other businesses. The total space in the building was 89,600 square feet. Originally, at the top of the building's dome, there was a flag pole surmounted by a beacon light for airplanes.

One of the treasures of the structure is a coffered, hand-painted plaster ceiling on the main floor. For many years certain office lights remained on at night during Easter Week, creating huge crosses on three sides of the building. Today, the structure's Corinthian columns recall another era to Fresnans who meet at the clock tower on the Fulton Mall.

Fresno Historical Society, R. W. Riggs Collection

In the early years of Fresno Station, before the city was incorporated, justice was rather loose. Disagreements were often settled by the parties themselves. This happened in the case of two members of the legal profession.

The year was 1884 and Grover Cleveland had been nominated for president on the Democratic ticket. However, the local Democratic party held differing opinions and decided that a meeting should be held to air these differences and formally ratify the candidate. The two lawyers, Walter Grady and Reel Terry, disagreed over who should chair the meeting.

On the evening of the ratification session, the hall of the Grady Opera House rapidly filled with voters of both parties. The local band began to play and the stage was graced by local dignitaries who were to speak. Grady held court near the entrance to the hall. Terry swaggered in, walked over to Grady, called him an insulting name and slapped his face. As Terry reached for his pistol, the weapon got stuck in the fabric of his coat and would not budge. Grady, who had already drawn his revolver, was shooting it in Terry's direction. Terry, trying to dodge the bullets, was dancing up and down while frantically trying to pull his pistol out of his pocket. A bullet struck his arm as Grady was overpowered by the onlookers.

As much as this strange one-sided duel smacked of slapstick comedy, perhaps the real comedy could be found elsewhere in the room. The band, on hearing the first shots, had dived through the orchestra doorways, wrecking their expensive instruments in their haste to flee. But, even the resulting tangle of reeds and brass left scattered about was nothing compared to the sight of grown men scrambling through the open windows fleeing into the night and running through the streets of Fresno as though the furies were after them.

For the few people who immediately recognized that Grady was aiming only at one man who did not have a prayer of fighting back and decided to watch the goings on from a safe vantage point, the spectacle was probably more memorable than any mere political meeting could ever hope to be.

It takes many things to create the sounds of a city. The peal of church bells, the laughter in a schoolyard, the lyrical singing of birds on a spring morning, the whistle of a train as it approaches a crossing, the scream of sirens, the noise of traffic—all these and more blend together in a symphony of sounds that create the music that is Fresno.

In one Fresno neighborhood in the late 1920s, however, a sound could be heard six days a week that was so unusual that it stood apart from all others. Was it a whistle? No, it could not be. A whistle blew only one note. But, this—whatever it was—sounded not just one note, but a whole octave and sharps and flats as well! This sound might have been a mystery to residents of other parts of Fresno, but for those who lived near H and Santa Clara streets there was no mystery at all. The music did come from a regular police whistle; but, in the hands of postman Andrew Weir, the humble whistle became an instrument that serenaded those on his route. The strains of "La Paloma," "In a Little Spanish Town," "Moonlight and Roses," "When Johnny Comes Marching Home," and "Stars and Stripes Forever" wafted through the streets of this downtown neighborhood as he delivered the mail.

How did he do it? After serving as a bugler in the Spanish-American War, he decided to master the whistle. It posed quite a challenge. But he eventually found that by placing his thumb and first finger on the vent of the whistle and moving them into different positions he could create a vast range of tones. This allowed him to create a whole repertoire of music for his postal route. Today, the sounds of our city are, perhaps, a little noisier. But on a hot summer night when the city is still, there are those who say that, if one listens carefully, the strains of "La Paloma" can still be heard drifting across the downtown streets, borne on the gentle, cooling breeze that Fresnans love so well.

The Pioneer Women of Fresno

The roots of our city lie not in the dreams of a railroad entrepreneur, but in the toil, sweat and commitment of a small group of untiring people who came to a vast open space where three creeks converged onto the plains of the central San Joaquin Valley. They began to arrive in April of 1872—that most beautiful of months—when the Valley became a carpet of wildflowers stretching as far as the eye could see. The hogwallows, that would later test a developer's skill, were home to horned toads and rattlesnakes. Squirrels and owls nested on the ground and herds of antelope and elk swept across the plain. Mother Nature blessed the Valley in spring.

But, for those who came to Fresno Station in those first months, life was hard. By June, Mrs. Russell Fleming was creating the first home in Fresno for her husband and children. The thin walls of her home gave little respite from the heat of summer. She had to cook all the family meals on an iron stove fired by wood that had to be brought from the foothills. Water was available, if she cared to go out to the back yard and pump it by hand—in the stifling heat of summer and the freezing cold of winter—and then carry it to the kitchen. Every article of clothing was washed by hand. A heavy flat iron was heated on the wood stove, then brought to a blanket-covered table where the business of ironing all the starched clothes took place. Mrs. Fleming had little opportunity to rest or to complain. Her day was too full. Instead, she concentrated on her family's needs and put all her strength into creating her home.

It was Mrs. Fleming and the other women who came to Fresno Station in that first year who set down the firm roots of our community. Their husbands established businesses and are remembered. But these pioneer women are rarely thought of; indeed, most have been forgotten. Perhaps, it may be fitting from our vantage point to pause and to remember their contributions which created the foundation on which Fresno is built.

Fresno Pioneer Families

LIZZIE. ANNIE. JULIA. RUSSELL. WILL. FLEMING. MRS. FLEMIN. ISABELL. GEORGE. ROSE. ALICE. FLORENCE. RUSSELL JR.

RWRiggs
Fotografer.

The Russell Fleming family. In this composite, all the members of the family are identified by their first names with the exception of Mrs. Fleming who is known only as "Mrs. Fleming." Russell Fleming was the first postmaster in Fresno Station. Mrs. Fleming was the first homemaker.

Fresno Historical Society Archives, R.W. Riggs Collection

Fresno's War Hero

At the end of World War II, there was such great rejoicing on Fulton Street that only a healthy dose of tear gas could calm the jubilant throng! Indeed, Fresno has rarely seen such community excitement as that experienced on V-J Day, August 15, 1945. Fresnans were overjoyed that the terrible war was over. Along with their rejoicing, there was also a tremendous sense of pride in the young men from Fresno who had served with such distinction. Although many believed that one of these young men was the most decorated U. S. Marine in World War II, it could be said with certainty that he was Fresno's most decorated military hero. A participant in the battles of Tinian, Saipan and Makin Island, Lieutenant Victor Maghakian was awarded the Navy Cross, the Purple Heart with a gold cluster, the Gold Star, two Silver Stars, the Defense Medal, a second Purple Heart and the Presidential Citation of his division.

Serving his country was not new to Maghakian. Prior to World War II, he had enlisted in the Marine Corps for four years, serving in every port in the Far East. During the early part of the Sino-Japanese war, he was a member of the expeditionary force in Shanghai. At the time of his discharge in February 1940, he was awarded a good conduct medal. In November of that same year, he was ordered to report to active duty once again. On December 9, he reported to the Marine Barracks on Mare Island.

From that date on, once again he served his country with great distinction. Two of his brothers, Harry and Michael Maghakian, also served in the armed forces during the war. Like so many other Fresno families who sent their sons to war, the Maghakians lived for several years with mixed feelings of pride and concern. When our boys from Fresno came home, the community poured out its feelings in a celebration. As at the end of World War I, Fresnans were united in their feelings of thanksgiving and happiness.

For as many years as Fresno has existed, the city's central plaza has been Courthouse Park. Long the center of Fresno County's government, it has been, until fairly recently, a social center as well. In the earliest years of our city, before the trees were even planted, evangelists pitched their tents in the shadow of the original box-shaped Courthouse building. As the city grew, the Courthouse did as well, acquiring wings, columns and a more impressive dome.

By the turn of the century, Sunday band concerts were held in the park, couples courted walking its shaded paths, and on hot summer evenings, the park was filled with most of the city's inhabitants, walking, visiting, and enjoying the cool respite the large trees offered.

On important occasions Courthouse Park drew Fresno's residents into its familiar landscape. The end of World War I, the funeral of Dr. Chester Rowell, and the triumphant return of Young Corbett III were just a few of the times that Fresnans came in huge numbers to give thanks, grieve or rejoice near the steps of the majestic, old Courthouse. The building provided a fitting backdrop. It seemed so timeless, so permanent that just by its very existence, it offered comfort and strength.

Today, Courthouse Park, without its majestic building, has changed. Within its confines, many memorials may be found, but not as many people. Dr. Rowell looks down from his comfortable chair on a city he might not recognize.

Although changed, Courthouse Park still plays an important role in the life of Fresno. It is one of the few places left that one can look to and feel some essence of what once was. On the east side of the new Courthouse, just as one emerges from the walk-through, there is a large marker. Standing before it, if one tries to imagine the Valley as it is described here, for a timeless moment the years melt away.

In 1948 Fresno received distinction as one of the twelve best cities in the nation. In an article in the *American* magazine titled "Is Your Town Fit To Live In?," a consultant on city planning named Guy Greer reported on a study made at Columbia University. In this study, E. L. Thorndike and his staff conducted a survey of 310 cities across the country. They considered: schools, parks, sanitation, literacy, home ownership, crime, traffic conditions and hospitals.

Twelve cities were selected as the best. Pasadena was rated the top city. The other top towns were Montclair, New Jersey; Cleveland Heights, Ohio; Springfield, Massachusetts; Grand Rapids, Michigan; Minneapolis, Minnesota; Rochester, New York; Seattle, Washington; Madison, Wisconsin; and three other California cities: Fresno, Los Angeles and San Diego. According to the article, these twelve cities were where "the goodness of life abounds." Fresno was selected, the authors said, not only because it had all of the material qualifications in great abundance, but also because it had a climate that was nearly ideal. They cited the relatively low humidity as an important factor in good health and comfortability.

As we reflect on this article written nearly fifty years ago, we cannot help wishing for the time when our city was still a small town, unaffected by big city woes. However, one thing does remain fairly constant—the Fresno climate. Often the subject of complaints when the thermometer soars over 110 degrees or the tule fog sets in—it might be pointed out that there are few places outside of our Valley where you can enjoy the glorious reds and golds of autumn without having to shovel snow a few weeks later; where, on many days of the year, the grandeur of the Sierra is unveiled in all its breathtaking splendor; and where, in springtime, the blossoms of the orchards create sweeping vistas of pink and white and fill the soft air with subtle fragrances. At these times, the 100-degree temperatures and the tules seem a small price to pay for the privilege of living in a place where nature's beauty is all around us, without asking for too much in return.

Gordon G. Dunn

In February of 1948, the citizens of Fresno knew they were entering a new era of politics in local government. The streets were buzzing with speculation about the man who had just announced he was running for mayor.

Gordon G. Dunn was the son of a pioneer family. His grandfather, Thomas Dunn, had served on the city council. His father, William, had been a deputy city clerk in 1910 and was manager of the Associated Oil Company's Fresno division. Although he was no stranger to local politics, Dunn was running in a municipal election for the first time.

Gordon Dunn, at age thirty-six, had already had an eventful life. A graduate of Stanford University, he had distinguished himself as a discus thrower while attending that institution. He participated in the Olympic games in Berlin in 1936 and won the silver medal in the discus event. He had won fifteen gold watches competing in the West Coast Relays over a number of years. His feats won him the name "Slinger Dunn."

He served in the United States Navy during World War II and, after the war was over, actively participated in the American Legion, the Navy Club and the organization for the Naval Reserve officers, holding offices in these groups. He also served as president of the Fresno chapter of the Stanford Alumni Association.

After the war, he went to work for his father's company, Associated Oil. Six years later, he joined West Coast Aggregates, Incorporated. Having such a distinguished background prepared him for the office he sought. Everyone was proud of his achievements and looked forward to hearing his platform statement. However, few were prepared for the upheaval that was to come and was to earn him the sobriquet "No Fun Dunn."

A few days after Gordon G. Dunn announced his candidacy for mayor of Fresno, he issued his platform statement. He would, if elected, work to attract more industries to Fresno. He vowed that he would strive for more efficient use of police and fire department personnel to clean up vice and crime in Fresno. He would create more recreational facilities to keep young people off the streets and would use the Memorial Auditorium for public recreational purposes.

He called for closer cooperation between the citizens of Fresno and local government and for a liaison between city and county government. He stressed the need to maintain the mayor's office in such a way that all groups would have an equal hearing. He said, "I want to make Fresno a better place for your children and mine. I want to clean it up and administer it so that all its citizens can point with pride to our city, Queen of the Valley."

Some of these platform statements had been heard before; but, to the citizens of post-World War II Fresno, the focus on cleaning up the town, especially the Tenderloin district, had a welcoming ring to it. Dunn accused the police department, which was directly controlled by incumbent mayor Glenn DeVore, of being graft-ridden. He also portrayed Fresno as being known throughout the state as a notoriously open town.

The campaign was unpleasant. On election day, 63 percent of the registered voters of Fresno turned out at the precincts. Gordon Dunn was elected mayor of Fresno, the youngest in the history of the city. His first order of business was to shake up the police department as it had never been shaken up before. The fun was just beginning.

The first item on newly-elected mayor Gordon Dunn's agenda was to "clean-up" the police and fire departments. He charged the police and fire chiefs with seriously mismanaging their departments and demanded their resignations and that of their key officers. He appointed men to replace them.

Then he called in the State Attorney General's office to investigate the corruption and vice that he alleged ran rampant through both departments. This attracted the attention of both the Internal Revenue Service and Washington columnist Drew Pearson. Pearson alleged in his nationally syndicated column that the Fresno police chief had been accepting payoffs. The end result was that the former police chief was convicted of income tax evasion, fined $10,000, and sentenced to two years in prison.

Dunn's next target were the brothels and cheap bars that had added a certain local color to an area of downtown since the city was founded. Once again columnist Pearson came to his aid, and listed Fresno's bawdy houses in his Washington newspaper. The *Fresno Bee* picked up the story, which listed each establishment by name and address. A few were located on F, G and H streets, but most were either on Broadway or Tulare Street. The names ran the gamut from the Sly Rooms and Jade Rooms to the more respectable sounding Ritz Rooms and the Fairmont Hotel. Raids were ordered and the bawdy houses were shut down. Regular inspections assured the mayor that these places of business had become respectable and had not returned to their former practices.

This constituted quite an upheaval for a city that had its roots deep in the traditions of the pioneer West. Most of the populace applauded the mayor's efforts. Others were not so sure. However, on one matter both sides agreed. The mayor's new nickname was well-earned. Henceforth he was known to one and all as "No Fun Dunn."

As we continue with the story of Mayor Gordon Dunn, we find that his 1949 policy to "clean up the town" was gaining support from many different quarters. According to an article in the January 16, 1950, issue of the *Fresno Bee*, the West Fresno Chamber of Commerce commended him for "making an earnest effort to give to Fresno a civic government of the highest type, free of all political influence. While this may not be the opinion of certain elements; it is the consensus of decent, law-abiding people."

Two years later, in an article in *Pageant* magazine, author Al Stump declared that Gordon Dunn was the "toughest mayor in the United States." The article reviewed Dunn's election campaign and quoted the report given by the state vice agent that Fresno was "clean as a whistle" with no "evidence of rackets operating." In his conclusion, Stump declared that "Fresno, California, in 1952, is a model for the whole country to observe." And then he asked the question, "Will it stay that way?" In 1952, Fresnans felt sure it would.

In the campaign of 1953, Dunn ran on his record of reform against anti-reform forces, which were composed of real estate and vice interests. These groups mounted a well-financed radio and newspaper advertising package. It did not have much effect. Dunn won the election by a margin of two to one.

The election also had another result. One of the items on the ballot was to have a new city charter which would end the commission form of government and replace it with a strong mayor. A board of freeholders who would work out the details also was elected. The vote on this issue was 4 to 1. However, a year later a special election was called over this issue. The voters did not like the plan the freeholders drew up, but they did approve enlarging the membership of the city commission. The charter issue would be raised again during the next four years.

L ife in the mining camps of Central California was not easy. Men eked out a living with the toil of their hands and the sweat of their brow. Only a few lucky ones struck it rich. Most made just enough to live on and just enough to make them think that the next time their pick hit the ground, it might strike gold.

When people are living under such conditions, the social structure changes. The social niceties are usually nonexistent. And so it was at Fine Gold Gulch, nestled in the hills just east of the great Central Valley.

Whenever a new wagon came to a mining town, the men, who probably had not seen a young woman in some time, would look at the new arrivals and choose a wife. Many times, the young woman was a small child. In this case, the man would form a friendship with the family while he waited for her to grow old enough to marry. Then there were other instances when the young woman took matters into her own hands.

Mary Agnes Lewis, daughter of Malvina and "Doc" Lewis, lived in Fine Gold Gulch with her family. One day she overheard Joseph Burns, who owned a ranch and mining business in Coarsegold, ask her parents for her hand in marriage. Her mother disapproved, but her father said yes. Mary Agnes, who was just fourteen years old, donned her best dress, went outside and hid until Joseph came outside.

When she saw him walk to his horse, she stepped out of her hiding place and confronted him. She told him that she would marry him if the marriage could take place on that very day. He lifted her onto the back of his horse and together they rode off to Coarsegold. Justice of the Peace J. William Maughlin wrote out the marriage license and performed the ceremony, the first recorded marriage in the new county of Fresno.

Fresno's Scots Bell

Those among us whose memories go long into the history of Fresno may remember a lady who had such a powerful and distinctive speaking voice that if she entered a crowded room it was impossible not to be aware of her presence. As she spoke, the most mundane conversation became poetry—such was the magic that her voice produced.

She was born in Glasgow, Scotland, in 1873. Her parents immigrated to San Francisco and then to Fresno where her father engaged in farming. She went to local schools and graduated from the University of California at Berkeley with a bachelor of arts degree in English and Latin. Her first love had always been music, and after graduation she began to study voice in San Francisco, New York and London. In London, she worked with the great voice teacher, Plunkett Greene, studying the folk songs of Scotland, the Hebrides and England. Her concerts in England and California won her praise for her powerful voice and dramatic style.

In 1905, she helped to form the Fresno Musical Club. Eight years later she began a thirteen-year term as president of that organization. It was she who suggested presenting a public subscription series that enabled the club to bring outstanding artists to Fresno for many years. She oversaw the development of the Musical Club as it grew to become one of the largest organizations of its kind in the state.

She was a charter member of the American Association of University Women's Fresno branch, and was selected the Foreign Born Citizen of the Year in 1964. After she ended her singing career, she presented readings to local groups and continued to teach voice and elocution. She lived to the age of ninety-seven. Scholarships are given each year at the San Joaquin Regional Metropolitan Opera auditions in her memory. These are possible because of her generous bequest to the Fresno Musical Club.

Those who remember Miss Bell Thompson Ritchie and voice students who have been the recipient of her generosity know that Fresno is a richer place because she lived here.

Bell Thompson Ritchie. Remembered for her service to the Fresno Musical Club which, during her tenure as president, began subscription concerts that for many years brought the finest musicians in the world to Fresno.
Fresno Historical Society Archives

A Squirrel Named Jimmie

For many years, indeed from the time our grand old Courthouse was built in 1874 until well into the 1950s, some kind of tank house or water tower had graced Courthouse Park. In the earliest years of our city, a two-story windmill pump brought water from the ground. Townsfolk took their buckets to the park, filled them with water and carried them home. For many Fresnans, this was the main source of water.

In later years, a more imposing water tower sat on the M Street side of Courthouse Park, between the south wing of the Courthouse and the Hall of Records. It was part of the water system for the buildings in the park, but it served another purpose as well. Living in the park were dozens of bushy-tailed squirrels. These little fellows spent their time begging for food from park-goers and scampering up and down the park's many trees.

One squirrel stood out from all the rest. Fourteen-year-old Jimmie was not content with merely climbing trees; he made a habit of climbing the water tower as well. All day long he would play with the other squirrels, but when darkness began to fall, he would race up the steel rungs of the 100-foot water tower to the very top without missing a step. Here he built his nest and resided in a kind of comfort unknown to the other squirrels. When morning came, instead of descending the steel rungs, he would leap from the top of the water tower to nearby trees and scamper down onto the grass. The other squirrels would not be far behind.

But, it was always Jimmie who was first in line when Park Officer James Ross handed out the daily ration of cracked almonds to the park's small inhabitants. Everyone knew Jimmie, but it was only Officer Ross who received Jimmie's affection. For those who spent time in Courthouse Park in the 1930s and 1940s, one of the most unforgettable sights was of one rather large bushy-tailed squirrel sitting on Officer Ross' knee. It was a special friendship that, in its own way, is worthy of chronicling in the legends of the Valley.

New Year's Eve – 1883

On New Year's Eve in 1883, the Odd Fellows Hall became the setting for an amazingly diverse assemblage of people. For the uninvited guest who wandered into this throng, the sight was awesome. As his eyes surveyed the room, he recognized Cardinal Richelieu, President Washington, Othello, Aunt Dinah (of popcorn fame), clowns of various nationalities, a beggar woman, a wheelbarrow man, women in dominoes, royal princes and princesses, elegantly attired men and women, and a number of buffoons. After blinking several times, the guest no doubt realized that he had happened on one of the grandest costume parties ever in the history of the young city.

The evening festivities began at 9:00 P.M. with the entrance of Grand Marshal Leopold Gundelfinger, who led the assemblage in the Grand March. Never had so many plumes graced so many elegantly coiffed ladies. Never had so many handsome gentlemen bowed which such grace. At midnight, the masks came off and prizes were given for the best costumes, amid much applause and laughter. Then supper was announced and the guests paraded to the French Hotel where a lavish banquet awaited. The music of Boyle's Band enticed those who wished to dance. The party lasted until dawn. And that is how many of the citizens of Fresno ushered in the New Year of 1884.

Permelia E. Baley

The stories of the people of our Valley vary as much as their special personalities. However, there are a few people who seem set apart from all the others. Such is the person of Permelia E. Baley.

In 1858, Mrs. Baley left Jackson County, Missouri, with her husband, children, three-week-old baby, and other members of the family to travel in a wagon train headed west to California. The trip was fraught with hardships few modern women could imagine, including a battle with Indians, the loss of their livestock and wagons, and a long walk to Arizona where they stayed for seven months trying to recoup their losses.

They started out again for California, arriving at Millerton in 1860. Here she made a home for her family. Meals were cooked in an open fireplace, dishes were washed in an iron pot on the hearth, all the family's clothes were made by hand and washed with soap she made from oak-ash lye and scraps of fat. When her daughter, Elizabeth, died in 1872, leaving five children and a baby scarcely a month old, she took the baby into her home and raised it as her own child.

When the county seat moved to Fresno in 1874, her family moved there also. Her life became a little easier in a material way, but tragedy seemed ever present. In the diphtheria epidemic of 1878, five of her grandchildren and her youngest child, Lewis, who was just seventeen, died of the terrible disease. Her husband was a respected judge and founder of Fresno's first church, much of which he built with his own hands.

After the collapse of the 1887 boom, the Baleys lost their home. The judge died soon after. Mrs. Baley lived until 1906. The tribute in the *Fresno Morning Republican* praised this noble woman, who was beloved and respected as one of the pioneers who built Fresno County. Perhaps an even greater tribute was paid at her funeral. Six of her grandsons carried her casket to the Methodist Episcopal Church South at Fresno and L streets. After the service, her casket was carried, by one of Fresno's last horse-drawn funeral carriages, to the foothill community of Academy. Her body was laid to rest next to that of her husband in a small plot surrounded by an iron fence.

The peace of this lovely site belies her difficult life. Her story is testament to all the pioneer women who laid the foundation that made our county great.

Permelia E. Baley, wife of Gillum Baley.
Courtesy of Willetta Pokorny and Charles W. Baley

Ex-mayor Parker Lyon, who had ruled Fresno with a toughness softened by his flair for the ridiculous, left Fresno under a bit of a cloud to spend the rest of his life running a museum. For those who remember Mayor Lyon and his escapades with such local celebrities as Moocow Molly, it would be safe to assume that any museum run by Lyon would be unusual, to say the least.

His celebrated venture, the Pony Express Museum, was located in Arcadia, California. His first museum was built just behind his mansion. As his collections grew, he moved to a new site right across the street from the Santa Anita race track. This building contained over one million items, including the contents of a country store of the 1890s exhibited in a store setting. Red flannel underwear and chewing tobacco figured prominently in this display. Fire engines dating back to 1858, old carriages and a narrow gauge train given to him by the Southern Pacific Railroad were prized exhibits and were loaned to motion picture studios for props.

In an article in the *Fresno Bee* on September 19, 1947, Lyon declared that the museum had kept him active and had helped to prolong his life. At the age of eighty-two, he still put in a full day showing folks his collections. Some of the more prominent items recalled his days in Fresno. Brass signs from his Fresno furniture store were always pointed out to visitors. More poignant, however, was a framed copy of the *Fresno Evening Democrat* of April 11, 1905, which heralded his sweeping victory in the mayoral election.

His turbulent, albeit fun-filled term in office, which ended in his sad departure from Fresno, overshadowed his achievements for the city he truly loved and tried, in his own way, to serve. Fresno's first City Hall, first sewer system, an underpass at Fresno Street and the Southern Pacific railroad tracks, the paving of Tulare Street and the reduction of gas and electric rates were some of his major accomplishments. Not a bad list for any era.

With the advent of spring, one's thoughts may turn to gardens and outdoor activities—or to social events, including luncheons and teas. For some of the Fresno women of 1889, that was not quite enough. At the suggestion of Mrs. Jesse Church, the Wednesday Club was formed. The members wrote and presented papers dealing with a chosen theme. Limited to a membership of twenty-five, this study club is still active today.

In 1894, three women's clubs were founded. The Leisure Hour Club, Fresno's second women's study club, had as its purpose the study of literature and the arts to foster the improvement of the mind. The club motto was "How Good To Live and Learn." The club met twice a month for a leisurely hour to listen to a learned talk.

The Query Club members explored topics of antiquity as well as subjects of current interest.

The Parlor Lecture Club's founding meeting, as well as subsequent meetings, was held in a parlor of the Hughes Hotel, hence its name. Two of the club rules were that ladies must remove their hats before the meeting began and that no whispering take place during the program.

The Friday Club was founded on October 6, 1902. The club motto reads, "To glean what is best in the past; to keep a listening ear to the message of the future."

Other study clubs were created as more women wanted to combine cultural pursuits with a social hour.

The Parlor Lecture Club, with a larger membership than the other clubs, was involved in community service. The members assisted in the founding of the Fresno Nutritional Home.

From the earliest days of our city, the women have striven to improve their minds through study and exposure to fine music and literature. In a frontier community with more than a few rough edges, it became important to provide a balance and to create a cultural environment in which children could develop an appreciation for the arts. One of ways they accomplished this was through study clubs. The fact that these groups have stood the test of time is a tribute to the vision and determination of the women, both past and present, who created the clubs and have loyally kept them active.

Lewis Swift Eaton

One of Fresno's secret strengths lies in its pioneer families, those strong, stalwart folks who, in the 1870s, arrived in a little place called Fresno Station and whose descendants have chosen to remain in the city it has become 120 years later. The initial commitment to come to this tiny train stop required courage and strong determination—of the kind that through the generations grows into something even stronger—a deep love of place, a clear vision for the future of that place, and a commitment to make that place richer for the next generation. And so it was for the gentleman we speak of.

He was born in 1919 in the home his parents built at Franklin and Ferger avenues. His paternal grandfather arrived in Fresno in 1874 and was one of Fresno's pioneer merchants and bankers. His maternal grandfather, Lewis Swift, along with C. B. Shaver, established the Fresno Flume and Irrigation Company and, in the late 1890s, built a large sawmill at what is now Shaver Lake. In 1919, his father, Edwin Eaton, founded Guarantee Savings, which would grow in later years into one of the premier financial institutions in California.

After attending local schools and graduating from Stanford University, he served as a captain in the Army during World War II. He returned to Fresno to work for his father's savings and loan company and began many years of public service which resulted in such benefits for Fresno as a major museum downtown, a stadium at the university and a beautiful park along the San Joaquin River.

But it is not just for these that he will be remembered. A warm and generous man who possessed that rare combination of intelligence, humility and grace, Lewis Swift Eaton will be remembered for his unwavering commitment to his vision for Fresno—a vision that came from a deep love of and dedication to his community—a vision that inspired Fresnans to reach upward and to work tirelessly to bring beauty and culture to our city—a vision that, ultimately, has enriched not only our community, but the lives of us all.

A. T. Stevens, Cleo Stevens, Lou Denny Stevens, and Roy Denny, Lou's son by a previous marriage. c. mid-1890s.
Author's collection

Fresno in the 1880s was a hub for travel and commerce. People and goods arrived on the train and then it was the stage-coach that was called into use to provide the important means of getting both the people and the goods to their ultimate destination. There were a number of stage lines in Fresno, but one is of particular note.

Soon after the founding of our community, two brothers, A. T. and Clark Stevens, built the Black Hawk Stables at the corner of Fresno and L streets. They purchased their 125- by 150-foot lot from Charles Crocker of the Central Pacific Railroad for $562.50. The livery stable and feed yard provided room for a large number of horses. The Stevens brothers had a diversified trade. Their horses and wagons were leased by local businesses who wished to take their goods

Clara Shanklin Stevens, Leta Stevens and Clark Azro Stevens. c. mid-1890s.
Author's collection

door to door. Thus, the butcher, baker, and produce man could provide fresh goods to the Fresno homemaker by coming to her front door. Fresnans who needed to rent a horse and buggy by the hour also did business here.

But, more important, the Stevens brothers had the task of delivering mail to the mountain areas adjacent to Toll House and Shaver Lake. Travelers rode along with the mail. It was a harrowing ride. The Toll House grade was so steep that on the return trip to the Valley, a log was tied onto the stage as a braking device. The Stevenses also took private parties by stage to Yosemite—another memorable experience since the stage road was narrow, winding and primitive. In many places, streams had to be forded. It was not a journey for the faint of heart.

The stage, indeed, played an important role in everyday life in those years before the advent of the automobile. Travelers were often unprotected from the elements and arrived at their destinations rumpled and either very hot or freezing cold, depending on the season. Rather than the stuff of romance, the stage was a practical, albeit uncomfortable, part of everyday life in the Old West.

Fresno's First Businesses

With the establishment of Fresno Station in 1872 and the influx of people that followed, businesses developed at a rapid rate. James Faber's general store was the first. The next stores were housed in tents like Faber's. Soon wooden structures were built, and by the early 1880s business "blocks" were constructed. These buildings had glass windows on the bottom floor so merchants could display their goods. The second floor was used for offices. These structures often took the name of their owners, the Winchell Block, for example.

With the increasing population, hotels were sorely needed. Rooms at the Star Hotel, the California Hotel and the International were so in demand that as early as 1874 the traveler had to make reservations at least a day in advance. Saloons could be found on every corner and general stores did a thriving business. One such operation, owned by William Vellguth, not only sold household items and clothing, but included a bath house and barbershop on the premises. Mrs. Vellguth created hats, which she sold in a corner of her husband's store. Other women opened millinery shops as well. By 1884, one of these featured imported chapeaux from France.

In the early years, Fresno could boast five banks and five newspapers. Dr. H. C. Coley was the first doctor, setting up his practice in 1874. Later that year Anna Cramer, a nurse and midwife, arrived in Fresno. Dr. Lewis Leach and Dr. Chester Rowell arrived soon after. Fresno's first lawyer was A. C. Bradford, who set up his practice in March of 1874. Within two years, five other lawyers had established offices—all in the Fresno County Courthouse.

By the time Fresno was incorporated in 1885, the little railroad stop of Fresno Station had grown into a thriving city with businesses and professional offices throughout the downtown area. The tents had disappeared and in their place was a city of beautiful Victorian structures, Queen Anne buildings, large trees and a beautifully landscaped Courthouse Park.

Mr. Cearley & His Store

Shoppers on J Street (now Fulton Mall) in downtown Fresno in the 1890s rarely walked past the store of C. T. Cearley without going inside. The pristine white counters topped with glass cabinets were welcoming, and the merchandise neatly stacked on shelves against the wall contained all manner of things to interest the shopper. Every item in the stationery line imaginable could be purchased here—paper, pencils, pens, legal pads, blotters, and sealing wax, to name a few. But this was not what brought Fresnans to his door. It was the huge selection of books, newspapers and periodicals from all over the world that drew people inside. Indeed, one could visit every corner of the globe just by glancing through the wealth of reading material in the store.

Mr. Cearley himself was also worth a visit. A charming, learned man, he enjoyed having his customers drop by to chat about the latest book, current event or news-maker of the day. His patrons enjoyed Cearley's enthusiasm and ability to speak intelligently on any subject. His store was a gathering place for those who loved books and the people and events that made news. It was not only the news of the world that interested Cearley, however. Like so many of the business people in 1890s Fresno, he was, above all, concerned about the development of our city.

The fact that Fresno grew and prospered as quickly as it did was due, in no small part, to the commitment, enthusiasm and hard work of so many of the early businessmen like C. T. Cearley, who added that extra measure of interest and congeniality that brought customers flocking to their doors.

Mr. Taylor & Mr. Wheeler

A drive through the older neighborhoods of Fresno takes the traveler past many homes that possess a distinctive style. Usually such a home is built in a Monterey-colonial or Spanish revival-style, featuring a low-pitched red tile or shingle roof. The homes often had long, second-floor, cantilevered balconies as well. These features set them apart from other Fresno homes that were built during the 1930s and 1940s. When the owner of such a home is asked who built it, the answer is—"Why, Taylor and Wheeler, of course."

Orville Taylor came to Fresno from Indiana in 1919. He was a draftsman and salesman for the Routt Lumber Company. One of his customers was Dennis Wheeler, a contractor. Wheeler had lived in Fresno since he was ten years old. He graduated from Fresno High School and the University of California at Berkeley. In 1927, the two men formed a partnership and began constructing homes throughout the Central Valley. Wheeler was the business manager and supervised construction; Taylor did the design work until 1936 when they hired architect Allen Collins.

During the latter part of the 1930s, the three men began to construct homes in the Cape Cod style, although the Monterey-colonial and Spanish revival remained their trademark. At the time the firm began its Terrace Avenue subdivision, truckloads of red tile were brought to Fresno. Another kind of tile for the interior was trucked here as well. Custom-made in the Bay Area, it was used for many of the master bathrooms in the Terrace Avenue homes. Featuring earth tones ranging from brown to green interspersed with decorative tiles, this tile grows more beautiful with age.

During the 1930s and 1940s the names of Taylor and Wheeler were synonymous with distinctive, quality homes. In our era, young families are discovering these Taylor-Wheeler homes and are choosing to raise their families within the lathe and plaster walls that evoke a sense of quality and permanence. As these older neighborhoods in our city begin a new generation of ownership, another chapter in the history of our community is written.

Horse Cars & Homemakers

In the late 1880s, Fresno was beginning to grow beyond its original boundaries. For the residents who lived at the eastern edge of the city, on U Street, it was quite a distance to walk to work or to shopping. To solve this problem, Fresno's first public transportation system was established.

The Fresno Street Railroad began operation on January 25, 1889. Track was laid from H Street along Mariposa Street, down K Street (now Van Ness Avenue) to Tulare Street, and along Tulare to U Street. Two other lines were developed at the same time. These lines went north and east, well beyond the city limits. The streetcars that traveled these tracks were drawn by horses and mules, earning the system the nickname, the "horse car lines." The system worked rather well. The horses and mules were agreeable and became so knowledgeable about the schedule and route that the driver had little to do but to greet the passengers.

The housewives of Fresno, noticing that the horse cars came by their homes on a regular basis throughout the day, decided that this could be used to great advantage. As the horse cars rode by, Mrs. A could wave from her front porch and call out prettily to the driver, asking him to bring her twenty-five cents worth of mutton chops on his next trip. Mrs. B, hearing the clop, clop of the horses' hooves, would venture out to her porch, hail the driver, and ask him to please have a prescription filled for her sick baby. Mrs. C, over on T Street, would walk to the track as the horse car approached and hand the driver a spool of thread, asking him to please drop it off at Mrs. D's house on O Street on his return trip. These errands would be dispatched in an efficient manner.

The passengers would usually arrive at their destinations on time. If they were a little late, at least they had the satisfaction of a journey that was interesting. As the city grew larger and the pace of life increased, the horse cars were replaced by electrically operated streetcars. The pioneer town was on its way to becoming a real city. And the homemakers of Fresno were deprived of a most interesting delivery service.

On the night of July 29, 1895, downtown Fresno was the scene of a fire that would live in the memory of its citizens. In 1893, a copper dome had been added to the Fresno County Courthouse. Just looking at this imposing addition filled Fresnans with pride.

However, at 9:30 on this hot July evening, fire was sighted in the roof of the Courthouse next to the dome. The fire alarm sounded, bringing not only fire trucks and volunteers, but most of Fresno's citizens as well. The fire spread rapidly and soon the dome was involved. Flames shot up in all directions and then, with the intense heat, the copper began to melt. Red liquid poured down in streams onto the water being shot up from below by the firemen. Then came a heart-wrenching crash as the dome fell.

The sight of such a spectacle brought tears to the eyes of those watching, that such a grand building that symbolized so much should suffer this destruction. The firemen did not give up. They raced inside—risking their lives to save the building. Hoses were dragged up the stairs. Nozzlemen were stationed around the building, pouring water on it.

As the firemen reached the second floor, the timbers under the fallen dome were burning furiously. The spiral tongues of red hot flames roared upward, fanned by the rushing currents of air racing through the open archways below. Water was applied to the flames and, within a short time, the fire was reduced to smoldering embers. Three courtrooms on the upper story were destroyed, but the rest of the building was saved.

The cause of the fire was a subject of debate. Arson and a cigar stump were mentioned as possible culprits. Much to the delight of Fresno's citizens, the building was rebuilt and continued to be the centerpiece of community life. At least until 1966, when redevelopment projects and unfeeling government leaders accomplished what a fiery conflagration could not. They tore down the grand old building and in so doing tore the heart of the city asunder.

The year was 1921. Fresno State Normal School became Fresno State Teachers College. The new school had a football team, but did not have two necessary ingredients for success - a name or a mascot.

Student Body President Warren Moody became aware of a tough-looking bulldog who showed up on campus every day at noon, hoping to share lunch with students. They adopted him, thinking that he might be an excellent mascot for their team.

In November 1921, the _Fresno Morning Republican_ referred to Fresno State as "The Bulldogs" for the first time. The college's first official mascot arrived in Fresno from Alameda in 1935. He was a solid white purebred English bulldog named Touchdown. Finding himself unwelcome at his fraternity house home because he loved to chew up featherbeds, he was moved to the home of Frances and Arthur Safstrom. For the next thirty-five years, Frances Safstrom would serve as the master of five bulldog mascots.

In 1957, when the campus moved north to its present location, Moose I, who served as mascot after Touchdown, proudly chewed apart the ribbon to open the Kennel Bookstore. Moose II, fondly called "Winnie," was an outgoing, football-loving mascot. When making public appearances, he arrived in his own wagon, with his own personal fire hydrant. Moose III was shy and was unnerved by the cannon that was shot off when touchdowns were made. He finally retired. Moose IV tried hard to be a good mascot, but fell victim to student disinterest during the latter 1960s and early 1970s.

For several years the football team did not have a mascot. Then Halftime, an energetic and enthusiastic bulldog, won the hearts of Bulldog fans. Literally raised in the athletic department offices, he was a CSUF mascot in the truest sense. After his death, another English bulldog named C. B. took his place. His story, a Valley legend in the truest sense, will be told at another time.

Fresno, Fires & Fire Trucks

In July of 1872, a burning mail bag was the first recorded fire in Fresno. At that time, the only protection the city had was one Babcock extinguisher at the Jacob & Co. Store and that was later made ineffective by a local tinker. There was no fire department.

Sighting a fire, a man would pull out his gun and fire it into the sky. Whoever heard it would fire his gun and so on until enough men were rounded up to fight the blaze. By the time a bucket brigade formed, it was usually too late to save the burning structure. Needless to say, a major portion of the town burned down several times.

Finally, the Fresno Hook & Ladder Company was formed in 1877. They bought a hook and ladder truck which was supposed to contain the latest in modern fire fighting equipment. It was stored in Magnolia Hall. However, when a fire broke out which consumed three buildings, the truck could not be used because its wheels were fastened to the floor and no one was able to move it.

In another ironic twist of fate, in 1882, the truck was destroyed in a fire that leveled Magnolia Hall and several other buildings. It seems that because, once again, no one could unfasten the wheels and get it out of the building, the fire truck became the ultimate victim of the fires that plagued Fresno.

During the first twelve years of Fresno's existence, a string of natural disasters plagued the town.

A series of earthquakes made the year of Fresno's birth, 1872, memorable. Centered on the east side of the Sierra, they were called the Owen's Valley Earthquakes and were said to be the worst in California's history. There were five of these seismic eruptions between February and October. The worst of these shocks lasted for nine minutes and was followed by two hours of quivering motions and many aftershocks.

The summers of 1872, 1874 and 1876 experienced heat waves so terrible that the *Fresno Expositor* newspaper ran an article that applauded the citizens of Fresno for their patience and fortitude in dealing with the heat by the liberal use of ice water, lemonade, ice cream and whiskey.

In April of 1884 a tornado ripped up a house, a warehouse and two barns.

However, the most destructive of all the natural phenomena to plague the city was the Great Flood of 1884. In February of that year, heavy rains caused the Red Bank, Dog and Dry creeks to overflow and dump rushing streams of water on Fresno. Because there was no drainage system and no dams had been built, the "Sinks of Dry Creek" filled up. Establishments with basements were the hardest hit, with water flooding to the ceiling and furniture floating at the water line. For a time Fresnans were ferried to their businesses in flatboats. What a sight it made, seeing small boats cruising through downtown Fresno!

H Street (Broadway) looking east on Mariposa to the Courthouse during the flood of 1884. Kutner, Goldstein & Company is on the left corner.
Courtesy of William L. Eaton

The Colony System—
The Dream That Became a Reality

In 1875, the first colony in Fresno County was established. Bounded by North, South, East and West avenues, the tract also contained five broad avenues named Fruit, Walnut, Fig, Elm and Cherry. These streets were lined with trees which corresponded to their names.

The Central California Colony, as this parcel of land was called, was the brainchild of a newcomer to Fresno who had been inspired by a speech he heard at a grange convention in Stockton. The speaker talked about how land and water rights could be purchased cheaply in Fresno County and how an investor could profit by buying a large parcel, subdividing it and offering buyers land that had water rights. The colony system had never been tried in Fresno County, but this man was sure it would work. He talked one of the largest landowners in the area, W. S. Chapman, into investing in his scheme. William Martin and M. Theo Kearney joined up also.

During the first year problems developed and some of the investors pulled out. However, the dreamer held fast to his dream. The second year brought great results—the vineyards began to flourish and all the land had been sold. Other colonies began to develop and were successful as well.

Who was this man who became known as the Father of the Colony System? Bernard Marks, for whom Marks Avenue is named.

California's First Raisin Baron

In March of 1869, a mysterious gentleman, traveling by stage-coach from San Francisco, made his first visit to Fresno County. From his lodgings at Jones Ferry on the San Joaquin River, he was able to visit the 8,640-acre parcel of land he had purchased some distance from the future Fresno Station.

A proper Bostonian with impeccable manners, this gentleman who called himself a "capitalist" was associated with William S. Chapman, a San Francisco land speculator. The two men became partners with Bernard Marks in the successful development of the Central California Colony in 1875.

In 1883, this man, whose wealth had increased dramatically with his land speculations, purchased 6,800 acres of rich agricultural land west of Fresno. It was on this land, called the Fruit Vale Estate, that his empire would be built.

The enigmatic Bostonian, whose background was a source of speculation and whispering among the citizens of Fresno, easily passed himself off as an English aristocrat. He traveled with the socially elite in Europe six months of each year. The rest of the time was spent overseeing the development of his Fruit Vale Estate. Although the estate grew a diversity of crops, efforts were focused on raisin production. Despite some setbacks, his raisin crops flourished. His success in agriculture and his efforts to unite the raisin growers into a cooperative association caused M. Theo Kearney to be known as California's first "raisin baron."

Fresno's finest early-day hostelry was the Grand Central Hotel which stood at the corner of Mariposa and J streets (now Fulton Mall). Built in 1882, it was the most modern hotel between San Francisco and Los Angeles and became the pride of Fresno. It had wide, covered verandas at the second-story level, so guests could enjoy cool breezes and the sights and sounds of the passing parade of life in Fresno. Two years after it was built, the Grand Central Hotel was sold.

The new owner, a native of Maine, had come to California in 1851 at the age of seventeen. He settled in San Francisco where he established himself as a colorful figure in local parades. Riding on a white horse and costumed in a white Spanish don's outfit with a red sash and a huge sombrero, he stood out in the crowd. A rather uninhibited prankster, he was known to ride his horse into the bar of the Lick House on Montgomery Street after these events.

His move to Fresno in 1884 provided the town with a lively, colorful personage. He ran the Grand Central Hotel with flair and panache. His wife redecorated the rooms with excellent taste. Electricity and baths were added. A steam laundry was set up so guests would not have to suffer clammy towels or linens. The cost of a meal in the dining room was lowered from fifty to twenty-five cents. He cut costs by raising fruits, vegetables and meat for the hotel on his farm west of Fresno. With prices cut, mealtime customers increased and the hotel did extremely well.

The hotel owner died suddenly in 1910. As he wished, his funeral was highlighted by a lively parade headed by a brass band playing, "There'll Be A Hot Time In The Old Town Tonight." When it was time for the city fathers to rename J Street, they named it Fulton Street in honor of Fulton G. Berry, the owner of the Grand Central Hotel and one of Fresno's most memorable characters.

Fulton G. Berry, owner of the Grand Central Hotel, was one of Fresno's most colorful citizens. Fulton Street was named in his memory.
Fresno Historical Society Archives

On November 11, 1919, the first anniversary of the signing of the Armistice that ended World War I, the members of the newly formed American Legion led a parade through downtown Fresno. Then official ceremonies were held in Courthouse Park to welcome home Fresno's soldiers and to pay respects to her 165 servicemen who were killed in the war.

Two weeks later a rousing concert was held at the White Theater. While not connected with the local celebrations marking the return of Fresno's sons from war, it was timely, nonetheless, for it served as an opportunity for Fresnans to enjoy the music of a man whose compositions brought out patriotic feelings in every American. As the curtain went up, John Philip Sousa walked out onto the stage of the theater, lifted his baton and led his renowned band in the overture from *Mignon*.

As the evening progressed, the music gradually moved from the classical to the patriotic. When the band played Sousa's composition, "The Golden Star," which he dedicated to Mrs. Theodore Roosevelt, four of whose sons had served in the war, with one dying in battle, the stateliness of the music failed to completely overcome the feelings of grief that the music engendered.

Then, one by one, the rousing marches began. "Bullets and Bayonets," "El Capitan," "U.S. Field Artillery March," "Manhattan Beach," and "Stars and Stripes Forever" created excitement in the audience, building a wave of patriotic fervor.

As the majestic strains of the "Star Spangled Banner" brought everyone to their feet, there were few in the audience who had not been caught up in the magic of the evening. For a city that had just welcomed home her sons from battle and had mourned those who did not return, John Philip Sousa and his band and their special brand of musical enchantment had arrived in Fresno at just the right time.

In the early 1890s, a young man joined a dry-goods business in which his father-in-law was part owner. The highly respected store was called Kutner, Goldstein & Company. As he gained new responsibilities, first as merchandise manager and then as general manager, he began to consider opening his own business.

A chance conversation with T. W. Patterson at the Forsythe Barber Shop opened the door for his dream. Patterson offered to lease him 31,000 square feet of floor space in his new office building at Tulare and J streets (now Fulton Mall). Several family members joined the new business, adding their capital to help the venture get started. Advance advertising in the *Fresno Morning Republican* drew huge crowds to the store's opening on September 17, 1904.

The new store carried the highest quality millinery, cloaks, yardage, trims and dress goods. It featured a candy department, something new for Fresno. Service was the byword. The store remained open on Saturday night until the last customer went home, even if it was nearly midnight. A horse-and-carriage service guaranteed delivery of even the smallest item to a customer's front door.

As his business and profits grew, the store's owner began to purchase property at Kern and J streets, the site of an old stagecoach stop. In 1914, he began construction of a new store at that location. When it opened in the fall of that year, it featured one special modern amenity—water-cooled air-conditioning. It also offered the finest merchandise from the East and from Europe. Employees wore hats and gloves. Sales clerks only helped customers select merchandise. Cashiers, sitting on high platforms, handled the financial transactions. As the business grew, branch stores were opened in Fresno and in other California cities. Today, the grandnephews of Emil Gottschalk carry on the tradition of service that has drawn customers to their stores for over ninety years.

Fresno's First Theater

L ocated halfway between San Francisco and Los Angeles, Fresno made a perfect overnight stop for musicians and touring companies visiting the West Coast. To accommodate these quality performers, Fresno needed a theater.

In 1890, the Barton Opera House and Armory Hall was built on the northeast corner of Fulton and Fresno streets. The brainchild of vineyardist Robert Barton, who acquired his fortune during the Comstock Lode era in Nevada, the Opera House was beautifully decorated and had excellent acoustics. This first true theater in Fresno contained eight box seats and regular and loge seating for 1,600 people. Prior to the opening on September 29, 1890, boxes and seats were auctioned off to those wishing to have season tickets.

In succeeding years, the finest talent in America and Europe graced the Barton's stage—Lillie Langtry, John and Ethel Barrymore, Sarah Bernhardt, George M. Cohan, Mme. Ernestine Schumann-Heink, Otis Skinner, Nellie Melba and Eddie Foy among them. With the advent of the Barton Opera House, Fresno truly became a cultural center.

Other important events were held there as well. Fresno High School graduations and amateur theatricals played a part in the theater's history. The Armory Hall, the site of many popular dancing parties and teas, still stands; but it has been converted to a commercial building.

The Opera House, which over the years was known by many different names, most recently the Sequoia Theater, is gone. Like so many of Fresno's historic buildings, today its site is a parking lot.

Fresno's First Woman of Agriculture

Improvements in the agricultural industry in Fresno in the 1880s were due in large part to the efforts of Minnie Eshleman, a woman from Philadelphia. When her father's failing health forced the family to move west in 1877, they settled in Oakland. For a time her father speculated in mining stocks and made a profitable income. The market declined and, thinking his stocks worthless, he bundled them together and tossed them into the fireplace. His daughter entered the room and quickly retrieved them. After several years, the value of the stocks increased and he gave the money to his daughter as a gift.

Miss Eshleman used the money to purchase 640 acres of farm land in Fresno. Here she planted emperor and muscat grapes, olives and peaches. She became fascinated with raising crops and experimenting with new varieties. She pioneered in the shipment of table grapes to New York. As she became more successful, she bought more land and built a large home surrounded by eucalyptus trees. She named her estate "Minnewawa," a word which means wind in the trees. Next, she began breeding a strain of Holstein cattle that drew buyers from all over the country.

Miss Eshleman's greatest contribution to Fresno was her pioneering efforts in the dairy industry. In the 1880s, dairy products in Fresno were not always safe to eat. The butter, cream and milk from the Minnewawa dairy were of superior quality due to scientific methods of processing and cleanliness in every stage of the operation. Her accomplishments led Governor Hiram Johnson to appoint Minnie Eshleman to the board of regents of the University of California.

D r. Frank Vincent and his wife, Annie, were having marital problems. They moved to Fresno in 1885, hoping to start a new life. However, the marriage continued to be unhappy. The doctor began drinking and became very depressed. Unable to put up with her husband's behavior any longer, Annie Vincent separated from him and filed for divorce.

The situation was fairly calm until Dr. Vincent was served with divorce papers on December 18, 1890. When the papers were handed to him, he went berserk. In a fit of rage he went to her home and demanded to know if she was determined to divorce him. She said she was. He tried to force her to take poison. When she resisted, he shot her four times. A policeman heard the shots and rushed into the house in time to keep Vincent from drinking the poison himself. The police rushed Vincent to the Fresno jail to save him from the lynch mob that was forming in the streets.

It was several months before the case came to trial. His lawyer tried to prove insanity, but Dr. Vincent was convicted of murder and sentenced to hang. The appeals process ran out in 1893.

The execution was set for October 27. Printed invitations were mailed to local citizens and a scaffold was set up outside the jail in Courthouse Park. The morning of October 27 found 600 people crowded into the enclosure near the scaffold. At noon on that day, the only legal hanging in the history of Fresno County took place.

Fresno County Sheriff Jay Scott (left) and L. P. Timmons (right), pose on the scaffold that was built for the hanging of Dr. Frank O. Vincent in 1893. The invitation was issued to many of Fresno's citizens, requesting their presence at the execution of Dr. Vincent.
Courtesy of William B. Secrest, Sr., Collection

When Fresno Station was founded in 1872, water was brought to the settlement in tanks from the San Joaquin River. Later, Fresno's first well was dug at Mariposa Street and Broadway. About 1876, a two-story windmill pump was installed in Courthouse Park, enabling residents to fill their buckets there. Some businesses and well-off homeowners installed hand-operated pumps on their property. Pumping and fetching the water was considered women's work. It was not long until housewives began to complain about these primitive conditions. Some of the wells were so close together and so deep that the walls threatened to collapse. Clearly something had to be done.

In June of 1876, George McCullough and Lyman Andrews founded the Fresno Water Works on Fresno Street where the Guarantee Savings Building now stands. They bored a single well 100 feet deep and found what to them seemed an inexhaustible supply of water. A steam engine pumped the water through a seven-inch pipe up to a 23,000-gallon storage tank. The tank was three stories high. At this height, it could provide enough gravitational pressure to fight rooftop fires. The tank was encased in an octagonal structure which was praised for its architectural symmetry.

By the winter of 1876, water was being pumped to Fresno households. Customers were billed by the month: $1.50 for a family of five, 10 cents for each additional person, $1.50 for a garden, and 50 cents for the family cow.

Fresno's boom era in the 1880s saw the construction of many architecturally important buildings. Commercial blocks, banks and hotels began to dot the skyline. One of the most interesting of these was the Hughes Hotel which, for many years, was Fresno's finest.

Built in 1888 and representing an investment of $300,000, the Hughes Hotel was unequalled in any California city outside of San Francisco and Los Angeles. The design featured a large court in the center of the building, decorated with orange trees and flowers which grew luxuriantly. A peacock, named Admiral Dewey, held court there and could be viewed from the second and third floor balconies which opened onto the court. Tastefully decorated reception rooms and parlors invited guests to linger and socialize. The architectural design of the building allowed each of the 200 rooms an outside view.

Modern in every way, the hotel boasted hot and cold running water, electricity, and large air shafts that kept the building well-ventilated and cool. The hotel had its own waterworks. It consisted of a twenty-five-horsepower engine fired by two cords of wood a day which pumped 8,000 gallons of water an hour from a 300-foot well. All of these modern conveniences insured that each guest would be provided with the finest service.

Gradually, other, newer hotels became more popular and, by the end of the 1920s, the Hughes had fallen into disrepair. The hotel that was once Fresno's showcase fell victim to an arsonist on July 10, 1953, when ten buildings were set on fire on one of the most spectacular and terrifying days in the history of downtown Fresno.

An Assassination Attempt

In 1929, the year of the stock market crash, the citizens of Fresno elected a new mayor. This gentleman was described as being honest and enlightened as well as the most experienced politician elected to City Hall since Dr. Chester Rowell. He had a colorful history as well.

Born in Pennsylvania in 1883, he was a muleskinner at age seven and, at fifteen, ran away from home to cast his lot with Colonel Theodore Roosevelt's Rough Riders during the Spanish-American War. He first was the unit's "mascot," but rose in the ranks to become Roosevelt's personal orderly. During the battles of Bloody Creek and San Juan Hill, he was wounded twice and cited for bravery in the field. After the war, he finished his schooling at the University of Pennsylvania. He was a teacher in the East before coming to Fresno High School in 1915 to teach civics and history. He served in the infantry in World War I and then returned to Fresno High, eventually becoming vice principal.

In 1926, he was elected to the state assembly, leaving that office after three years to become mayor of Fresno. The times were difficult and, sometimes, cruel. On October 28, 1929, a mysterious gunman tried twice to assassinate the new mayor. The gunman was never apprehended. The next day the stock market crashed. The *Fresno Bee* ran stories on the mayor's close encounter with death, the heavy losses on the stock market and an article citing charges of a liquor conspiracy involving three people in west Fresno and members of the police department.

In spite of this difficult beginning, Zeke Leymel served two terms as mayor. During this time he kept the city relatively free of organized crime, made a strong start on developing the civic center, and made garbage disposal a municipal program.

Baseball has a long history in Fresno. In 1883, the Fresno Stars Club was formed and played competition games on Fresno's first baseball park, at the Southern Pacific Railroad reservation on Ventura Avenue. The first "kids" team was the *Fresno Evening Expositor* Club. Included among its members was Frank Chance, who in later years would join the Chicago Cubs as player and manager of the team until 1912. The Fresno Tigers in the 1890s and 1900s and the Fresno Reds in the 1910s competed as semipro clubs with other Valley teams.

Fresno entered the professional arena in 1908 with a team called the Fresno State League Club, which was fondly called the "Raisin Eaters." Later, the Fresno Tigers turned pro and were soon followed by a new club, the Fresno Acorns.

New ball clubs meant new playing fields and several were established. Robert Barton and C. L. Walter leased property near Belmont and Blackstone avenues for a baseball diamond. Recreation Park near the fairground, Frank Chance Field at Ventura and Cedar avenues, and Euless Park behind Ratcliffe Stadium helped fill the need for playing areas over the years.

In 1914, an amateur baseball program called the Fresno City Twilight League was organized by Raymond Quigley, Fresno City playground superintendent. It was one of the finest programs in the country and became a springboard for young people who showed promise and who later entered the minor and major leagues. The league's games were held until 1942, when World War II ended them.

After the war, baseball games began again. The Fresno Cardinals and the Fresno Giants were two major teams. Today, the city is pushing once again to bring professional baseball to Fresno and to build a new stadium. Ironically, the proposed stadium site is adjacent to Fresno's first ball park on Ventura Avenue. One might say that in the last hundred years, baseball in Fresno has come full circle.

Jim White's Bridge

In 1855, a town site sprang up on the south branch of the San Joaquin River, also known as the Fresno Slough. The town was called Fresno City and was located eight miles southeast of present-day Mendota. Fresno City was a station on the Butterfield Overland Stage line and the head of navigation for steamboats taking cargo and passengers to the northernmost point of the Fresno Slough. Plans to extend the ship canal southward were underway.

A store and hotel named Casa Blanca were built on the slough. Casa Blanca was a stopping point for the steamboats and provided overnight lodging. It became one of the few well-known landmarks on the west side of Fresno County.

The southern canals were never finished. The steamboat traffic decreased and, in 1865, Fresno City passed into history.

Six and one-half miles upstream from Fresno City, James R. White established a settlement. He built a hotel, a store and a warehouse and, in time, erected a bridge to replace the ferry. Steamers often stopped there. It became a sheep-shearing center. Travelers began to call it White's Bridge. Today, White's settlement has faded into history, but his name lives on, on the long highway that stretches from Fresno across the west side of Fresno County, White's Bridge Road.

The Land Boom of 1887

Fresno's real growth as a community began in 1878. New homes and business buildings were being constructed within the city; but, until 1885, most of the thousands of acres of land outside the city limits were still vacant.

With the incorporation of the city in 1885, Fresno began thriving and growing in all directions. A great percentage of the land outside the city had been purchased by speculators for as little as twenty-five cents an acre. As the city's growth began to spill over its boundaries, the developers saw an opportunity to trade in their land for cash. As their advertising campaigns spread throughout the country, people began arriving in Fresno by the thousands. The hotels were crowded. On a typical day in the summer of 1887, the clerks of the Grand Central Hotel were struggling to find room for two hundred and fifty guests in their eighty-bed establishment. Most of the newcomers bought land and prices began to soar. The boom of 1887 was well under way.

By late 1888, the peak had been reached and leveled off. One lasting memento of this period, that has always been a puzzle to locals and newcomers alike, is that the downtown area is aligned differently than the newer parts of Fresno. When Fresno Station was established, the Central Pacific Railroad laid out the streets so that they ran parallel to the railroad tracks. When development spread north of Divisadero Street, streets were established in a north-south direction, creating intersections that future generations would find interesting and, often, frustrating.

The man who was to become one of Fresno's most noted citizens was born in Illinois in 1849. His father had a mercantile business and the young man was raised with a good knowledge of commerce. His father's death caused him, at age eighteen, to go to work to help support his mother and sister. He was hired by a shoe merchant, Jacob Vogel, and, eventually, married Vogel's daughter, Anna. The young man began investing and trading sections of railroad land and prospered. He then decided to head west with his wife and family, which now consisted of two sons and a daughter.

In 1885, they arrived in Fresno. He purchased a large parcel of land south of the city. It became the first area to be annexed by the city of Fresno. In 1887, he was hired for the position of cashier at the First National Bank of Fresno. Within a year he had become the president of that institution. He continued to invest in land and subdivision projects in the Fresno area.

In 1890, he and Jacob Vogel helped organize the People's Savings Bank. By 1895, he was one of the wealthiest and most prominent citizens of the business community. Through his advertisements for land, he attracted hundreds of investors to Fresno County. After his First National Bank merged with the Bank of Italy, he shifted his role to an advisory capacity. He traveled extensively until his death in 1935.

The maxim by which he conducted his business life held true for him throughout his career. "Early to bed, early to rise; work like hell and advertise" typified the life of Oscar James Woodward.

The Fresno National Bank Building located at the corner
of Mariposa and K (now Van Ness) Streets. One of the many
new buildings built during the boom period of the 1880s.
Courtesy of William L. Eaton

In 1919, a new tract of land north of Fresno was developed by J. C. Forkner and Wylie Giffen. It was called Fig Garden. They hired landscape architect Horace Cotton to design the plantings for the new area. Cotton's plan called for lining the main street, which was called Van Ness Boulevard, with cedar trees. These cedars, which in the Middle East were called the "Timber of the Gods," gave Van Ness Boulevard the potential to become a beautiful scenic drive.

In December of 1920, Mrs. W. P. Winning decorated and lighted one of the cedars in memory of her son. The lighted tree was so beautiful and gave so much pleasure to those who saw it that the Fig Garden Woman's Club asked other residents of the boulevard if they would like to participate also. By 1928, ten families lighted trees in front of their homes. An appeal for financial contributions was successful and, in December of 1930, the first official Christmas Tree Lane opened with thirty lighted trees stretching one quarter of a mile. The number of decorated trees grew each year.

Today, as the trees have reached the size and beauty that Horace Cotton envisioned, the lane extends for over a mile and a half with over three hundred lighted trees. For sixty years, this special tradition has given added joy to the Fresno Christmas season. It has also provided a most memorable experience. When each car approaches the Herndon Canal, lights are dimmed, the crest of the bridge is reached and the lane stretches ahead in all its breathtaking beauty. Peace and goodwill prevail as Christmas Tree Lane adds its special joy to the celebration of the holiday season.

By 1910, Fresno had grown considerably. Twice the boundary lines had changed as areas were annexed into the city. A year later a subdivision developed by Billings, Fine & Meyering made history. Known as the Alta Vista tract, it was the first subdivision and third area to be annexed to the city. One of its major land owners was A. G. Wishon, pioneer of the electric power industry in the San Joaquin Valley and founder of the San Joaquin Light & Power Company. He and his associates planned the subdivision to illustrate how electricity could be used to make life easier.

Wishon also was manager of the Fresno Traction Company. He had the electric streetcar line extended so that it ran down the middle of Huntington Boulevard, the main street of the subdivision.

After Wishon built his Huntington Boulevard home, he put colored lights on a small redwood tree in his front yard to illustrate how electricity could be used to decorate. The year was 1918 and this was Fresno's first outdoor Christmas tree. He continued to light this tree every year until his death in 1935.

Today, the tradition lives on in the annual Candlelight Christmas on Huntington Boulevard. The one-mile boulevard greets the visitor with festive displays, colored lights and lamp posts which have been transformed into glistening red candles. The centerpiece of it all is Mr. Wishon's redwood tree. Now eight stories tall and decorated with dazzling lights, the oldest living Christmas tree in Fresno proudly stands, ushering in each holiday season.

The fig industry has a long history in the Fresno area. As early as 1888, the white Adriatic fig was being grown here and packed for market. Some of the pioneer fig growers were Emil Bretzner, Martin Denecke, Melcon and Henry Markarian, Samuel Mitrovich and John Seropian.

As the industry expanded, some difficulties arose. Most of them were overcome, but one great problem that seemed to have no solution was the inability to grow the Smyrna fig. This variety was the most flavorful and grew in great abundance in the Mediterranean region. However, in Fresno, the fruit would reach a certain size and then fall off the tree.

This phenomenon intrigued nurseryman George Roeding. He decided to find the answer to this mystery. He sent Stockton nurseryman W. C. West to Turkey to investigate the success of fig growers in that country. The answer turned out to be a rather surprising and simple one. In order to grow Smyrna figs, a wasp which visited the Capri fig had to pollinate the female Smyrna tree. This was done by placing cuttings from the Capri tree among groves of Smyrna trees at appropriate times of the year.

With this new information, Roeding began importing Capri figs which contained the insects. The cuttings were placed in bags and hung in branches of the Smyrna trees in an effort to pollinate the fig blossoms. Difficulties arose, but after receiving a number of shipments of Capri cuttings and experimenting further with pollination, Roeding began producing delicious Smyrna figs. The best variety had the Turkish name "hop Injir." In an effort to simplify the name, Roeding adopted the term "Calimryna" for his new product. Today, the Calimyrna fig is a delicacy enjoyed throughout the Central Valley.

In the early years of this century, a young Sicilian immigrant decided to make his home in Fresno. The hot, dry summers and cold, frosty winters were a hard adjustment for a gentleman accustomed to the mild Mediterranean climate. In an attempt to escape summer's scorching heat, he began to dig an underground refuge.

For the next forty years, he continued to sculpt a network of almost a hundred underground rooms, passageways, grottos, courts and patios, using only hand tools. To support the earth, he used Roman arches, domes and columns strengthened by mortar and cement. Within the rooms, he created interesting landscape areas, experimenting with growing many types of citrus trees. His efforts to produce citrus grafts were very successful. One tree carried eight varieties of fruit. These underground areas had a temperate, frost-free climate which did not vary more than ten degrees throughout the year.

As he sculpted the earth into his own designs, he learned how to control air and light. To visit his underground home and wander its passageways is to experience constant amazement and delight. Today, the Underground Gardens is listed in the National Register of Historic Places. This maze of rooms, created from the earth with a pick and shovel, stands as a tribute to the hard work and skill of Baldasare Forestiere, a man who created harmony from a hostile environment.

A Legacy of Music

During the early part of this century, a group of women who were all involved in the cultural life of Fresno began to talk of creating a meaningful forum for musical expression. They were enthusiastic and had great dreams. With the drafting of a constitution in 1905, this group became known as the Fresno Musical Club. Their stated purpose was to "cultivate the musical taste of the community, to raise the standards of music, to encourage local talent and to attract artists from abroad." From its inception, the club had active members, who were participating musicians, and associate members, who were subscribers to the concert series that developed.

Fresno's geographical location midway between San Francisco and Los Angeles allowed the finest musicians of the time an opportunity to perform in Fresno. The first concert season, in 1906 at the Barton Opera House, featured the Ernest Gamble Concert Party. The year 1907 brought MacKenzie Gordon, the great Scots tenor, and Mme. Ernestine Schumann-Heink, the German Wagnerian contralto, to the stage of the Barton.

As the number of subscribers grew, the concerts were moved to larger auditoriums. The White Theater, the Fresno High School Auditorium and the Warnors Theater were some of the concert sites.

Many memorable evenings were enjoyed by concert-goers. In 1915, violinist Fritz Kreisler performed at the White Theater, his final appearance before enlisting to fight for his native Austria in World War I. He left the stage in tears. During a performance by ballerina Anna Pavlova there was a power failure. Two cars were driven onto the stage of the White Theater. The light from their acetylene headlights allowed her to continue. In 1960, Eileen Farrel became ill and an unknown soprano, Anna Moffo, was introduced to Fresno audiences in one of her first concerts. Pianist Artur Rubinstein's fourth and final appearance, in 1973, elicited a prolonged and emotional standing ovation.

For over 75 years, the finest musicians in the world were brought to Fresno through the auspices of the Fresno Musical Club.

*Fresno Historical Society
Archives, R. W. Riggs Collection*

The history of Fresno's oldest family-owned business begins in Gilroy in 1867. In that year, Henry Conrad Warner, a watchmaker and optician, moved west to California. He opened a store in Gilroy which sold glasses, jewelry, watches, and stationery. He called his store The Golden Rule, a name which symbolized his business philosophy. The new store was doing well, but Warner had developed health problems. His doctors advised him to move to a warm climate. His neighbor, Henry Miller of Miller & Lux fame, suggested he move his family to Fresno.

By 1880, Fresno was growing rapidly. Warner decided to locate his business at 1809 Mariposa Street in the heart of Fresno's commercial district. The vault in Warner's store was popular with miners who came to town for a respite from the diggings. At that time, Fresno did not have a bank or a Wells Fargo Office so Warner's safe was the only secure place for the miners to store their gold dust.

By 1896, Albert Owen Warner had joined his father as a partner. Ten years later they incorporated the business under its present name, The Warner Company.

The business kept growing and moved to Fulton Street where it remained even after the Fulton Mall was constructed. Henry Warner's grandson joined the firm in 1921. Thirty years later his great-grandson, Albert "Bud" Warner, joined the business.

In 1987, one hundred and seven years after Henry Warner moved the business to Fresno, the store moved to a location in north Fresno. In that same year, Bud's daughter, Kathleen Warner, joined the business as the fifth generation member of the firm. In 1993, Warner's was sold to Casey Stephenson. A year later he moved the business to Fig Garden Village.

An Oil Baron's Mansion

Fresno has witnessed many success stories, but the saga of a German immigrant who made his way to California in the early 1880s is truly a story of the Horatio Alger variety. After losing both parents and his seven brothers and sisters in a cholera epidemic, this young man left his home in Germany and traveled to America. He came west to California, homesteaded in the Coalinga area, and started farming grain. Not succeeding in this effort, he went to Alaska to seek his fortune in the Yukon. The Alaska gold rush gave him a modest amount of money which he invested in oil properties on his return to Coalinga.

While he was gone, Coalinga had experienced an oil boom. His new investments made him a very wealthy man. By 1915, he and his associates had purchased 1,400 acres of oil land on the west side of Fresno County.

In 1903, he and his wife decided to make their residence in Fresno. After 1909, he began to invest in real estate in Fresno's downtown. The Hotel Fresno was one development project which he helped finance. After this death in 1915, his heirs fulfilled his dream of a multistory office building by erecting such a structure on Fulton Street in 1922. It still bears his name.

But his lasting contribution to Fresno is his mansion, which was built in the Italian villa style. Designed by architect Edward T. Foulkes in 1911, it is the only residence in Fresno planned in this elaborate architectural style. As you travel east on Fresno Street, leaving the downtown area, you cross R Street, and a blue and white mansion looms up on the right. It is the Brix Mansion, home of German immigrant Herman H. Brix, who rose from his humble beginnings to make a fortune in the oil fields of Coalinga and used a portion of that fortune to make Fresno a more beautiful city.

The year 1880 found the family of Melcon Markarian leaving their native Armenia to settle in Fresno. There were two sons who, when grown, joined their father in the raisin business. As the business prospered, they expanded their efforts to include packing raisins for the Eastern market. One of the sons, Henry, became the manager of this enterprise.

However, this son's interest extended beyond the raisin business. He was intrigued with the idea of expanding the cultivation of figs. The figs that grew in Fresno at this time were of high quality, but were mostly used as border trees. In 1894, he harvested and dried the figs that were grown on the family ranch and, along with those from other farms, shipped them to Saint Louis. These California figs were the first to be sent to an Eastern market. Not long after, he purchased land north of downtown Fresno and planted all of it in figs. Since the land was low and rather swampy, people were sure that his enterprise would fail. Instead, by 1910, it was flourishing and was called the "Fig Gardens." This was the first use of the term.

At this time, J. C. Forkner was beginning to develop his land farther north. He hired Henry Markarian to teach him the art of growing Smyrna figs. Markarian taught Forkner about the need to blast holes in the hardpan before planting to assure drainage for the trees, and about the pollination methods that were required to fertilize the Smyrna fig.

By the time of Markarian's death during a flu epidemic in November 1918, he and Forkner had transformed the barren land of northwest Fresno into a garden of Eden.

Today, Markarian's 160-acre ranch, bounded by Blackstone, Shields and Dakota avenues and Fresno Street, is the site of the Manchester Shopping Center.

In 1910, northwest Fresno was called the "hog wallow badlands," land that was cursed with an underlying stratum of adobe-like "hardpan" that was impenetrable and totally unsuitable for cultivation. The land flooded in the winter and was hard as stone in the heat of summer.

A real estate speculator arrived from Los Angeles that year. He took a one-year option to buy this land from E. E. Bullard, the owner. Fresnans were suspicious of the new arrival and, especially, of his claim that the land had the potential to grow the best figs outside of the Mediterranean and Adriatic areas. Suspicion turned to amusement. "It's impossible!" was the public sentiment.

However, the newcomer persisted. While tongues wagged, he busied himself with studying the land and learning the technique of blasting through the hardpan so that trees could be planted. He hired Henry Markarian as a consultant and learned from him the successful methods of propagating the Smyrna fig.

Land-leveling was another problem to be solved. Learning that Henry Ford was producing a new kind of tractor, this man ordered forty-eight of them. Ford was so impressed, he journeyed to Fresno to see them at work.

As time went by, the fig trees this man had planted began to produce figs in great abundance. Today, this land is called the Fig Gardens and extends north to the bluffs of the San Joaquin River. The success of this venture was due to the intelligence and tenacity of Jesse Clayton Forkner.

As you drive south on M Street from downtown, a structure reminiscent of the Old West can be seen in the distance. As you draw nearer, the illusion of another era becomes greater. When you reach the foot of M Street, the vision is complete, for there stands the Old Fresno Brewery, unaltered in its appearance since 1907.

Built entirely of brick, with black, fluted cast iron columns supporting a tin roof, the structure has had a colorful history. It was originally the business office and part of a larger complex that comprised Fresno's first and largest brewery, operating from 1900 to 1919. It employed over a thousand people during its most productive years. It supplied beer from Merced to Bakersfield and was one of Fresno's first large industries.

When the Prohibition Amendment was passed in 1919, the brewery stopped beer production. The owner, Ernest Eilert, being an innovative man, started bottling soft drinks and other beverages. When Prohibition ended in 1934, beer production began again. In 1955, the other buildings were demolished and, since that time, the Fresno Brewery building has stood alone.

Now listed in the National Register of Historic Places, the old building stands as a silent symbol of a colorful past. No doubt there are a few people in Fresno who also remember the brief period in the Roaring Twenties when it was also a popular and not too secret speakeasy.

Every seat, loge, and box of the Barton Opera House was filled on a magical Fresno night in 1902. As the house lights dimmed, a hush fell over the audience. Anticipation hung palpably in the air as the orchestra began the overture, the curtain began to rise, the cast of the road company of the opera *Princess Chic* swept onto the stage. Then the prima donna stepped forward to sing, and the audience stood cheering as Maude Lillian Berri, former Fresnan, bowed low. Her triumphal return to Fresno filled the natives with pride. Like her father, Fulton G. Berry, Maude had a charming personality that had made her well-liked by everyone.

Since her youthful days of singing in the choir of the First Presbyterian Church, the people of Fresno knew she had talent. She studied at the National Conservatory of Music in New York, and John Philip Sousa chose her as lead singer for his band. Soon after, she left his group to make her debut on Broadway.

Unlike most young actresses, Maude started at the top—her first role was as star of the comic opera, *Maid of Marblehead*. Many other roles followed, including one in the production of Victor Herbert's *Wizard of the Nile*.

Maude Lillian Berri returned to Fresno on April 8, 1910, for another appearance at the Barton Opera House. Once again playing the lead role, this time in a production called *The Rich Mr. Hoggenheimer*

Watching a man run down a track, plant the tip of the pole he is carrying on the ground and soar through the air is to witness grace in motion. Those who attended track and field events at Fresno State College in the mid-1930s had the opportunity to watch a young man from Hanford who later became known as one of the greatest pole vaulters of all time. Armed with his bamboo pole, Cornelius "Dutch" Warmerdam flew over the fifteen-foot barrier forty-three times.

His bamboo poles came from Asia in twenty-foot lengths and had to be cut down to sixteen feet. Oddly enough, the night he broke the world's pole vault record by soaring over the bar at 15 feet 3/8 inches, he was using a borrowed fourteen-foot pole. His had been lost on the flight to New York where the competition was held. The use of a fourteen-foot pole set a new standard of measurement.

In Chicago in 1943, after several years of competing in athletic events, including Fresno's West Coast Relays, Warmerdam attained his highest vault of 15 feet 8° inches.

After serving in the Navy during the last part of World War II, he was appointed assistant track coach at Stanford University. A year later, in 1947, he came to Fresno State where he served as a track coach until his retirement in 1980. His pole vault record stood for fifteen years. Over his long career, this outstanding athlete won the Sullivan Award in 1942 and was honored by inclusion in the National Track and Field Hall of Fame.

One of the truly great athletes of his time, "Dutch" Warmerdam and his soaring pole vaults will long be remembered in the legends of the Valley.

In 1841, a new order of Catholic nuns, called the Sisters of the Holy Cross, was founded in Le Mans, France. Their primary vocation was to heal the sick. Two years later, four Sisters journeyed to the United States, where the order attracted more members. During the Civil War their work in six Union hospitals earned them the name "Nuns of the Battlefield."

In 1894, the Sisters' work took on another dimension when nine members of their order opened a boarding and day school called Saint Augustine's Academy in Fresno. The school's facility was built near Saint John's Cathedral at Mariposa and R streets.

In 1926, Bishop John B. MacGinley asked the Sisters to establish the first Catholic hospital in Fresno. Ground breaking ceremonies were held on April 20, 1928. Bishop MacGinley blessed the site of the future hospital at Fruit and Floradora avenues and dedicated it to Saint Agnes, patroness of Fresno. Building began in earnest.

On the night before the opening ceremonies were to be held, the hospital opened early to admit a little boy, John Hammel, Jr., who required emergency surgery. The next day, August 5, 1929, the hospital officially opened with a staff of thirty-two in addition to eight Sisters and Sister Virginia, the Mother Superior. In the intervening years, the hospital continued to grow, never losing sight of its mission to care for the body and spirit of its patients.

Today, almost seventy years later, at its new location at Herndon and Millbrook avenues, the growth and outreach of Saint Agnes continues, symbolized by the outstretched arms of the statue of Christ at the entrance. After more than a hundred years, the dedication of the Sisters of the Holy Cross is still important to the life and well-being of the citizens of Fresno.

A Penthouse in the Sky

As you travel east on Tulare Street through downtown Fresno, you pass the Fulton Mall and Courthouse Park. In the next block the old Post Office building, called the "Pink Palace" because of its color, comes into view. Almost immediately your attention shifts to a classic building which stands across the street. As you look upward, a rather curious sight catches your eye, for perched on top of this stately structure is a rather modern-looking house. Your interest piqued, you may drive around the block for another look. "What is the story behind this unusual sight?" you wonder.

The Georgian revival building was built in 1911 by two prominent doctors. Planned as an apartment building, it had a distinguished address. At the time of its construction, an Otis elevator was installed. Today, it still transports people from floor to floor and is one of the oldest operating elevators west of the Mississippi.

But, what about the house on the roof? In 1947, the owner of the building, a superior court judge, built the wood-framed stucco penthouse on top of the building for his home. From this vantage point, he had a spectacular view of Fresno and the Sierra Nevadas in the distance. Today, this aerie serves as an office.

Built by Dr. J. L. Maupin and Dr. Dwight Trowbridge, Sr., the Maubridge Apartments is now listed in the National Register of Historic Places. Since 1911, it has added grandeur, elegance, and a little bit of a puzzle to downtown Fresno.

Pollasky, the Smooth-Talking Promoter

In 1891, a handsome young man named Marcus Pollasky arrived in Fresno. He was a promoter with a magnetic personality and a golden tongue. He immediately announced that he was going to build a railroad from Fresno to the present-day town of Friant, then known as Hamptonville. The train route would traverse the Barton Vineyard, run next to the Tarpey Winery, the new town site of Clovis and the Clovis Mill, ending at Hamptonville, which was now called Pollasky.

To accomplish this and to acquire a right-of-way, he brought together a group of influential Fresnans. These men, Thomas Hughes, Fulton G. Berry, and John Gray, became directors in his company, the San Joaquin Valley Railroad. Pollasky built a magnificent home at Tulare and U streets and began to entertain lavishly. He made quite a splash in Fresno society. He acted as though he had great wealth and could easily carry out his project. The hoped-for end result of his railroad was to turn the little town of Pollasky into a thriving city.

He got the necessary right-of-way, but had to build a railroad loop in south Fresno that connected with the Southern Pacific line to transport materials to the new line. Some of the materials were in crates marked "S.P." He said that the initials were those of his brother Sam.

The railroad was completed in 1892. To celebrate the event, guests were taken by rail to Pollasky for a barbecue. Oddly enough, the railcars said "S.P." also. There was a rumor that a buy-out had taken place. It was discovered that he had invested very little of his own money in his scheme. The town of Pollasky never prospered and the Southern Pacific Railroad took over the line.

And what about that smooth-talking promoter, Marcus Pollasky? He slipped out of town, leaving his investors, and went on to greener pastures. Pollasky Avenue in Clovis bears his name.

On the night of January 28, 1893, one of the wildest and most eventful meetings in the history of Fresno took place. For some time the citizens of the Madera region had been advocating separation from Fresno County and the formation of a county of their own. Their area was growing and prospering and, instead of representation on the board of supervisors in the person of one supervisor, they wanted their own county government. The first step in the process was a favorable vote from Fresno. If this was obtained, then Fresno's state senator would lend his support to the bill for separation that Assemblyman Mordecai of Madera had introduced in the state legislature.

The meeting was to be held in Kutner Hall on J Street. While most Fresnans were eating their dinner, a trainload of Maderans arrived and proceeded to Kutner Hall. By 7:30 P.M., the hall had filled. Suddenly, a fire alarm sounded. All the able-bodied Fresno men dashed out to answer the alarm, leaving their chairs vacant. These were quickly appropriated by the Maderans. During their absence a pro-separation chairman was elected to lead the meeting. Interestingly enough, the alarm turned out to be false.

The debate began. Fresno lawyer W. D. Grady led the arguments against separation. His talk grew lengthy as he bought time until the Fresno men returned. He said too much, however, bringing up the issue of secession and the Civil War in a community with strong Southern sympathies. Thomas Hughes, speaking in favor of separation, argued that Fresno was stagnant with a lack of initiative. The debate grew more and more heated. Finally, a motion was made which called for a division of the county. A standing vote was asked for. All of the chairs were filled with Maderans, which left the Fresnans standing. So, when the standing vote was called for, everyone in the room was standing up. To no one's surprise, the motion passed overwhelmingly. On February 28, 1893, the state legislature passed the bill which created Madera County.

In the fall of 1853, Charles Porter Converse started a ferry on the San Joaquin River south of Fort Miller, where today stands the town of Friant.

Converse was hired by the board of supervisors to build Fresno County's first Courthouse and jail at Millerton. The district attorney was instructed to oversee his work. Any disputes between the two were to be arbitrated by the county clerk and the sheriff. The Courthouse was completed in June of 1867. Three months later an election was held.

The sheriff's race had been especially bitter. J. Scott Ashman and James N. Walker, whom Converse supported, were the candidates. While waiting for the results to be tallied, Converse walked over to Payne's Saloon where an Ashman supporter, John Dwyer, threw a rock at him. Converse fell to the ground. Then another Ashman supporter, William Crowe, hit him on the back of the head. Converse rose and fired his gun, hitting Crowe between the eyes, killing him instantly. Converse was saved from a lynch mob that was forming and was placed in the jail he had built. He was its first prisoner.

After seventeen days he was brought to trial. The slick San Francisco lawyer Converse had hired to defend him stood before the judge. "Your Honor," he asked, "do you believe in the Bible?" The judge nodded. "Have you heard of the story of David and Goliath?" Again, the judge nodded. "Don't you agree, Your Honor, that when David confronted the giant, Goliath, and pulled out his slingshot to kill him, he acted in self-defense?" Another nod. "Was not the slingshot a lethal weapon?" Another nod. "David was cheered as a hero, was he not, Your Honor?" Another nod. "Like David," the lawyer continued, "Charles Converse used his weapon to strike at the enemy who tried to overwhelm him."

The case against Converse was dismissed. Charles Porter Converse left his jail and moved to a large basin of trees eight miles northeast of Dunlap. Not only did he leave a mixed legacy in Millerton, but the area where he lived is today called Converse Basin.

J esse Jansen, a Danish sea captain, left his ship to seek his fortune in the Gold Country of California. He became involved in farming and eventually, in 1889, moved to Reedley, the largest grain shipping area in the world. He soon became a grain agent as well as going into the real estate and insurance business.

In 1902, a major fire burned a two-block area of downtown Reedley, with the exception of one brick building. Jansen bought the four lots on which it stood at the corner of Tenth and G streets. After convincing local merchants that only brick should be used downtown, he led the effort by rebuilding the old brick structure. The new edifice contained Reedley's first bank, a drugstore, a harness shop and an opera house. In addition, Jansen constructed his own water works for the downtown area.

In 1903, the first performance in the Opera House took place. The play was *Uncle Tom's Cabin*, presented by a traveling company. The construction of the Opera House allowed it to be used for many purposes. It had portable seating which meant that it could be used for theatrical performances for an audience of three hundred or transformed to accommodate dancing, a church meeting or a boxing match.

For many years the Opera House served the Reedley community in many ways. It was the scene of high school graduations, grand balls, square dances, revival meetings, and, for four years, it was used by the local Catholic church for services.

Since it opened in 1903, the Reedley Opera House has been a gathering place for the citizens of that community. Today, it is listed in the National Register of Historic Places and continues to be one of the finest examples of brick commercial architecture in the Central Valley.

The Reedley Opera House.
Courtesy of Fresno County Free Library

The Republican Printery Building,
now the Downtown Club.
Courtesy of Fresno County Free Library

A Printing Press & Preservation

A walk east on Kern Street between the Fulton Mall and the Civic Center Square development takes you past a building that played an important role in Fresno history. Built in 1919 to create much needed space for the job printing division of the *Fresno Morning Republican*, this building was designed by architects Edward Glass and Charles Butner. A Spanish red tile canopy over the center of the structure denotes a Mediterranean style and adds a distinctive touch.

The *Fresno Morning Republican* was one of the most influential newspapers in the state and had outgrown its headquarters at Van Ness Avenue and Tulare Street. When the *Republican* was sold, William Glass, father of the architect and business manager of the *Republican*, assumed control of the job printing business. In 1925, he entered public service and turned control of the business over to his son-in-law, Leon Camy, who operated a commercial printing business in the building well into the 1970s.

In the late 1970s, Camy's son and daughter sold the building to Robert Klein, Jr., who was committed to restoring it in a way that would allow a new, but historically sensitive use. Klein found the building's interior to be a treasury of printers' artifacts. The oldest typeface was of wood and was dated 1856. It had been brought to Fresno by the owners of the *Republican*. All of the artifacts were appraised by and in cooperation with the Smithsonian Institution.

Today, the building's exterior remains intact, but the interior has been transformed into an elegant dining club. In one corner of the main dining room, an imposing printing press is preserved as a reminder of the building's historic use. The original saw-toothed skylights have been replicated and allow light into the building.

The bar area is dominated by an exquisitely carved back bar, dating from 1888, that had graced the Sing Chong Lung Kan Kee Company building on China Alley for many years. Today the Fresno Republican Printery building is listed in the National Register of Historic Places.

On the corner of M and Calaveras streets sits a lovely home that looks as if it was transported from England. It is an example of the influence that the Arts and Crafts Movement had on American architecture at the turn of the century. The quaint lines of the roof add to the romantic feeling of an English cottage. However, it is larger than a cottage and its setting makes one wonder about its history. Built in 1912 by banker and merchant Louis Einstein, it was, in its time, located well north of the business district in one of Fresno's upper-class neighborhoods.

Born in Germany in 1847, Einstein came to America at age eighteen. He first settled in Memphis, Tennessee. Later he came west and, by 1871, became an associate of Elias Jacob in Visalia. The two operated a general store under the name of Jacob & Einstein.

At this time, Jacob was operating a store in Kingston, a small town on the Kings River. He asked Einstein to take charge of this business. Soon after, Vasquez and his gang of bandits rode into Kingston with guns blazing. After shooting up the village, they tied up Einstein and rode off. For Einstein, it was a memorable and terrifying experience.

In 1874, the firm of Jacob & Einstein bought Otto Froelich's business in the new town of Fresno Station. The firm continued to expand and by 1888 had formed a stock corporation capitalized at $200,000. In 1887, Einstein founded the Bank of Central California and served as its president until his death in 1914.

Mr. Einstein was one of the most respected citizens of the Fresno community. Active in almost all phases of the economic growth of Fresno, he also was involved in the cultural life of the community. His impact on the community is still being felt as his descendants carry on his legacy of community service.

Today, his lovely home, designed by architect Edward Foulkes, is listed in the National Register of Historic Places and is owned by the YWCA.

Louis Einstein
Home located at
Calaveras and M
Streets.
*Kate Rehart Byerly
photograph*

One of Fresno's most famous adopted citizens was born in Papert, Armenia on November 7, 1903. In 1915, during the Armenian massacres, he saw his father killed and he was taken captive and placed in a Turkish prisoner-of-war camp. He was near death from inhumane treatment when he miraculously gained his freedom. In 1922, he boarded a ship for America.

His first glimpse of the Statue of Liberty sparked a love for America that he would share with others for the rest of his life. On his arrival at Ellis Island he took a shower which, he felt, washed away all that was rotten—hatred, wars and famine. He took a train to San Francisco, eating only potato salad because it was the only item he could read on the menu. He vowed that one day he would make a far better one. Settling in San Francisco, he got a twelve-dollar-a-week job as a dishwasher at Coffee Dan's.

In 1930 he moved to Fresno where he found a home in the Armenian community. He opened a lunch counter called Omar Khayyam's at 1129 Van Ness Avenue. In spite of the Depression, customers flocked to his restaurant to enjoy his delicious clam chowder, chili con carne and pot roast special. His dream was to instruct Americans in how to eat good food. Soon he had to find larger space. He moved his business to 1918 Mariposa Street and three years later to the Sequoia Hotel on Van Ness Avenue. By now his patrons were enjoying such Armenian dishes as shish-kebab and kouzou kzartma.

During these years, he had married a Fresno girl he had met at Fresno's Holy Trinity Armenian Apostolic Church. Throughout his life this would remain his church home.

In 1938, he decided to move his restaurant to San Francisco. The location he chose was the site of Coffee Dan's where he had washed dishes so long ago. The San Francisco Omar Khayyam's became world famous.

From 1942-1954, he served as a food consultant for the U.S. Army. For this he received commendations from Presidents Hoover, Truman and Eisenhower. In 1951, he received the Medal of Freedom.

When Ellis Island was declared a historic site, he was one of six Americans honored at the ceremony.

George Mardikian died on October 23, 1977. The Holy Trinity memorial service for this special man was filled to overflowing.

Fresno's Mission-Style Depot

As you travel on the Santa Fe Railroad line through the great Central Valley, you see vineyards, orchards, fields of crops stretching for many miles and, on a clear day, the great mountain ranges of the Sierra Nevadas and Coast Range looming in the distance. From time to time this vista is broken as a town is reached and the peaceful countryside is replaced by a bustling urban center. Most of these Valley towns have one thing in common—the railroad depots are built in a simple Mission style. The selection of this architectural style reminds the traveler of the era when California was a part of Spain and evokes a feeling of permanence.

Fresno's Santa Fe Depot was built in the Mission style in 1899, with two additions at a later time. Located at the corner of Tulare Street and Santa Fe Avenue, the depot was constructed three years after the Santa Fe Railroad line was built.

For a number of years the Central Pacific Railroad (now the Southern Pacific) had a monopoly on railroad access to the Valley. In response to the growing stranglehold that developed, a group of capitalists purchased subscriptions for a new line. The public responded enthusiastically and on October 5, 1896, the new line, originally called "The People's Railroad," reached Fresno.

Today, the Santa Fe Depot is no longer used for passengers, but houses executive offices. Listed in the National Register of Historic Places, it stands as a symbol of Fresno's growth as the nineteenth century reached its close.

The Gray Brick House

Kate Rehart Byerly photograph

A two-story gray brick house stands on the corner of S and Mariposa streets. Of Georgian Revival design, it is one of the few homes left in the once gracious and elite Cathedral District near downtown Fresno. The original owner, Frank Rehorn, was a pioneer building contractor and the first president of the Builder's Exchange, which was born out of anti-union sentiment during the time that he was designing and building his mansion. As a result of Rehorn's outspoken involvement, his home was the focal point for at least three union strikes, which caused delays in its completion.

On January 16, 1906, Mr. and Mrs. Rehorn gave a housewarming party to celebrate their new home. Among the guests was architect A. C. Swartz, who was responsible for the design of the impressive mansion.

After Mr. Rehorn died, the house was sold to H. H. Holland and underwent remodeling. Later the structure served as a convent for the Sisters of the Holy Cross until 1970. During those years, one of the rooms was converted into a chapel.

After standing vacant for several years, the building was purchased by architects Allen Lew and William Patnaude and became the focus of an extensive rehabilitation project. When the project was finished, the rope molding on the newel posts and bannisters of the entry hall's magnificent stairway, considered to be of museum quality, once again greeted visitors. Mill work throughout the home also reflects the sensitivity and care with which the restoration project was undertaken.

Today, housing a group of busy architects and a ghost named Sister Irenita, it is a reminder of an era when this downtown neighborhood was an elegant and gracious section of Fresno.

Soon after the turn of the century, the boundary of Fresno began to move across Divisadero Street in a northward direction that continues to this day. The stylish North Park subdivision, centering around Fulton Street and Van Ness Avenue, was developed first.

As the First World War drew to a close, the country entered the "flapper" era, followed by the Great Depression of the 1930s. In spite of the economic woes of the period, building continued and the area we know today as the Tower District came into existence.

The commercial district centered around the Tower Theatre at the corner of Wishon and Olive avenues and Van Ness Village to the north. As the residential area grew, homes of many different architectural styles emerged, ranging from Victorian to Craftsman Bungalow. This colorful, exciting neighborhood contained everything one might wish, even Fresno State College, all within walking distance—quite a boon during the gas rationing of World War II.

As the growth of Fresno raced northward in the 1960s and 1970s, the district became quieter. Some of the residential neighborhoods began to show signs of deterioration. Once grand North Park declined under the impact of an impending freeway. Lovely old homes, one by one, faced the onslaught. Some were purchased at auction and moved, others were demolished. The rest waited quietly by, hoping for better times.

The restoration of the Tower Theatre and the City Council's approval of the Tower District Specific Plan in the late 1980s brought a new community awareness to the commercial district. Merchants who had retained their commitment to the neighborhood were rewarded as new businesses opened. Young couples began to buy the district's still gracious older homes, their restoration projects giving the area a new life.

Today, the Tower District is a center for live theater, fine restaurants, antique shops, bookstores and coffeehouses. A unique and colorful neighborhood, it throbs with an exciting pace of life unlike any other part of Fresno.

The Temple Bar

From 1889 until the wrecker's ball leveled a good part of downtown Fresno in the mid-1960s, a remarkable building stood on the northwest corner of Mariposa Street and Van Ness Avenue. This ornate three-story structure had bay windows at the corner of the two upper floors and was topped by an elaborate cupola, also at the corner of the building. The imposing structure also had two large signs on the roof, one facing each street. Here the name of the building, flanked by the names of the owners, S. N. Griffith and R. B. Johnson, was proclaimed to all who looked upward. Atop each sign stood a large statue.

The proximity of the building to the Courthouse made it popular among the legal profession. Not long after it was finished, the entire second floor had become law offices. The third floor became a rooming house managed by an efficient woman named Mrs. Lundy. A store occupied the first floor, namely the Webster Drug Store, which was later sold to Casner's.

Many of the lawyers who inhabited the second floor of this building later became judges or went into politics. One of the most colorful tenants was Justice of the Peace George Washington Smith, whose court was in the building. He was well-known throughout Fresno as the marrying judge. He performed so many marriages that he was called often to provide the latest total for the newspapers. One tradition he always observed was to kiss the bride at the end of the ceremony. He also kept a large cuspidor outside his courtroom with a sign above it urging gentlemen who chewed tobacco to use it with caution and not to hit the wall.

When this building, appropriately named the Temple Bar, was razed in 1964, Fresno lost one of its most elaborate and colorful early office buildings.

TEMPLE BAR BLDG. 1887

The Temple Bar building was located on the northwest corner of Van Ness and Mariposa Streets. Many attorneys had their offices here because it was close to the courthouse.
Fresno Historical Society Archives.

An Eggs-Acting Contest

Fresno County, with its flat lands and open spaces, has in its history been the site of many kinds of races. The West Coast Relays brought the fleetest feet in the United States to compete in all kinds of track events. Auto, bicycle and motorcycle races also have been favorites over the years. But one rather unusual event that began in November of 1926 is not as well known—the Selma Egg-laying Race.

Local poultry men, hoping to put to rest the notion that the Central Valley was not a good place to raise chickens, decided to hold an egg-laying contest. Hens entered in the contest were brought to a plant in Selma where they were housed throughout the months of the competition. As each egg that the hens produced was tallied, the enthusiasm of local farmers grew. In May of 1927, a hen owned by Mrs. W. L. Griffith laid an egg a day for thirty-one days. Such an output gave the other hens a high mark for which to aim. The biddies rose to the occasion. By the time the first contest ended in the spring of 1927, Fresno County led the state in egg-laying capabilities and ranked eighth nationwide.

Encouraged by such a good result, the 1927-28 contest saw a larger number of entries. This year the goal was to compete more successfully with the records established in similar contests throughout the United States. In November of 1927, 235 hens were brought to Selma. They labored at their task with unstinting concentration. When the year was up, Fresno County hens and poultry men alike had much to crow about. The 1928 national championship had been won by Fresno County, leaving Texas as the runner-up.

With pride and production the bywords of the day, one biddy in particular deserves to be remembered. Owned by John Cox of Fresno, she laid 315 eggs in the 365-day competition, making her the "high hen" of the event. Tired, but triumphant, she made a special contribution to local history.

As you travel up and down the Central Valley, one feature of each community is easy to spot—the local historic water tank. Because water was necessary and not always easily obtainable, when water systems were installed these tanks became symbols of the resource that allowed a desert to be developed into rich agricultural land. Most of the water tanks look much alike. The tank stands tall on four steel legs, proudly bearing the name of the community in which it is located.

When Kingsburg's water tank was dedicated in 1912, it looked like all the others. Standing 122 feet above the town, with a capacity of 60,000 gallons of water, it could be seen from all over Kingsburg. For a number of years, a flag was flown from atop the structure on special holidays, but the practice was abandoned after it was decided that it was dangerous for the person who had to install it.

The original water tank continued to tower over the community until 1974 when it was decided that it needed refurbishing. Donations for the project came from many sources, but it was the generous gift from Myrtle Sandell Hoeffler that made completion possible. Today a plaque honoring Mrs. Hoeffler's gift has been placed on one leg of the tower.

When the refinished water tank was unveiled, it had been converted to a giant Swedish coffeepot. What better symbol for a coffee-loving community that today has become a Swedish village. The citizens of this charming town can point to their water tank with a real sense of pride.

Original College Pharmacy building across Van Ness Avenue from its present location
Courtesy of Charles Alstrom

Van Ness Village, located in the 1400 block of North Van Ness Avenue in Fresno's Tower District, is a charming enclave of shops. At its heart is a family-owned business that has been an important part of Fresno history for more than half a century.

One of the founders of this enterprise, Edward John Alstrom, moved to Fresno from St. Paul, Minnesota, in 1926 at the age of eighteen. He was hired by the Owl Drug Store to make deliveries, a job which paid $12.50 a week. A year later he became an apprentice pharmacist, moving up to assistant and, in 1933, he passed his state board exams and became a licensed pharmacist.

During his years at the Owl Drug Store, Alstrom met Ben Wiebe. The two men decided to each put up $1,500 and form their own business.

On December 6, 1937, the College Pharmacy opened its doors.

Although the economy was beginning to pull out of the Great Depression, it took courage and determination to start a new business. For the first six months neither man drew a salary, investing everything in their enterprise. Open seven days a week, the new store was primarily a pharmacy, but it had a soda fountain that soon drew customers from nearby Fresno State College and the surrounding neighborhood. A post office in the back corner of the store served the Tower District as a postal substation until the present one was built on Fern Avenue.

The business flourished to such an extent that the two partners built a new building a short distance north and moved the soda fountain there. Today that building houses a laundromat, but the initials of the two men, A and W, are still in the walk in front of the entrance. Their plan to purchase the lots between the two buildings did not materialize.

In 1950, they bought a building from Aram Saroyan that is located just across the street at 1429 North Van Ness. Two years later Ben Wiebe died. Ed Alstrom purchased Wiebe's half of the business.

Today, Ed's son, Charles, is owner of the College Pharmacy. He maintains his father's philosophy of looking on each customer as a friend. Customers are greeted by name and receive courteous, friendly, old-fashioned service. It is this sense of caring that brings his customers back even after they have moved from the neighborhood.

Charles Alstrom's choice of a new logo in the late 1970s underscores his belief in traditional values. It pictures a horse-drawn wagon bearing a pharmacist's symbol. The College Pharmacy does not bring a horse-drawn wagon to your door, but it does offer free delivery.

The Twin Sisters

If you choose to leave downtown Fresno by traveling north on N Street, you will see the Memorial Auditorium on the northeast corner of Fresno and N streets. Continuing north, you cross Merced Street and, if you look to the right, you might look again and, thinking that you are seeing double, turn the corner, go around the block and look again. For there, set back from the street, are two charming identical Victorian houses. Right down to each elaborate bracket, boxed cornice, hand-turned spool and decorative spindle, these two homes are alike in every detail. Why would two such exquisite twin houses of Eastlake design sit side by side?

Early in the century, William F. McVey, who was the vice-president of the Fresno National Bank, wanted to build homes for his daughters, Pansy and Maud. He purchased the adjoining properties on N Street and decided to build homes that would be identical in every way. The women lived in them for a number of years.

Both homes were sold, but have been occupied on a continuous basis ever since. Well-cared-for and still beautiful, they do make you wonder why Mr. McVey made such an effort to be sure they were identical. Perhaps, even ninety years ago, fathers had to be careful not to play favorites where daughters were concerned. Whatever the reason, he left a special architectural legacy to the citizens of Fresno.

The area of Fresno known as west Fresno holds many hidden architectural treasures. Driving through the area, one must be on the lookout for something wonderful, and often fascinating, around each corner. Such is the case at Tulare and C streets, for on the northwest corner of this intersection, hidden among the trees, is one of Fresno's architectural gems, Saint Genevieve's Chinese Catholic Church.

As you look at the brick structure, it is evident that the concept of the building was to use Western design combined with Eastern themes. Built using a basilica plan, as in the early Christian churches, the tower is capped with a cross. The wood trim is painted in red and green with upturned eaves at the roof line in the Chinese style.

Saint Genevieve's was built in 1938 as a part of a dream of members of the Chinese community who were of the Catholic faith. The dream was more completely realized when the parish was able to hire a Chinese-speaking priest. It has now been more than twenty-five years since Father Francis Chung arrived in Fresno to serve the parish of Saint Genevieve's. During this time he has revitalized the parish greatly.

At services each Sunday, Father Chung delivered his homily in both Chinese and English. Part of the liturgy of the Mass was sung in Chinese, also. This was very meaningful to the older members of the parish and gave the younger people an opportunity to hear their ancient language and to carry on the traditions of their culture.

Father Chung has since died. Father Vincent Lau is now serving as Saint Genevieve's priest.

Aside from its importance to the Chinese community of Fresno, Saint Genevieve's has another distinction as well. The entire parish includes the church building, the parking lot and the house next door. The inhabitants of the house are the only people who live within the parish. It has the distinction of being the smallest parish in the world.

In the 1870s, as the town of Fresno Station began to grow west of the Southern Pacific Railroad, a colorful neighborhood developed. Settled by peoples of many nationalities, one of the largest of these groups was the Chinese. Many had moved from Millerton where they had been traders and shopkeepers.

As they established a community in the new town, they formed associations, called tongs. The tong was made up either of people from the same province in China or it consisted of members of the same family with the same surname. The tongs gave newcomers housing until they could find jobs and assimilate into the community. The tongs were located mostly on China Alley, a colorful two-block byway between Kern and Fresno streets.

By the late 1880s, there were six tongs which, together with other clubs, composed the Chinese Consolidated Benevolent Association of Fresno. It was the elders of this group who governed the Chinese community. They settled disputes and meted out justice. They took care of their own.

Today, two tong buildings remain in Chinatown. The Bing Kong Tong Association building is the only structure remaining on China Alley. It has been a center of Chinese culture for almost a hundred years. Here Chinese opera and speeches can still be heard and enjoyed.

The Bow On Association has a frontage on F Street with an exterior entrance on China Alley. Here men gather to play mahjong and, at the time of the Chinese New Year, members of the association stand before the Joss House, their temple altar, to pay respects to their ancestors.

As Fresno nears the twenty-first century, there are those in this community who have not forgotten their heritage. It is interesting and, perhaps reassuring, to note that not far from the bustle of the downtown commercial district, in the quiet of their historic settings, the ancient traditions of the Chinese in Fresno are kept.

Chinatown as it appeared just after the turn of the century. The view is looking east, towards the railroad tracks and the main part of town towards the upper left hand corner. G Street intersects with Tulare at the upper right. Fagin's, or China, Alley is just behind the tall smokestack in the middle foreground. The alley was really more of a street in the early days as indicated by the awnings all along the route.
Courtesy of William B. Secrest, Sr., Collection

On the southwest corner of Tulare Street and Waterman Avenue, in a residential neighborhood of west Fresno, sits a large modernistic building with an obvious Chinese influence. In fact, the two-story building has a wide span of roof that is shaped like the Chinese word for "man." This imposing structure, built in 1961, houses the Confucius Church and Chinese Consolidated Benevolent Association. It also is the location of the Chinese School of Confucius.

However, this is not the first building to house this important component of Chinese culture in Fresno. In the early 1900s, the elders of the Chinese community established a Chinese school to give their young people insight into Chinese history, language, culture, philosophy and literature. They felt that it was their responsibility to teach their children about their heritage. The first school was in the middle of the 1000 block of G Street.

After several moves, a new building was completed at 1040 D Street in 1936. This new facility housed both the school and the Chinese Consolidated Benevolent Association, the latter being the parent organization for the Chinese family associations and clubs in Fresno. Classes were held after public school let out. On Monday through Friday, classes met from 5 to 8 P.M. and on Saturday morning from 9 A.M. to noon. Grades were kindergarten through ninth. At this point in its history, the school had an enrollment of 120 to 150 students and two teachers. As the school continued to grow, extracurricular activities were added. Of all these, the Drum and Bugle Corps was the most popular.

In 1955, the school was forced to look for a new site as an expansion of Highway 99 cut a swath through west Fresno and their structure was torn down. In 1961, the school reopened in its new building on Tulare Street and Waterman Avenue. Over a thousand people attended the dedication ceremony on November 18, 1962. The building, which was designed by architect Allen Y. Lew, won an award of excellence from the San Joaquin Chapter of the American Institute of Architects.

Today, even though most of the Chinese community has moved from Chinatown, the school is still thriving and draws young people from all over Fresno. Every Saturday morning they come to their historic neighborhood to learn to read and write in Chinese, to study the teachings of Confucius and to learn Chinese folk dancing. For a few hours each week the laughter of children fills the air of historic Chinatown once again.

The Mosgrove Home

In the Echo/Carmen area of Fresno's Tower District can be found a wealth of historic homes. In this neighborhood of varied architectural styles, Spanish revival, English Tudor and Craftsman Bungalow homes provide an aesthetically beautiful environment.

Near the southern edge of this enclave, a cozy, unpretentious bungalow sits, nestled amid trees and shrubbery. Obviously of an earlier period than the surrounding homes, it has a pioneer flavor. Built in 1910 by Mr. and Mrs. William Mosgrove, it is, indeed, the first home constructed in this area and one of the first built north of Olive Avenue. The architect, Frank Faulkner of Missouri, was Mrs. Mosgrove's brother. He designed the house according to her specifications. She requested a storm cellar like those in the Midwest which was reached by outside doors that had an upward slant toward the house. This cellar door provided a special treat for the three Mosgrove boys. A "cookie window" just above the cellar door had a wide shelf that extended outside. On baking day, fresh cookies could always be found cooling on the windows wide ledge. The sloping door provided the perfect means for climbing up to reach the cookies.

Today, the Mosgrove home is in the heart of Fresno surrounded by homes and nearby businesses. In 1910, when the house was completed, vast open land provided a view of the Sierra mountains. It also provided another kind of vantage point. When Mr. Mosgrove took the Santa Fe train to San Francisco, he could see Mrs. Mosgrove waving to him from the front porch.

The Prescott Mansion

As the wrecker's ball hit structure after structure in downtown Fresno during the 1950s and 1960s, much of Fresno's architectural heritage began to vanish. Broadway as Fresnans knew it virtually disappeared. Victorian neighborhoods were ravaged as homes one by one were torn down to make way for medical offices, businesses or, most tragic of all, parking lots.

One of Fresno's early prestigious neighborhoods, near Saint John's Cathedral, felt the onslaught most keenly. Established just after the turn of the century, this area of elegant homes was bounded by Fresno, U, Tulare and Q streets. At its heart was a home that, at the time it was built in 1888, was the most elegant and expensive in Fresno. Situated at the corner of Tulare and Q streets, it was of Queen Anne design, two stories high with a large corner cupola that soared above the roof line. The bay windows featured colored, leaded glass that was custom-made in the East. The formal rooms boasted rosewood paneling from France. A large, covered veranda graced two sides of the main floor. Topping this spectacular house was a widow's walk.

Seven years after the house was built, it was purchased by Robert Kennedy, whose daughter and son-in-law, Jessie and Fred Prescott, would eventually live in it. The year after Kennedy acquired the house, in 1896, the Santa Fe Railroad was built down the middle of Q Street. Suddenly, this beautiful street was no longer a pleasant place to live.

Kennedy bought lots three blocks away on the northeast corner of Mariposa and S streets and proceeded to move his huge home. The monumental task was accomplished by jacking up the house and setting it on heavy timbers. Using horses, the house was pulled along inch by inch on wooden rollers, a process which took several days. Eventually it was placed on its new foundation. In its S Street setting, it added to the beauty of this gracious neighborhood for over seventy years.

In the 1960s, the funerals of both Mr. and Mrs. Fred Prescott, who had years earlier moved into the house with their two daughters, were held in the house, as had been the custom in prior times. The house stood lonely and silent until it was torn down a few years later. With its demise, a priceless Fresno legacy was lost.

Fresno's oldest family-owned newspaper began its existence in 1886. It was called the *Daily Real Estate Report & Abstract of Records* and was the brainchild of Bruce Cavit, a local lawyer. Its purpose was to provide Fresnans with a daily log of real estate transactions, recorder's documents and reports of Municipal and Superior Court civil actions.

Two years later the newspaper, experiencing financial difficulties, was purchased by Morris Shelby Webster. Webster, a native of Contra Costa County, had come to the Fresno area for the first time at age fifteen to herd sheep on Potter's Ridge near Huntington Lake. Ten years later, in 1886, he moved to Fresno and began to work in real estate and banking. This background led him to purchase the fiscally troubled newspaper. At first Webster hand-copied court records, set the type and printed the paper in his home. As the business grew, his son, Norman, began working for his father as a reporter and took over the business when his father died in 1937.

The years have seen small changes as the paper strove to serve the Fresno community. These changes have been reflected in the name, which has been the *Fresno Daily Legal Report & Abstract of Records, Fresno Daily Legal Report*, and *Fresno Daily Report*. Today, under its new name, the *Fresno Business Journal*, Fresnans are given a publication that contains not only legal reports, but also the latest business news along with stories from United Press International.

As the years went by, Norman's son Gordon, and grandchildren, Gordon, Jr., Norman and Laura, joined the family firm. The newspaper flourished and expanded as they purchased their own typesetting business and eventually Mid-Cal Printing.

Even when two fires caused extensive damage to their plant, the Webster family provided the citizens of Fresno County with continuous and uninterrupted publication of the community's legal transactions.

After Gordon, Sr. retired, Gordon, Jr. and Norman bought out each other's interests. Norman operates Mid-Cal Printing which he soon expanded by buying another printing company, California Color, from Fresno book publisher Stephen Blake Mettee.

Gordon, Jr. runs the newspaper. Two of Gordon's sons work part-time for the paper so perhaps, one day, a fifth generation will be at the helm of this longtime Fresno success story.

The Cocktail Napkin Policy

Many business deals are made after work, when people gather at the end of the day to relax. One deal that changed the course of business insurance writing all over the world occurred in the spring of 1936. Until that time businesses that wanted maximum liability coverage had to carry as many as a dozen policies from several different companies because many of the standard policies had gaps in the coverage offered. Often this resulted in overlapping protection. Not only that, this method of insurance coverage was very expensive.

On a spring evening in 1936 two men, Grover Cleveland Appleton, of Shepherd-Knapp-Appleton Insurance, and J. W. Reynolds, could be seen deep in conversation in the bar of the Hotel Fresno. They were discussing the problems that arose from this situation. It was then that Cleve Appleton offered an idea he had been considering for some time. He envisioned a liability policy that would be all-inclusive. He had talked to a number of companies, but they rejected his idea as dangerous and impractical. As Appleton talked, Reynolds, who was president of United Pacific Insurance Company, became enthusiastic about his idea. Many meetings followed this initial conversation.

After working out all the many necessary details, the first comprehensive liability policy was printed on August 25, 1936, revolutionizing the liability insurance business in the United States. It all was initially written out on a cocktail napkin in the bar of the Hotel Fresno by Grover Cleveland Appleton, thus adding one more important chapter to the history of Fresno.

For a number of years Fresnans have watched with sorrow as the historic North Park area of the city has been torn away bit by bit. Each drive down Fulton Street or Van Ness Avenue south of Belmont Avenue brought the view of another vacant lot as homes were torn down or relocated. All of this activity was to accommodate a new freeway which would link Highway 99 and the Freeway 41/180 interchange.

On March 26, 1991, the Tower District Specific Plan was adopted by the city council. This led Caltrans to do a further study, called the GAP Project, of the remaining structures in the neighborhood affected by the freeway. As a result of this study, thirteen structures were deemed eligible for the National Register of Historic Places. It was then decided that six of these structures would be moved to sites within the neighborhood.

Although a great deal of work remains to be done, a drive down Fulton Street today is a much happier experience. Just north of Mildreda Street two brown-shingled structures, the Porter and McIndoo houses, have been moved from Van Ness to this site. They have been situated so they face the same direction and, thus, remain eligible for the National Register. In the next block the Brooks home, having been moved one block from its original site, sits on pilings waiting to be put in place. Suddenly, the vacant lots that loomed so starkly are filled with homes that, because they were built for the neighborhood, look appropriate in their new setting. Caltrans plans to place these homes on foundations and to landscape the yards.

The homes, when restored, will create a lovely neighborhood that will constitute a potential historic district. After chronicling the stories of so many of the historic buildings that have been lost to our community, one must say—Hats off to Caltrans and to the City of Fresno for having the imagination and commitment to endeavor to preserve history and create beauty once again in North Park.

O ver the years many debates have been heard in the governmental chambers of Fresno's City Hall, but on August 23, 1939, one of the most unusual discussions in the city's history took place. As reported the following day in the *Fresno Evening Herald*, the argument centered on whether or not a popular dance called the "jitterbug" should be allowed at public dances in the Memorial Auditorium. Also at issue was another popular activity among the young, "necking."

Sparking the controversy was the owner of the Rainbow Ballroom, who would not allow the jitterbug to be performed in his establishment. He argued that this dance was dangerous. Not only did it inflict bruises, he claimed that flying feet would also cut women's stockings. The dance also offended his gentler customers.

After much debate and reflection, City Commissioner James S. Rankin, Sr., made what turned out to be the definitive statement on the matter. "I see nothing immoral about jitterbugging, although I do not and could not do it myself. And, as to necking, we have had it since Adam and Eve, and even some of you (commissioners) did it in your horse and buggy days."

This seemed to settle the matter. The commissioners decided to allow the jitterbug to be a part of Friday evening community dances. This endeared the city fathers to the younger generation, who loved nothing better than to spend Friday nights "cutting a rug" at the Memorial Auditorium. As to the issue of necking, it seems the city fathers decided there were some issues that could not be effectively legislated.

Otto Froelich was Fresno Station's second businessman and resident.
Fresno Historical Society Archives, R. W. Riggs Collection

The man who was to become Fresno's second merchant was a Danish immigrant who found his way to Millerton in the early 1860s. Here he established an express and store in the frontier town. He gained a certain standing in the life of Millerton and on October 25, 1869, he was named postmaster. He served in this post until April 4, 1872. In that month Fresno Station was established.

The ex-postmaster packed up his family and his belongings and moved immediately to the new town, thus beginning the exodus of Millerton residents to Fresno Station which would be the death knell of the frontier mining community.

As soon as he and his family arrived in Fresno, he set up his Pioneer Store across Front Street from James Faber's business. Although only a few days old, Fresno Station now had its first example of capitalistic competition.

In May of 1872, Fresno's newest entrepreneur became the town's first Wells Fargo agent. As the years went by he would serve as a school district trustee, postmaster and a partner in Fresno's first bank. He also, in partnership with Dr. Lewis Leach, would operate a winery and distillery.

A respected member of the early community of Fresno Station, Otto Froelich was a man of many talents and interests.

Miniature Golf Indoors

On the evening of October 1, 1930, Fresno residents were all atwitter. This excitement was generated by the opening of Fresno's first indoor miniature golf course. The proprietor of this establishment, Harry Hoffman, had made a study of the latest design ideas for miniature courses throughout California. As a result, his new facility featured the very latest hazards, traps and unusual shots to be offered at a miniature course anywhere in the state.

Those who attended the opening were greeted by the sight of not only the eighteen-hole course, but also of a large man-made lake, cactus beds, artificial flowers and elaborate ceiling decorations. On one wall, a huge stone fireplace drew attention. Flanked by overstuffed chairs and sofas, this area would provide a respite for tired golfers. Another wall was devoted to a refreshment center. Here a soda fountain and lunch stand would draw hungry and thirsty patrons.

With the strains of an orchestra providing background music, opening night guests strolled amid these surroundings that would provide countless fun-filled hours for Fresnans. As they gazed at the marvelous sights, they might also have reflected on the fact that the building in which these entertainments were housed, at 334 North Broadway, was owned by former heavyweight champion of the world Jack Dempsey.

In this or any election year, one of the real disappointments on election day is the usual low voter turnout. It is often forgotten that the privilege of voting was not always granted to everyone.

In the early days of our country, only those who owned property could vote. And it was not until this century was a number of years old that women were granted this right through a Constitutional amendment.

In October of 1911, the *Fresno Morning Republican* ran several articles about the great changes that were taking place regarding this matter. In a statewide election on October 12, Fresno County voters passed the amendment for women's suffrage. This vote was greeted with great enthusiasm.

Two days later, Mrs. Cecilia Cameron, wife of the Associated Press operator in Fresno, was the first woman to register to vote in Fresno. An active suffragette, she made it a point to sign her name to the registration form at the first opportunity. Not only was she the first female registered voter in the city of Fresno, but she was probably the first suffragette in California to qualify to vote as well.

An interesting sidelight to this story is that her husband, Frank, well aware of her involvement in the women's suffrage movement, called her the moment that he received an Associated Press dispatch from Sacramento saying that women could now register to vote. She immediately went to County Clerk Barnwell's office where he cheerfully handed her the registration papers.

As one remembers her story from the vantage point of the 1990s, one can probably be quite certain that Cecelia Cameron, well aware of the struggle to gain the important right to vote, never failed to go to the polls on election day.

A Fair Beginning

In the year 1882, just before the city of Fresno was incorporated, something rather wonderful happened. The central San Joaquin Valley had become an agricultural paradise and there had been a lot of discussion about showing examples of its finest produce. It was thought that a little friendly competition among growers might create interest as well. So, a number of Fresno County ranchers and businessmen formed the Fresno Fair Grounds Association. On December 26, 1882, they incorporated and named Dr. Lewis Leach their first president.

In February 1883, one hundred acres was purchased from Thomas Hughes for $5,000. The land was just two miles east of what was then called Fresno Colony. With the land purchased and an association in place, the first Fresno County Fair became more than just a dream.

After a great deal of planning and hard work, the fair opened on October 7, 1884. It was not a large event, but it was impressive. For five days, visitors could see horse races, view livestock and examine exhibits of produce. On opening day, admission was free; during the next four days a small fee was charged. The fair association noted that attendance was not as good on the days that visitors had to pay. The fair did not make a large profit that first year, but Fresnans enjoyed it and the association promised to hold another one the following year. And, happily for Valley residents, so they have for over one hundred years.

There is a neighborhood just north of downtown and west of Blackstone Avenue that contains a number of homes built prior to 1900. One such home is a two-story 1892 Eastlake Victorian on Glenn Avenue. It has a cross-gabled roof and remnants of Victorian gingerbread features, although many of those components have been removed, rendering the house less distinctive. However, the facade of the structure is not nearly as important as the human story that began within its walls.

In 1893, lawyer Walter Thompson, his wife and two daughters arrived in Fresno and purchased the house. One of the daughters, Marguerite, showed an early interest in art. When she graduated from Fresno High School in 1906, she listed her paintbrush as her best friend. Following graduation, she went to Paris with her aunt. By the time she returned in 1912, she was termed a "post impressionist painter" by a San Francisco newspaper. Her family, in an effort to inhibit her rather modernistic artistic aspirations, hid her paints. She was not so easily dissuaded. She painted the Sierra on a summer camping trip and held her first show at the Royal Galleries in Los Angeles. The exhibit was later shown at the Parlor Lecture Club in Fresno.

Marguerite married William Zorach, a fellow Paris art student, and moved to New York. Here she turned her attention to producing tapestries in wool. They were a tremendous success. Many years later, in 1949, she created a tapestry called, *My Home in Fresno*. In it she depicted the Victorian home of her childhood. She filled the canvas with her family and memories of her youth. Today, this tapestry hangs in the National Collection of Fine Arts at the Smithsonian Institution in Washington, D. C., thus preserving, in a special way, the home of her youth.

On the west wide of the great Central Valley, just as the flat arid land begins its gradual climb to join the Coast Range, lie the fabled Big Blue Hills. Flowing out of the mountains just north of the hills is the Cantua Creek. This area was made famous by Joaquin Murrieta and his sidekick, Three-Fingered Jack—for it was here that they met their fate in the person of Captain Harry Love. However, in 1890, another event of momentous proportions occurred in this small, barren corner of Fresno County.

For many years it had been said that in millenniums past giants had roamed the Valley around Cantua Creek. The legend was such a part of the fabric of life that one would have thought that when the petrified remains of a giant man were discovered by two farmers, everyone would have shrugged their shoulders and said, "Of course." Instead, it became the focus of conversation as far away as Fresno.

On December 17, 1890, the *Fresno Expositor* ran a headline asking, "Is It Genuine?" The story beneath the headline described the Cantua Man, as he became known, as weighing five hundred pounds, having a height of seven feet, and being blessed with the features of a Greek god.

The farmers who made this discovery, S. L. Packwood and R. L. Barrett, sold their giant petrified man to two Fresno businessmen who intended to exhibit him on the East Coast. Before they could profit from this venture, a petrified woman was found near Coalinga. A livery stable in Selma was traded for this latest discovery.

Then a petrified boy was found near Los Gatos. As he was being readied for shipping, his leg broke off. To the amazement of all, he was made of plaster of Paris. It was quickly discovered that the giant and the woman also were constructed of this material. Thus ended the hoax of the Cantua Man and the colorful legend of the giants of Cantua Creek.

Justice in the 1880s

Tracking down desperate criminals in the 1880s was not an easy business. One notorious bandit and murderer, Juan Galindo, had been on the wanted list for several years for crimes committed in a number of coastal counties. His ability to evade capture had become legendary and had led him to boast that no officer would ever be able to take him alive. He had not reckoned with a certain deputy sheriff from Fresno County named Ledyard Winchell.

Winchell had learned of Galindo's whereabouts and set up his plan of action. On a dark, moonless night, Winchell and his associate, O. J. Meade, hitched up their horse and buggy and set out on their lonely mission. They drove the horses hard through the night. At first light they set up camp at a secluded area at the mouth of Silver Canyon.

When nightfall came, they set out again, arriving at the New Idria quicksilver mine within a few hours. They found a small door that led to a cabin. Inside they could hear several people drinking and gambling. Opening the door, they burst inside, ordered the men to put their hands up and covered them with their six-shooters. Meade continued to cover the men with his gun while Winchell disarmed the criminal, Galindo, of his Colt .45. He handcuffed Galindo while his hands were still above his head. Winchell and Meade pushed Galindo through the door, tied him in a buckboard, and brought him to Fresno. He was put in jail, tried, found guilty, and sentenced to life in prison.

Thus was the legendary criminal Galindo brought to justice by a man who had been born in 1859 in one of the colorful buildings of old Fort Miller.

Vartanian's Block

In a neighborhood deep in the heart of west Fresno there is a complex of buildings constructed around 1894. A Victorian house, a barn, a water tank, and an outhouse still stand on their original parcel of land. This grouping of structures represents a microcosm of life in 1894 Fresno.

Before Fresno's first water system was built, every home had its own well. Water had to be pumped by hand. Those who had enough land built water tanks which were usually topped by a windmill. These were built high enough so that they would provide adequate pressure to bring the water to the faucet. One of the additional benefits of the water tank was that, if one stretched out underneath the tank, it provided a wonderfully cool spot to sleep on hot summer nights.

The barn, of course, was used to house the family's horse, and, possibly, buggy as well. The outhouse harkens back to the time when indoor plumbing did not exist.

The gentleman who built the house, Henry Vartanian, owned a jewelry store where the Hotel Fresno now stands. The house is of Victorian Stick design with a bay window embellished with colored glass. Fish scale shingles decorate the gable above.

Today, the house is the oldest home in the area of Fresno west of the Southern Pacific tracks. Given to Poverello House by Frank and Florence Caglia, the house has a new life as offices after a sensitive restoration project.

It is tempting, from the vantage point of the 1990s, to think of the days of steamboats paddling up and down the rivers of the Valley as a romantic time. Visions of a slower pace of life, unspoiled land, clear air filled with scents of wildflowers and herds of wild elk all create an illusion that is almost irresistible. However, into even the best of lives a little rain must fall.

For the family of William H. Parker, who lived at a hotel named the Casa Blanca on the Fresno Slough, January of 1868 brought more than a little rain; it brought a major flood. As the waters of the San Joaquin River continued to rise, so did the waters of the slough, one of its tributaries. Since the Casa Blanca was located adjacent to the waterway, the Parker family soon realized that, as the river rose, they should begin to move all their worldly goods to the second floor. By the time the move was accomplished, the flood waters began to pour into the structure. Soon the first floor was totally engulfed.

After several days of being stranded, the family was greeted by the welcome sight of a steamboat. As the steamer, called the *Empire City*, reached the Casa Blanca, its captain witnessed the plight of the Parkers and swung his boat into position next to the structure. Cables were run through the windows and fastened in place, making the upper deck of the steamer level with the upstairs windows of the Casa Blanca. The Parkers merely had to step out of the windows and onto the boat with all their belongings.

When people and goods were safely aboard, the steamer cast off and traveled down the Fresno Slough to the San Joaquin River. As they sailed away, their minds were certainly filled with thoughts other than romance, wildflowers and wild elk.

Autumn in Fresno

During autumn in Fresno one is aware of many things—the shorter, but still hot days, with increased humidity, that old-timers for some reason call Indian summer; the cooler mornings, with a decided nip in the air, that give hope that summer will truly end; the awareness that the leaves are beginning to change color, reminding us that soon the trees of Fresno will be a symphony of dazzling red and gold; and the completion of the grape harvest. The trays have been emptied into huge boxes and hauled off to the packers, and the wineries are in full production, their juicy fruit beginning the ancient process of turning into wine.

For those who call the Central Valley home, autumn is a special time of year. With the end of the grape harvest, for a short time the vineyards will stand silent. Each year, as more agricultural land becomes tract housing developments, it is tempting to wonder how many more generations will have the privilege of watching the seasonal changes in our rich farmland.

In 1930, Gustav Eisen, a scientist and wine expert, penned a letter to L. A. Winchell, vice-president of the Historical Society, describing his memories of Fresno when the city was small and surrounded by farmland.

He wrote, "I thank God that I saw the country before the flowers had been plowed under, before the Antelopes and Elk had been killed off, before the trees in the mountains had been cut to any extent, before the millions of wild ducks and geese had been vanquished, before the ground squirrels had been exterminated and while the Beaver built his dams in the Kings River canyon. Those are the things that I loved in life. Few now living saw it as I did."

For those of us fortunate enough to live in this place, perhaps we also should savor the special qualities of our area so that we too can remember and share our recollections with those who come later.

In a city like Fresno, with a history that encompasses more than 120 years, there are a variety of stories to be told concerning its architecture. Many of Fresno's wonderful structures fell victim to the wrecker's ball and are still mourned by those who appreciate fine design and history. For those buildings, still standing, that relate to a much earlier era there are some success stories and then there are stories that evoke only feelings of sadness. This is the story of one such building.

In the days after the turn of the century, Broadway buzzed with activity. Businesses of many kinds, hotels, and Fresno's first City Hall all drew people to this colorful street. The Pleasanton Restaurant, with its curtained booths, was a popular eatery. The 1,227-seat White Theater, the stately Carnegie Library, and the grand Hughes Hotel also graced this wide street. Many of the buildings had the name of the owner and the date of construction emblazoned on the uppermost facade, giving visitors a sense of history and continuity.

In 1913, a new hotel was built at 1257 Broadway. Designed in a modified Renaissance revival style, it rose seven stories high and was capped by an ornate cornice. It definitely made a statement of permanence to the young city.

Visitors to the new hotel were treated to a breathtaking experience for, when they entered the lobby, they looked up to the incredible skylight two and one-half stories above. A pipe organ sat against the west wall, its pipes blending into the decor. A balcony ringed the mezzanine, which overlooked the lobby. Public rooms opened off the balcony and, it was here that many organizations held meetings, including sororities from Fresno State College. For many years the college held its dances in the large lobby, and it is safe to say that many courtships began in that elegant setting. The dining room to the right of the lobby was Fresno's finest. Here waiters attired in tuxedos served beautifully appointed meals to diners seated at tables which were topped with fine linen cloths. The pipe organ provided dinner music.

Fresnans who had enjoyed the elegance of this hotel for many years took it for granted. Most thought that nothing would ever change. However, the whole face of the city changed in the late 1950s. Broadway suddenly was redeveloped out of existence—only two short blocks were left. The hotel became a home for senior citizens and then was abandoned and left defenseless.

Today, the Hotel Fresno sits vacant—alone on an island surrounded by asphalt. Its future uncertain, it stands as a stark reminder that nothing should be taken for granted, least of all something that brought beauty and elegance into our lives.

The Watchmaker & His Clock

The story of one of Fresno's oldest jewelry stores is bound up in the story of a clock—not a small wall clock or even a desk model, but a beautiful, rather magnificent twenty-foot-tall clock.

The story begins in a modest way. In 1908, a young Danish immigrant named Iver Eriksen settled in Salinas and began work as a waiter at the Bon Ton Restaurant. He formed a friendship with a man named Neilsen who worked in the jewelry store next door. Within three years both men had come to Fresno and, in 1911, they began their own jewelry business, Eriksen & Neilsen. Every week Eriksen visited the mountain lumber camps to sell watches, walking up Toll House Grade to get there. He would take watches back to the store for Neilsen to repair, returning them on his trip the following week.

The partnership later broke up.

Having taught himself the watch repair business, Eriksen moved to the 1100 block of Fulton Street and opened his own store. About 1919, he decided to purchase a large, rather rare clock, made by Mayer Brothers, for about $1,800. The clock, which came from Seattle, was installed outside his store. It stood twenty feet tall and, being made of cast iron, weighed 5,000 pounds. The face of the clock was made in Italy of galazzo glass. It had to be wound every seven days.

During the next forty-four years the clock moved to two other sites along with the business. For a brief time it sat next to the Mason Building and then moved to 1145 Fulton Street, where it is best remembered. Because of a city ordinance that required any sign advertising a business to be a certain number of feet from the store front and of a certain height, the name Eriksen & Company was inscribed on the face of the clock in letters only one inch high.

For years the clock was a landmark downtown. People set their watches by it, used it as a meeting place and, of course, were aware that it was a central part of the store's advertising, "Eriksen's, by the sign of the clock in the middle of the block."

When the Fulton Mall was built the developers felt the clock did not fit into the decor of the new street and asked Iver Eriksen, Jr., the second-generation owner of the business, to take it down. In

1977, when he moved his store to northwest Fresno, the owners of the shopping center where he moved felt it did not fit into their decor either.

And so, a once proud Fresno landmark, one that is fondly remembered by many Fresnans, sits silently in storage. One hopes that one day it will be allowed to emerge and once again grace a corner of Fresno, and take its rightful place as a proud part of Fresno's history.

Fresno's Electric House

Historic Huntington Boulevard, its broad expanse lined with sixty-five-year-old camphor trees, is a part of the Alta Vista Tract, Fresno's first subdivision outside of downtown. Many large homes of varying architecture grace this lovely neighborhood.

One of these, a two-story structure of Mediterranean revival design enhanced by a turret, made Fresno history.

In 1928, Abe Blum, treasurer of Gottschalks department store, decided that the new home he was planning to build on Huntington Boulevard should reflect the most modern conveniences available. The result was Fresno's first Red Seal all-electric home. It boasted an automatic heating system with a clock mechanism, which turned the unit on each morning and kept the house at a constant temperature all day. This was a truly revolutionary idea. Each bath also had individual electric heaters in the walls. Electric hot water heaters, lights, radio outlets and an all-electric kitchen with a Copeland refrigerator and an enameled freestanding range were all the most modern appliances for their time. An exhaust fan in the kitchen was also a new concept. Not only did it remove cooking odors, but Blum felt it helped to keep the kitchen cooler in the summer.

The electric features extended to the outdoors. In the front courtyard, a fountain played at night bathed in the rays of a lamp. This stately home not only had the newest conveniences, but it also reflected the craftsmanship of the period. Leaded glass windows, heavy oak doors, hand-wrought light fixtures and the living room's hand-hewn stenciled beams all reflected the era. In its revolutionary use of electricity throughout, it ushered in a new period in home comfort and design. Recently listed on the Local Register of Historic Resources, the Blum home is one of Fresno's special architectural treasures.

The name Rowell conjures up for many of Fresno's citizens a building downtown, a statue in Courthouse Park, a kindly doctor, and one of Fresno's earliest and most renowned pioneer families. However, there is another Rowell many Fresnans may not know by name. He was born in Woodsville, New Hampshire, to Jonathan and Cynthia Rowell, one of eight sons. The family moved to Illinois and, at the outbreak of the Civil War, he went off to join the Union Army with four of his brothers.

In 1883, he came west to Fresno County where his brother, Dr. Chester Rowell, was a prominent figure. Instead of settling in the city, he purchased property in the Washington Irrigated Colony near the small settlement of Easton. A year later he built a nine-room redwood house on his land. The redwood used in its construction was brought down from the mountains on horse-drawn wagons. He became involved in the development of farm properties in the Easton area. The first cooperative raisin association was another of his interests and he was very active in its formation. He also owned a cooperative packing house in Easton.

His fellow citizens looked to him as a leader in their community and elected him to the state legislature as the representative from the sixty-second district. At the request of his friend John Muir, he introduced a bill into the legislature to make Yosemite Valley a state park. A number of years later, in April of 1912, William Franklin Rowell died, just ten days before the death of his brother, Dr. Chester Rowell. He left a number of important legacies to his community, including six children who carried on the family tradition of community service.

However, William Franklin Rowell's most lasting contribution and the one that all those who love the beauty of the Sierra appreciate, was his successful effort to protect the priceless beauty of Yosemite Valley for generations to come.

The Legacy of Emma Miller

Situated on a tree-shaded lot on North Van Ness Avenue, as it wends its way through the Tower District of Fresno, is a two-story frame farmhouse. Not unlike many others of its vintage, this 1910 structure boasts a hipped roof, broken by a dormer. A deep porch across the front of the house often offered refuge during the hot Valley summers.

Those who venture down Van Ness now and spot this lovely old home would never guess that at one time it was turned a different direction. Originally, it faced Home Avenue, but in the early 1950s, it was relocated to its present site. Its rural origin sets it somewhat apart from its neighbors, yet it seems to blend into this architecturally diverse area.

The Miller family, who purchased the house in 1917, made significant contributions to Fresno. Dr. Walter Palmer Miller and his wife, Emma, left Maine in 1888 and settled in Sanger. Dr. Miller opened a medical practice and his wife began to pursue her interests by organizing a study club. Her great passion was the study of Shakespeare. Her knowledge of Latin, Greek and French gave her an excellent background for this pursuit. Her readings and interpretative talks attracted such interest that a Shakespeare Club was formed, which included women from other communities.

When the Millers moved to Fresno in 1891, Emma Miller joined the Wednesday Club. Soon, she was leading the study of great works of literature at meetings of the Parlor Lecture Club. As time went on, she began to review works of modern literature as well. She was a patron of the Wednesday Club, Leisure Hour Club, Query Club and Friday Club, the first four literary clubs in Fresno.

In 1925, the Query Club gave her a trip to Europe in appreciation of her contributions to the study of literature. On this trip, she had an audience with the pope. While she was on the trip, her friends formed the Emma Miller Study Club in her honor.

During the years 1911 to 1930, Emma Miller taught English and literature as a part-time faculty member at Fresno State College. The house on Van Ness was only two blocks from the school—her work was just a pleasant walk away.

Her legacy to Fresno is apparent in her contributions to the early study clubs in Fresno. She guided these groups of women in the

Mrs. W. P. (Emma) Miller c. 1900
Courtesy of Emma Ann Rue Kludt.

study of important literature and set the tone for the qualities of excellence that these clubs still possess. For that gift to her community, she will long be remembered.

A Bakery for the Valley

Around the corner from William Saroyan's "Red Brick Church" and one block south on M Street, stands a building that has played an important part in the culinary life of our city. When it was built in 1922, it was at the heart of Fresno's Armenian community. Time and development northward may have changed the neighborhood, but when Fresnans long for lahvosh and peda bread they happily drive to this special place to purchase it.

More than seventy years ago, Gazair Saghatelian began baking his own special creation, peda bread, in the ovens of his newly-opened bakery. His bread was unique among the round Middle Eastern varieties, because he made a circular cut in the center of the loaf and sprinkled sesame seeds on top. He also made lahvosh, a fifteen-inch, round, cracker-like bread, that, like the peda, was made from natural ingredients with no preservatives of any kind.

As the years progressed and the popularity of his breads spread beyond the Armenian community, his son, Sam, took over the business. After Sam's death in 1982, his sister, Janet, who had worked in the bakery since she was ten, became the owner.

Remaining faithful to the original recipes of her father, she has continued to produce the breads that have become staples in this community. However, she is adding her own special touch as well. In 1983, against everyone's advice, she began making lahvosh cut in heart shapes. This item is now the business' second largest seller.

Today, a third generation Saghatelian, Agnes, is working in the business. This is good news for all those Fresnans who grew up on peda bread and lahvosh. For them, the Valley Bakery is more than just a place to buy bread; it is an important Fresno tradition.

Fresno's Bank of Italy

In the years immediately following World War I, there was a sense of optimism about the future of Fresno's downtown. In 1918, A. P. Giannini and P. C. Hale, president and vice-president of the Bank of Italy, decided to invest in this area by building one of the most impressive structures that would ever grace Fulton Street. Of Italian Renaissance revival design, the eight-story steel and concrete building is faced with brick and ornate terra cotta. On its site on the northwest corner of Tulare and Fulton streets, the first floor window trim sets it apart from other structures in the area.

As impressive as the exterior may have seemed to the passerby, the interior truly was breathtaking with its twenty-five-foot decorative plaster ceiling. The ornate tellers' cages circled a portion of the room, etched brass elevator doors awaited those wishing to visit the offices upstairs, and stretching everywhere was a highly polished marble floor.

The visitor felt a sense of permanence, of stability. This was a bank that was solid, the building said to all who did business there.

A visit to the vault was memorable. Holding on to a solid mahogany railing, you descended marble stairs to the basement. There, a comfortable waiting room and an adjacent powder room were provided for the customers. The man in charge of the vault sat at a large roll-top desk. When he had checked the customer's name in the file, he then allowed access to the vault where the safe deposit boxes were housed. The vault was large—a sea of silver-colored boxes of all sizes built into the walls. After the completion of business, the customer climbed the marble stairs back to the first floor where everything bespoke elegance and professionalism.

Although the Bank of Italy building, later called the Bank of America, is listed in the National Register of Historic Places, today it stands empty and silent. Its elegance and function forgotten, it patiently waits for someone to bring it back to life.

The Expositor

The journalistic enterprise, the *Fresno Expositor*, had its beginnings in Millerton in 1870. Its editor, John William Ferguson, had traveled with his family from Louisiana to California during the Gold Rush. After holding a number of jobs in as many different fields, Ferguson became publisher of the Truckee *Tribune* for several years. Failing health caused him to move to Millerton where he hoped a drier climate would help his constitution. He launched his newspaper, with its Democratic editorial position, in this community of heavily pro-Southern sympathies, at a time when Millerton's first newspaper, the *Fresno Times*, had ceased operations.

Ferguson, his partner, Charles Heaton, and the boy who rolled ink onto the type lived in the stable which housed the printing plant. The first paper came off the press on April 27, 1870. Within two months the *Fresno Expositor* became the official county newspaper.

Three years later, in response to the agricultural problems local farmers faced trying to grow crops when cattle were allowed to roam freely, the newspaper backed the "No-Fence Law." Passage of this legislation would require farmers to build fences that would keep cattle on their grazing land. Cattlemen were outraged and organized a boycott of the *Expositor*. However, the law was passed and the *Expositor* emerged stronger than before.

When the county seat was moved to Fresno Station, Ferguson, like many others, dismantled his office and rebuilt in Fresno. The paper grew quickly, first becoming a daily newspaper and then, in 1890, the largest paper in the inland valley. It had a number of competitors, especially the *Fresno Morning Republican*. However, the *Expositor* continued to be a major journalistic influence in the growing city of Fresno. This lasted until the national election of 1896 when the Democratic party suffered many divisions. A number of Fresno Democrats withdrew their support from the *Expositor*. This, along with management problems, led to the newspaper's closure in September of 1898. With its demise, an important chapter in the history of Fresno came to a close.

The Other Prescott Mansion

A large, rather imposing structure of Georgian revival design sits in magnificent splendor on a corner lot at Tulare and T streets. If you can imagine how it looked before the Tulare Street addition was built, you could see that this was once one of Fresno's most beautiful mansions.

As is the case with most buildings, the story of the person who built it is often as interesting as the structure itself. In 1883, F. K. Prescott arrived in Fresno with his family and his wife's brother, C. S. Pierce, and his family. The two families made the train trip west looking for a warmer and more healthful climate than the one they left behind in Iowa. Their destination had been Fowler, where they had been assured there was a hotel, which, of course, there was not. The conductor was sympathetic and, seeing that the two couples had small children, urged them to stay on the train for another ten miles, without an increase in fare, and disembark in Fresno. They gratefully accepted the conductor's kindness.

After their arrival in Fresno, the two men established the Prescott & Pierce Lumber Company at Mono and H streets. They had been in business for several months when, one day, a stranger came to the lumberyard and proceeded to sit and whittle on a piece of wood all day. Finally he approached the partners and introduced himself as Return Roberts, owner of the Madera Flume & Trading Company. He offered to help them by supplying their needs on credit. The business prospered.

Later the partnership of the brothers-in-law was dissolved and each established his own lumber company.

In 1906, Prescott asked architect Eugene Mathewson to design the lovely brick home on Tulare and T streets. Since Prescott was a knowledgeable lumberman, the wood in the home was of the highest quality. Brazilian mahogany, black sequoia and clear pine graced the formal rooms. The exterior was constructed of brick with walls that are three feet thick at the base narrowing to nineteen inches at the third floor. Six Ionic columns support the portico and two octagonal towers support elaborate Eastlake dormers that add a sense of drama to the structure.

Today, the building houses the Palm-Colonial Funeral Chapel.

Nellie Boyd took a prominent role in the State Federation of Women's Clubs.
Fresno Historical Society Archives, R. W. Riggs Collection

In 1873, one year after Fresno Station was established, Conklin's Great United States Circus came to town, the first traveling troupe to do so. A year later Len Farrar built the Magnolia Hall on H Street, Fresno's first theater and town hall. Within ten years the Grady Opera House and the Barton Opera House were built and were able to accommodate the finest artists of the time as well as touring companies from New York.

One New York star who came west in the latter half of the nineteenth century became the first woman to organize and manage her own touring company. Her troupe made its first visit to Fresno in October of 1880. She was enchanted with the autumn weather and returned a number of times. Three years later she purchased a twenty-acre vineyard in the Central California Colony. Her parents and her sister moved to Fresno as well and she made Fresno the center of her operations. Within three years, she retired from the theater and concentrated on her vineyard.

Soon, she was much sought after by amateur theatrical groups. She was happy to participate and each year directed the Fresno High School play. One of her most notable contributions to her community was the Parlor Lecture Club, which she organized and led as its first president. She also took an active role in preparing Fresno County's exhibit in the 1893 World's Fair in Chicago.

The community of Fresno appreciated the role Nellie Boyd played in the development of the young city. But, it was also for her character, generosity, and charming disposition that she will long be remembered.

The Collins Home

A charming home of Eastlake design sits at the corner of R and Mariposa streets. The eaves on the cross-gabled roof reflect the elaborate gingerbread elements of the period, while a bay window with leaded glass diamond-shaped panes lends elegance to the Mariposa Street vista. The house was built in 1905 by Dave Cowan for James Darwin Collins, one of Fresno County's pioneers.

Collins was born in Tennessee in 1843. After serving in the Confederate Army during the Civil War and spending three years in a Union prison, he came west to Fresno County. He settled in the Big Dry Creek area and was instrumental in the development of its Academy school. He and his wife, Ann, were the Academy's first teachers. Mr. Collins was elected to the California Assembly in 1876 and in 1898 was elected Fresno County sheriff.

When he died, he had eight surviving children. His son, Dr. Clinton Collins, who lived in the house for many years, served as president of the Fresno County Medical Society and also was president of the Community Hospital staff. William Collins, another son, served seven consecutive four-year terms on the Fresno County Board of Supervisors—twenty-eight years in all.

Through the years, the home was the site of many happy family events, including weddings. More recently, during the 1970s, it was the Symphony League Decorator House and was featured on the La Paloma Heritage Home Tour. During its conversion to a restaurant, in the decade of the 1980s, it underwent many interior changes. Now in use as a law office, this structure, which is listed on the Local List of Historic Resources, is an important reminder of a pioneer family whose members contributed a great deal to the development of Fresno County.

The Swift Home

Remnants of one of the most beautiful of Fresno's early residential neighborhoods can still be seen as you drive down L Street just north of downtown Fresno. Of the mansions that remain, one in particular catches the eye. On a raised lot at the corner of L and Calaveras streets, a magnificent home of Georgian revival design transports the viewer to an era of graciousness and gentility. Built by lumberman Harvey Swift in 1905, the home contains some of the most beautifully detailed elements of any home in Fresno. Six Ionic columns rise to the roof level above the second story to support an open portico above the front door. Beveled glass entry panels; rich, carved moldings; dark, glowing wood—all attest to Mr. Swift's success. The ballroom in the basement was the site of many elegant parties in the years before World War I. Costume balls, birthday parties and formal dances drew guests from the cream of Fresno society.

Today, the home still retains the elegance of former years. It was purchased by the Lisle family for use as a mortuary, with additions made to the northern and southern ends of the home. These additions were built with care and every attempt to match the existing facade of the original part of the home was made. As a result, more than a hundred years after it was built, the home maintains its timeless quality.

In this case of a preservation story with a most happy ending, the citizens of Fresno can be grateful to two pioneer families—to the Swifts for constructing a home of such beauty and to the Lisles for appreciating the home's special qualities and making it possible for future generations of Fresno to enjoy this important reminder of our past.

Lee's Theater

On October 8, 1987, a select group of preservationists, architects, interior designers and community supporters gathered in the lobby of the Tower Theatre to sip wine, enjoy hors d'oeuvres and view the beginnings of an ambitious restoration project. Conversation centered around the building itself—memories of its glittering past, of milestones that took place in the old theater (a first date, a first kiss), and the most sincere and often voiced question, "Can it be brought back to life?"

With the entrance of the theater owner, Dottie Abbate, looking spectacular in a vibrant red dress, everyone anticipated the arrival of the evening's special guest. A hush fell over the gathering as a white limousine pulled up in front of the theater. As Mrs. Abbate walked to the curb, a distinguished, silver-haired man stepped out of the limo to an enthusiastic welcome. As they walked into the theater, everyone waited for an introduction to this distinguished gentleman, S. Charles Lee, the architect who designed the Tower Theatre.

Mr. Lee, then eighty-nine years old, had not seen the building since it opened in 1939. As he mingled with the guests he was pleased that so many people were interested in restoring the building. Later in the evening he was honored for his contributions to art deco design.

For those in attendance, it was a memorable night—a night when Dottie Abbate shared her dream of a theater for the performing arts in a beautifully restored building. Those who heard her speak that night wished for her dream to come true. And, indeed it has.

In the words of Ron Eichman, first general manager of the restored theater, "We have taken an incredible building that has been restored and has now become a centerpiece of cultural life in Fresno. It is a vibrant example of the arts working creatively and financially. The building is more successful today than in its long history. It has made its presence felt."

Hattie May Hammat

Growing up in Fresno in the 1940s and 1950s was a happy experience. The city still had a small town atmosphere. Those who lived in the Tower District and attended Heaton Elementary School carry special memories of that time.

Heaton School was housed in a large, two-story brick building that faced on McKinley Avenue. One block away was Fresno State College. Its campus also consisted of old brick buildings covered with ivy. In fact, in those years, Fresno State seemed to beckon to the young students at Heaton, inspiring them to excel so they could attend college on that campus.

And excel they did. Not only because a beautiful campus was nearby, but also because seated at the principal's desk at Heaton was a petite woman who ran her school with a determination and authority that belied her small stature. Her teaching staff was hand-picked. They taught the three R's with little foolishness and taught them well.

Discipline was not a problem. A bench outside the principal's office awaited offenders. As they sat there contemplating the swift and sure justice that they knew they would endure, they usually determined never to misbehave again. For those who behaved well, but had trouble adjusting to school, a kind, sympathetic friend who believed that the needs of each child should be considered awaited in the principal's office. In this atmosphere, education flourished. It is a tribute to Hattie May Hammat that most of her students completed school and went on to higher education.

After her retirement from the school system, she entered politics and was elected to the commission that governed the city of Fresno, becoming the first woman to serve in that capacity. She served the city well, but it was the children of Fresno who were her major concern. She dedicated thirty-eight years of her life to their well-being. Those children, who are now adults, remember Hattie May Hammat with gratitude for caring enough to make sure they received an excellent education in an environment that encouraged learning—a rich legacy.

Fresno's First Artist

In the summer of 1868, a girl was born in the town of Millerton. Her parents, Otto and Sine Bloss Froelich, were Danish and had arrived in this tiny frontier town a few years earlier. Her father was named postmaster. When Fresno Station was established, her family was the first to leave Millerton and settle in the new community.

The barren landscape and the rather wild social climate of these two towns were not the usual environment in which a creative spirit would develop. However, by age eight, this young girl was drawing so well that a number of people felt she had genuine talent. Her parents sent her to the finest schools—first to Mills Seminary and then to the Mark Hopkins Art Institute in San Francisco. Her artistic achievements were such that she was sent to Europe where she studied with leading painters in France and Italy.

One of her oil paintings, *The Chinese Robe*, was exhibited in San Francisco art galleries and eventually was bought by a collector of fine art. Her work also was exhibited in the Columbian Exposition in Chicago in 1892-93 and in the Panama-Pacific International Exposition in 1915. Her paintings are even today a part of the permanent collections of two great museums, the Oakland Museum and the National Gallery in Washington, D.C., which has six of her works.

From her birth in the small mining camp of Millerton to her adulthood recognition as an artist of national stature, Maren Froelich, Fresno County's first native-born artist, left a proud legacy to her community.

An Actress Named Berry

Every seat, loge, and box of the Barton Opera House was filled on a magical Fresno night in 1902. As the house lights dimmed, a hush fell over the audience. Anticipation hung palpably in the air as the orchestra began the overture, the curtain began to rise, the cast of the road company of the opera *Princess Chic* swept onto the stage. Then the prima donna stepped forward to sing, and the audience stood cheering as Maude Lillian Berry, former Fresnan, bowed low. Her triumphal return to Fresno filled the natives with pride. Like her father, Fulton G. Berry, Maude had a charming personality that had made her well-liked by everyone.

Since her youthful days of singing in the choir of the First Presbyterian Church, the people of Fresno knew she had talent. She studied at the National Conservatory of Music in New York, and John Philip Sousa chose her as lead singer for his band. Soon after, she left his group to make her debut on Broadway.

Unlike most young actresses, Maude started at the top—her first role was as star of the comic opera, *Maid of Marblehead*. Many other roles followed, including one in the production of Victor Herbert's *Wizard of the Nile*.

Maude Lillian Berry returned to Fresno on April 8, 1910, for another appearance at the Barton Opera House. Once again playing the lead role, this time in a production called *The Rich Mr. Hoggenheimer*, she was a great hit and the source of tremendous pride for her father. He sent a huge floral piece to the theater which bore the inscription "To Our Lillian."

The next day Fulton G. Berry died, the victim of a sudden heart attack. His lighthearted funeral contained all the elements of the practical jokes he had loved in life. At the cemetery, the large floral piece he had sent to the theater was placed on his grave. Now, in an ironic, sad twist of fate, it had become a tribute from his daughter.

Sarah McCardle

From her birth at Millerton in 1873 until her death in Fresno in 1952, this granddaughter of Judge Gillum Baley made her life one of meaningful purpose. Educated in local schools, she graduated from Fresno High School and furthered her education in a school of library science.

She went to work in the Fresno County Free Library in 1908. Within three years, she advanced to assistant librarian and then, in 1911, she became the county librarian. She saw her new position as an opportunity to expand the library and its services. Her first goal was to establish branches throughout the county, first in schools and then in separate library buildings. By 1915, forty-five branch libraries had been established throughout the county. Three years later the board of supervisors bought an automobile for her use so that she could visit the branches more frequently. However, the branch at Ockenden in the Sierra was still reachable only by a rather interesting ride on a logging wagon.

She began holding annual meetings for the custodians who administered the branches. She also set up strict rules for her librarians. They must be unmarried and be hatted and gloved when arriving and leaving work.

Under her administration, the Fresno Country Free Library grew into one of the largest library systems in California. Not only had the branch system developed, but the library had acquired an excellent reference collection, built a circulation collection to meet the needs of the patrons, and built a collection of children's books. "From a small room above the librarian's office, the Fresno County Free Library had grown to a system of 196 distributing stations, including 54 branches, and 152 elementary and high school libraries."

When she retired in 1945, she was hopeful that a new library would soon be built to meet the ever expanding needs of local citizens. Seven years after her death in 1952, a new library opened at Mariposa and N streets. In honor of her service, its new community room was named for her—the Sarah McCardle Room.

Mr. Wishon's Building

The history of the development of hydroelectric power in Fresno County began over a hundred years ago. It was then that the San Joaquin Electric Company built Powerhouse No. 1 on the north fork of the San Joaquin River. Soon forced into bankruptcy, the fledgling company was purchased by W. C. Kerckhoff and A. C. Balch, who incorporated their several small companies into the San Joaquin Power Company. A. G. Wishon was appointed manager.

The company grew steadily and, by 1905, was reincorporated as the San Joaquin Light and Power Company. By 1930, it had grown to such an extent that it became a part of the Pacific Gas & Electric Company network.

In the early years, as the company grew, the business offices moved several times. By 1922, the departments of the business were in seven different locations. Finally, in 1922, with Mr. Wishon working the controls of a steam shovel, ground was broken for a ten-story building at the corner of Fulton and Tuolumne streets. Eighteen months later the structure, designed by architects of the R. F. Felchlin Company, was completed. Its prominent position in the Fresno skyline was even more evident at night—it was touted as the best lighted building in the world, with forty-five or more different color schemes possible with its lighting effects. A modern heating and cooling system kept the building comfortable year round. A ventilating system assured those in the building pure air at all times.

The building has graced the north end of the Fulton Mall for seventy years and served the community well. Several years ago, the Pacific Gas & Electric Company moved to a new building in another part of downtown Fresno.

The old building stood empty. Many wondered whether it would be another sad story of demolition and regret. But, happily, it has a new owner. Home to the U. S. International Trade Center, the building is beginning a new life. Fortunately for the citizens of Fresno and for downtown, this historic building seems destined to be an important part of the architectural heritage of Fresno well into the next century.

In the early days of Fresno's acquaintance with airplanes, there was a romance to flying. Suddenly our vocabulary was filled with new words like "jennies" and "barnstormers." A jenny was a small training aircraft, and a barnstormer was a pilot who earned his living doing exhibition stunts.

Of all those who thrilled the crowds with his daring stunts, none was more famous than Loxla Thornton. Not only was Thornton one of the finest acrobatic aviators in the county, he was also one of the West's best pilots. This, in itself, is a remarkable achievement, but what made it an amazing one was that Thornton had no arms.

In May of 1918, while working as a brakeman for the Southern Pacific Railroad, Thornton fell between two railroad cars. The accident resulted in the loss of his arms. Not one to allow this disability to stand in his way, Thornton learned to fly with a mechanical arm which he clamped to the stick control of his plane. He used his shoulder on the switch and gas throttle. Using this technique, he went on to make aviation history. By 1925, he had logged 1,000 flying hours, had taught many young men how to fly and had never had an accident of any note.

Crowds flocked to see the barnstorming performances of the man who was the world's only armless aviator. His career ended in the late 1920s when the government began requiring pilots to be licensed. There were no provisions for someone with Thornton's disability, and he decided not to press the issue.

He turned his attention to his business, the Thornton Machine Works. He also perfected a new type of artificial arm which was available by mail order to people all over the world. His courage and determination in the face of hardship endeared Loxla Thornton to the citizens of Fresno. They also could never forget the soaring, daring stunts of his barnstorming. A legend in the truest sense was Loxla Thornton.

The Wishon Home

Huntington Boulevard east from First Street is one of the loveliest historic areas of Fresno. Tree-lined sidewalks and a vast expanse of lawn down the center of the avenue make a drive down this street a pleasant one indeed. Each home seems to be special unto itself, but there is one that will give the visitor reason to take another look.

Set back from the street and surrounded by a well-kept lawn and large trees, this home evokes quiet gentility and charm. The tile roof and stucco walls, so reminiscent of warm climates, share the architectural stage with bay windows, a hipped and gabled roof, and a pergola with fluted Doric columns. This is covered with a magnificent wisteria vine.

Built in 1915 by Albert Graves Wishon, who pioneered the electric power industry in the San Joaquin Valley, the house has two sleeping porches, a real necessity during Fresno summers before air-conditioning. The house also contains a library, solarium, and, like many of the homes in this neighborhood, servants' quarters. In the front yard of this home is a huge redwood tree on which, in 1918, Mr. Wishon put colored lights to show how electricity could be used to decorate.

Today, the tree is eight stories tall and is lighted each year as a central part of Huntington Boulevard's Candlelight Christmas celebration. As the oldest living Christmas tree in Fresno, it is enjoyed by everyone, decorated or not, throughout the year.

The Sun-Maid Girl

Long before the dancing raisins took their message to America's vast television audience, another symbol of the Valley crop found its way all over the world. It all happened quite by chance on a warm May afternoon in 1915.

On that day in Fresno, one of the girls who was representing the California Associated Raisin Company at the San Francisco Panama-Pacific International Exhibition had returned home for the Raisin Day parade and had just finished washing her long black hair. As was her custom, after her mother had set her hair in eight curls, she donned a red bonnet to hold them in place and sat in the sun while they dried. While relaxing on the front porch, a group of visitors, including a Sun-Maid executive, called on the family. Seeing how the red bonnet dazzled in the sun, he was struck by an idea for the perfect trademark for his company.

For the next two weeks, the young woman posed at a woman's art studio in San Francisco. Wearing the red bonnet, with her black curls cascading beneath, she held a tray overflowing with grapes. The finished painting showed her surrounded by a glowing sunburst. It was almost as bright as her winsome smile.

Such was the beginning of Sun-Maid Raisin's world famous trademark. Although it has been modernized over the years, the original painting always has been the basis for any changes that have been made. The Sun-Maid girl, Lorraine Collett Petersen, became one of the best-known advertising symbols in America and found her way into the hearts of people all over the world.

The original Sun-Maid girl trademark and Lorraine Collett Petersen at age 18, the year she posed for the painting.
Photos courtesy Sun-Maid Raisin

The Games Yokuts Play

Have you ever given thought to what our local Indians did when they had leisure time? Probably not. Most of us think of the life of Native Americans before the advent of the white man as one filled with hunting, gathering food, making baskets, and, mainly, spending time dealing with the all-consuming work of survival.

Therefore, it is interesting to learn that our local tribes had a number of games that they played. They fell into two categories: games of chance and games of dexterity.

One gambling game played by women was called *u-chu ʹ-us.* It involved walnut or acorn shells that had been cut in half, filled with pitch and charcoal and inlaid with tiny pieces of abalone shells. These shells were used like dice. A tightly woven basket tray that was almost flat became the gaming board. Four women sat around the basket. As a fifth woman kept score, the game began. Using eight shells, each player in turn scooped up the shells in her hand and threw them onto the basket, acquiring one point when two or five flat surfaces landed upright. Then the next woman scooped up the shells and took her turn. As the game progressed, the play went faster and faster.

The men who lived along the Tule River played a game using two balls and sticks that were spoon-shaped at one end. The balls were placed on the ground at one end of the playing field. Dividing into two teams, each with three men and a captain, the game began. The captains scooped up the balls with their spoon-shaped sticks and tossed them to the nearest teammate who, in turn, tossed them to another player. The team that made it around the 1,200-yard course and back to the goal first won. These were only two of many games that the Indians played.

At the turn of the century a report by the Bureau of American Ethnology listed 809 pages of games played by California Indians. It seems that California, the land of sunshine and cloudless skies, has always instilled in its inhabitants a desire to play as well as work.

In 1930, a professional children's librarian arrived in Fresno to become the director of the children's department of the Fresno County Free Library. She not only had impeccable educational credentials, but was an author and gifted storyteller as well. Having been raised in a home where literature was appreciated and enjoyed, she knew the importance of introducing children to fine books. She visited schools throughout the county, including schools for migrant children, telling stories and encouraging an interest in reading.

In 1936, KMJ Radio donated time for a series of forty weekly children's programs featuring this talented lady. She presented topics from fairy tales to biographies in a format children could enjoy. These programs helped to increase the popularity of the library's children's room.

By 1940, the children's collection had almost outgrown its space. In this same year, this woman published her second book, *Blue Willow*, the story of two migrant farm girls in the San Joaquin Valley, and was invited to join the faculty of San Jose State College, where she taught children's literature and storytelling. Her writing career continued. She authored eighteen children's books and seven textbooks.

In 1969, the children's room of the Fresno County Library's central branch on Mariposa Street was named the "Doris Gates Room" in her honor. This wonderful room and the exciting treasures it holds will continue to provide enjoyment for the children of Fresno County for many years to come. It is a fitting tribute to Doris Gates, who did so much to inspire a love of reading among the children of our community.

A Park for Mr. Kearney

In 1844, when John C. Fremont and Kit Carson rode their horses across the great Central Valley where today Chateau Fresno intersects with California Avenue and White's Bridge Road, the land was flat and fairly devoid of vegetation.

For the traveler of 1891, a journey to this part of Fresno County's west side would have disclosed a remarkably unchanged vista, with the exception of a boulevard being built by developer M. Theo Kearney from Fresno westward.

Returning fifteen years later the same traveler would have been awestruck by the beauty of the park that awaited six miles down the boulevard. The traveler would be amazed that the flat arid desert could have been transformed in so short a time. How had it been accomplished?

Having hired premier landscape architect Rudolph Ulrich, M. Theo Kearney began working with him to create an orderly design that would turn the flat landscape into a work of art. They planted trees in such a fashion that no matter where you stood in the park, you would think you were not in a flat area. You would either find yourself in a dense grove of trees or in an open space where, by looking in any direction, your eyes would see a graduated growth of shrubs and trees, thus producing the illusion of a hilly landscape. Each road within the park was curved so that new vistas were always opening up. The superintendent's lodge was built far back in the park so that the approach to it could be as long as possible. The lodge was half hidden among eucalyptus, cypress and palm trees, creating a romantic effect. The final sweep of drive leading to the lodge curved to expose a vista of five acres of open space backed by a grove of tall eucalyptus trees. Everywhere was beauty and grace.

Visitors from all over the world experience the same vistas today as they drive through Kearney Park. One of the few parks in the country to be designated a National Register site, it stands as a tribute to a man who transformed a desert into a garden paradise.

On the morning of September 21, 1931, at ten o'clock in the morning, the "Prosperity Special" pulled out of Pinedale amid great ceremony. A parade of Pinedale school children marching to the accompaniment of Falkenstein's band, a military escort, and an effigy of "Old Man Gloom," which was suitably hanged and burned, preceded the departure of the special train. With a send-off by Mayor Z. S. Leymel and railroad officials from the Southern Pacific and Santa Fe companies, onlookers knew they were participating in an important event.

All of the excitement was generated by the train's 108 cars of sugar pine lumber loaded by the Pinedale company of the same name. It was the longest train ever to leave one lumber mill and it carried one of the longest trainloads of lumber that had ever been shipped from a single mill. More than 2.8 million board feet of sugar pine valued at over $140,000 was on board. The shipments were going to fifty-eight cities in twenty states and Canada.

The efforts by the Sugar Pine Lumber Company to stimulate commerce were applauded by Secretary of Commerce R. P. Lamont. On behalf of the president of the United States, Lamont sent a congratulatory telegram to Arthur H. Fleming, a company official.

The lumber was to be used in different ways. Some would be used in foundries and casting works to make patterns for sand molds. Molten metal would be poured into such molds to form machinery parts. The remainder of the lumber would be used in the construction of homes and buildings. The amount of lumber on the train represented one week's cut at the Pinedale mill.

The mill and its subsidiary, the Yosemite Lumber Company, Ltd., produced one-third of the California sugar pine sold in the United States. It was estimated that one year's cut from these two mills would fill 8,000 cars. What a special train that would have been.

It may come as a surprise to Fresnans of today, but, in 1897, Fresno was touted as "The Electric City." According to a brochure published in that year by the San Francisco and San Joaquin Valley Railroad Company, Fresno gained this reputation because its San Joaquin Electric company excelled all other plants in the world in transmitting hydroelectric power to its customers, for a reasonable cost. Because of the abundance of power, the brochure stated that Fresno offered the best opportunities for new manufacturing industries on the Pacific Coast.

This publication also offered some fascinating bits of information on life in Fresno in 1897. The city's population was 10,818. Fresno had six banks, two daily and several weekly newspapers, an elegant opera house, three streetcar lines, and all the improvements of a modern city. A brand new high school building, costing $50,000, had just opened and a local steam flour mill exported flour to China.

However, the automobile had not yet been introduced; therefore, it took eight hours to drive from the civic center to the mountains. Anyone who wished to journey from San Francisco to Fresno by the Santa Fe rail line was first required to take a river boat to Stockton. The overnight trip was twelve hours. Then they boarded the train at Stockton and reached Fresno three and a half hours later. On the Southern Pacific line, a train from San Francisco to Fresno took eight hours and twenty-five minutes.

When one becomes nostalgic about the "good old days," a gentle reminder that life was once lived at a much, much slower pace usually makes one less likely to long to return to those times.

The Railroad & the Overripe Eggs

For the farmers of Fresno County in 1883, the railroad was a necessary evil. It was the railroad that transported produce to markets outside of Fresno, but it was the railroad bosses who set the rates for shipping. The railroad was a monopoly and no one could forget that fact.

In June of 1883, one Fresno County farmer by the name of C. W. Ayers decided to journey to San Francisco to attend a meeting of the State Railroad Commission. The commission was going to listen to arguments, both pro and con, on the proposed reduction of railroad freight and passenger rates. As Ayers packed, he decided to take along some of the mature produce from his farm in case it was needed to make a point.

The meeting was long. The debate was one-sided and that side definitely did not favor the farmer. The longer Ayers listened, the more angry he became. Unable to contain himself any longer, he stood up and launched into a tirade that seemed to have no end. The gavel banged on the table, but the farmer could not hear it so intent was he on his mission. Finally, in desperation, one of the commissioners appealed to him to stop.

Ayers was suddenly silent. Then, eyeing the men at the table who had such power, he reached carefully inside his coat and drew out the mature produce he had brought along for the occasion. Taking careful aim, he hurled a fistful of overripe eggs straight at the commissioners.

The events of that meeting, not to mention the smells that permeated the commission room, were long remembered by those in attendance. The farmer was promptly arrested, but he was not prosecuted. And, although they could not applaud his methods, it was not a secret that many of the local farmers were a little jealous that they had not been a part of that memorable meeting.

The Wrong Christopher

In 1887, one of the most noted lawyers in California, Fresnan Milus K. Harris, was appointed a superior court judge. Not only did he serve his community in this capacity, but, during his long career, he also would be a member of the board of education and would serve as president of the board of freeholders who had the responsibility of drawing up Fresno's first city charter. In the election of 1888, Judge Harris won a full six-year term on the superior court.

During the next several years, the Southern Pacific Railroad was the target of a series of train robberies. The men accused of masterminding these crimes, John Sontag and Christopher Evans, hid out in the foothills of the Sierra. There they played a cat-and-mouse game with marshals, railroad detectives and sheriffs for months, much to the delight of local residents who hated the monopoly the railroad exerted over business and politics. Finally, at a shootout at Stone Corral, Sontag was killed and Evans captured.

One night, with the help of a friend, Evans escaped from the Fresno jail and hid out in the mountains, until he was captured once again. His trial, which later would be referred to as one of the most famous criminal trials in California history, was held in the court of Judge Harris. The jury found Evans guilty of the murder of a United States marshal.

On February 20, 1894, his forty-seventh birthday, Evans stood before Judge Harris awaiting his sentence. A hush fell over the courtroom. "Christopher Evans," Judge Harris intoned, "you have been tried and found guilty of murder in the first degree. Do you have anything to say?" Evans shook his head. "Then it is the judgment of this court that you, Christopher Columbus, be confined in Folsom Prison for the period of your natural life." Silent shock was followed by laughter that shook the walls of the courtroom. Evans laughed with the crowd and even the dignified judge could not help but smile at his mistake. Then, he repeated the sentence, this time with the correct name, and with his gavel closed the proceedings.

Fort Miller, located on the south bank of the San Joaquin River in the shadow of the Sierra Nevada Mountains, was the only military installation in Fresno County. In 1855, the woman who was to become the first schoolteacher in the city of Fresno was born at the fort. Her parents had been residents of this primitive outpost for only a year, having arrived there while still on their honeymoon.

By 1860, there were enough children at the fort and in the nearby town of Millerton to make a local school necessary. In the absence of a proper building, the first school in Fresno County met in the dining room of the Winchell family. Our future teacher was now five years old and was part of this first class.

As the years progressed, she left Millerton to attend San Jose Normal School. The year of her graduation was also the year of the founding of Fresno Station, 1872. The new town needed a teacher and she was chosen for the job. Her classroom was the upper floor of B. S. Booker's store at Tulare and H streets. The new school was by private subscription since a school had to be operating for three months before it could be recognized as a public school.

In the election of 1874, a school bond was passed so that a proper school could be built. A new teacher had to found, however, because our young lady had returned to Fort Miller to marry John C. Hoxie. They soon returned to Fresno where Mrs. Hoxie became an important influence in the intellectual lives of Fresno women. She helped to organize the Catholic Church. She also served as president of the Leisure Hour and Parlor Lecture clubs.

From her beginnings in the foothills of the Sierra throughout her life in the young community of Fresno, Mary McKenzie Hoxie left an important legacy. Her key role in the development of local education paved the way for others. That so many followed suit is a tribute to the intellectual strength of the pioneer women of Fresno County.

Malvina & "Doc"

The stories of the Valley have often told of the hardships of those hardy pioneers whose courage and strength were the basis of the firm foundation on which our community was built. One such tale centers on Malvina Akers Lewis, who, until 1855, was the first white woman to permanently reside in the region between the San Joaquin River and Mariposa.

Malvina's life had been difficult. She was born in Kentucky, the first child of Henry and Delilah Akers. She received no formal education and could neither read nor write. She married at age thirteen. Within a few months, her husband was killed and she returned to her parents' home. The Akers family decided to journey west and traveled by wagon train as far as Texas.

Two years later, in 1841, Malvina married James Henry Lewis, who was a carpenter by trade and a herbalist by inclination. The book of herbal remedies that he always carried earned him the nickname "Doc."

Nine years later the Akers family headed west again. This time the size of the party had grown. Two hundred oxen-drawn covered wagons left Austin, bound for Millerton, California. A lack of water, food, and feed for the animals, illness and the ever-present danger of Indian attacks made such a trip difficult and often frightening.

The major tragedy of this journey was the death of Malvina and "Doc's" two-year-old daughter, Amanda. After succumbing to an illness, she was buried in the middle of the road. The wagons ran over the spot several times so the Indians would not find the grave.

By 1853, four of the wagons reached the Kings River, where Malvina gave birth to her seventh child. Then they continued on to Millerton. It was not long before Malvina and "Doc" decided that the wide-open, lawless town was not a good place to raise their family and they left, settling in Fine Gold Gulch. There "Doc" operated a boarding house, store and saloon, and Malvina made tailored shirts which she sold for five dollars each. Five more children were born to the couple. The younger girls helped earn money for the family by dancing on top of the bar in their father's saloon. Miners tossed bags of gold dust to them in appreciation.

As the years went by, the family moved to a ranch north of the Kings River. There "Doc" and Malvina lived until their deaths in 1892 and 1901 respectively.

A Plethora of Laws

The city of Fresno had so many laws in 1938 that according to Police Chief Frank Truax, it would take every citizen acting as a policeman and calling upon the National Guard and Supreme Court as well to enforce them. Two thousand, three hundred and sixty-three laws were on the Fresno list as the country came out of the Great Depression and headed into World War II.

It was against the law to ride a roller coaster in the business district.

Women were required by law to take off their hats in a theater or church, if the offending chapeau blocked someone's view.

One must never frighten a horse and if one threw tacks, broken glass or a sharp object on the street that would cause said horse injury, one might find that one's next home was in the county jail. Riding on the fender or running board of a car was forbidden. So was alighting from or boarding a moving vehicle.

One must not own a cow or a goat in the city, and if one kept pigeons or chickens, they must be kept out of the neighbors' yards.

If one persisted in ringing bells and that ringing was proven to be harmful to the health of a nervous person within earshot, the health officer had the power to arrest the bell-ringer.

The curfew law had not been enforced in many years, but according to that law young people under fourteen years of age had to be off the streets by nine o'clock in summer and eight o'clock in winter. If caught, their parents would be prosecuted. Minors also could be arrested if they were caught smoking behind the woodshed or anywhere else for that matter.

Our city has changed tremendously since 1938. Laws have changed as well. But, when we long for the good old days, perhaps we might long for some of the good old laws as well.

The Rat Patrol

As the United States struggled to make its way out of the Great Depression many interesting ways were found to put people to work. The WPA, Works Progress Administration, was the principal agency formed for that purpose.

Under the PWA, Public Works Administration, many new buildings were constructed in Fresno. The Memorial Auditorium, the Tulare Street Post Office and the Hall of Records were built at that time. These structures are tangible, visible reminders of that era.

However, in the latter part of the 1930s, there were some other problems as well. One, in particular, had to be dealt with immediately—the infestation of the downtown area by rats. Armed with traps and poison, a select group of WPA men were deputized by the city commission to eradicate the rats in a program bearing the rather odd name of "The 1,000 Rat Control Program." The only concern voiced by the city fathers was about their liability if the use of poison caused problems. A collective sigh of relief was audible when they were told that the poison would be used only under the direct supervision of W. O. Deal, of the state health department.

The deputies marched through the city rooting out the rascally rodents, using the tried and true methods that the program specified. Of course the rats were caught. Of course the WPA men were successful. And, of course, the rats that inhabited downtown became history for at least a short while, thus ending one of more unusual chapters in the stories of the Valley.

William H. Henderson

In 1919, a young man named William Henderson took a class in horticulture at Fresno Technical High School. It held such a fascination for him that he wrote a letter to Luther Burbank, a man renowned for his experiments in this field. Burbank, delighted to read his enthusiastic letter, invited him to come to his home in Santa Rosa. The result was that Henderson dropped out of school, moved to Santa Rosa, and worked with Burbank until the great man's death in 1925. Mrs. Burbank asked him to close the growing operations for her. Henderson did so and then returned to Fresno.

In 1926, he began his own experimental gardens at 2760 South Orange Avenue near the town of Oleander, where he was born. As the years progressed, he continued the work he loved. He enriched the dry Valley soil by using cover crops, and then, by using hybridization and long experimentation, he was able to create new varieties of plants. He also introduced plants from all over the world, experimenting and adapting them through hybridization to our Valley climate.

In 1955, a new, wider Highway 99 cut through the middle of his gardens. Forced to move, he selected a site on Fowler Avenue on the east side of Fresno, far from encroaching freeways. Today his work is carried on at Henderson's Experimental Gardens by Don Kleim, who joined him in 1946, later became his partner and, after Henderson's death in 1976, took over the operation.

However, on old Highway 99, one legacy of his gardens remains. A large Paradox walnut tree, its huge root system intact, still stands along the right-of-way—a reminder of the once-beautiful gardens that graced this portion of our Valley.

When the new town of Fresno Station was first drawn on a map by the staff of the Central Pacific Railroad, the town was laid out so that the streets would run parallel to the railroad track. Each of these parallel streets was given the name of a letter of the alphabet—A, B, C and so forth.

The streets that intersected and ran east and west were named for the counties of California. Hence, today, going south from Divisadero Street we have—Amador, San Joaquin, Calaveras, Stanislaus, Tuolumne, Merced, Fresno, Mariposa, Tulare, Kern, Inyo, Mono, and Ventura—a name that is derived from the Spanish *buenaventura*, meaning good luck.

At the point where Ventura curves in west Fresno it becomes California Avenue. The Spanish conquistadores, possibly Cortez, gave the name California to the land which would become our state. It was the name of an imaginary earthly paradise in a Spanish romance novel written in 1510.

On January 6, 1805, a Spanish lieutenant named Gabriel Moraga, who was conducting an exploration of our interior valley to see if it would be a good place to built a permanent settlement, discovered a river. He named it *Rio de los Santos Reyes*, the River of the Holy Kings, in remembrance of the Wise Men whose feast day he was honoring. The name was later shortened to the Kings River.

In 1940, a new park was opened in the mountains east of Fresno. It was named Kings Canyon National Park because it contained the headwaters of the Kings River, which flowed through the park. In 1953, the street which carried travelers to the park was named Kings Canyon Boulevard. Thus, the name of the park and the name of the street honored that day almost two hundred years ago when Lieutenant Moraga knelt at the banks of the newly discovered river and paid tribute to the Wise Men who had brought gifts to the Christ Child two thousand years ago.

The Munger/Porteous Home

On a street corner in Fresno's Tower District sits an imposing two-story wood frame home with a hipped, gabled roof. Four Ionic columns soar to support the roof as well as the second floor balcony. Built by Albert Munger in 1911, it was the northernmost home on Van Ness Avenue. He hired Hans Hansen, a builder who was responsible for many of Fresno's finest homes, to construct his residence.

Munger was a member of the first graduating class of Fresno High School. In 1889, he was a founding member of the Fresno High Senate, where he served as the senator from Michigan, a seat his grandson would also hold many years later. In 1898, he and Milo Edwin Rowell went to work for Hobbs-Parsons Company. Later, the two would become owners of the business.

In 1916, Munger sold his home to James Porteous, the owner of the Fresno Agricultural Works and inventor of the Fresno Scraper. Porteous, a Scots immigrant, was a prolific inventor. Over two hundred patents are registered in his name with the United States Patent Office. The Fresno Scraper revolutionized farming in the Central Valley, dug trenches in World War I, and played an important role in building the Panama Canal.

After Mr. Porteous died in 1922, the family sold the home. Over the years it has been a rooming house, a rest home and the Valley headquarters for the Sequoia Council of the Boy Scouts of America. Today, it houses a business office.

Still stately in appearance, it is an important reminder of Fresno's past not only because of the two families which lived within its walls, but also because it is a part of the beautiful, historic neighborhood that still exists between Olive and Belmont avenues.

La Paloma Guild

Over twenty years ago, on one of those cold, foggy December mornings when the trees along Kearney Boulevard are completely hidden from the view of those driving on that historic roadway, twenty-some intrepid women braved the elements of a Fresno winter to journey to Kearney Mansion.

The lights of the mansion shone through the thick fog as the final turn in the road brought them to their destination. Mabelle Selland, director of the Fresno City and County Historical Society, opened the mansion door and welcomed them inside. Over cups of steaming hot Christmas punch, the assembled group decided that, yes, they wanted to form a support group for the historical society. On such a morning anything seemed possible, and dreams and ideas bounced from the mansion's walls.

A month later, the women met at the Chamber of Commerce building to formalize their commitment. Officers were elected, committees were formed, and La Paloma Guild was officially launched. By summer, the group held its first fund raiser, "Moonlight & Memories," an evening of nostalgia and fun at Kearney Mansion.

Then the ladies decided on a very different fund-raising activity—a tour of historic homes. It was hoped that it would both raise funds and heighten community awareness for historic preservation. Over the years, these goals have been successful to a degree which members hardly dared dream. Not only has Fresno undergone a renaissance as far as preservation projects are concerned, but guild members have been heartened to see their initial efforts play a major role in acquainting the Fresno community with the possibilities that exist within our historic architecture.

Funds raised by the guild have benefited the historical society in many ways, including restoration of the "Goddesses of Justice" statues that graced the old Fresno County Courthouse, restoration of the Paul Hutchison glass negative collection, interior restoration of Kearney Mansion, and restoration of the mansion's butler's pantry and kitchen.

A New Depot for Fresno

In the spring of 1888 there was a great deal of speculation about a new building that was being designed for downtown Fresno. A number of new buildings were being constructed during this period, but it seemed to be the consensus that this building had to be special. In fact, it had to be as grand in its own way as the Courthouse.

Finally, one of the worried populace decided the best way to find out what this new building was going to look like was to visit the Oakland offices of the company which owned the property on which this new building would sit, and find out just what was planned. The gentleman made the trip, and when he returned to Fresno, much to the relief of everyone, he had good news. He looked at the plans, he said, and they showed that "it would be a much larger building than anyone here imagines and will be a very beautiful structure and superbly finished." Also, he added, "some of the superb appointments would include stationary washstands and bathrooms for the employees."

It may seem curious from the vantage point of the 1990s that Fresnans were so concerned about this particular new building. Perhaps we can be grateful that they were. When this new structure was completed in 1889, it was magnificent—and when one considers that it was built on the site of Fresno's birthplace, one can understand the symbolism that it held for the community. Ironically, it is the building that out-lasted the Courthouse and many other grand structures. Today, the Southern Pacific Depot is the oldest commercial building in the city. It has stood the test of time and remains an endearing part of the heritage of Fresno.

The legends of the Valley hold many strange tales, but perhaps none more unusual than the story of Emma Piearson Paxton. Born into slavery in Missouri, she was one of seventy-five slaves living on her master's property. As a child, she worked in the fields doing the same work as the boys. After the signing of the Emancipation Proclamation, she moved into the home of her master where she was treated like one of the family.

At the age of twenty, she moved to Saint Louis and worked as a cook in a private home. Forced to wear a dress, she left after one year. She had always longed to be a boy like her twin brother. So, donning the clothes of a man and using the name Jim, she began to work like a man also.

Before coming west to Fresno, she worked as a coachman for Missouri Congressman Champ Clark.

When she arrived in Fresno, she went to work as the foreman for most of the Santa Fe Railroad ranch properties in the Fresno area. She worked side by side with the men. She preferred her tobacco strong—big black cigars, a pipe or chewing scrap tobacco suited her, but she did not like cigarettes.

When her death came at the age of eighty-five, her funeral was arranged by the granddaughter of the family who had owned the plantation where she was born. Her last request was to be dressed in her best suit of men's clothes and cremated, with her ashes to be strewn over Indian Creek in Missouri where she had played as a child. Her wishes were carried out with quiet dignity, and thus ended one of the more unusual stories of the Valley.

Fresno has been blessed with many individuals who have given of their time, talents and fortunes to create a better community. Three Fresno women, who married into the same family, not only made significant contributions during their lives, but left important legacies to Fresno as well.

Lulu, Mrs. Herbert Gundelfinger, was born in 1890 and was a graduate of the University of California at Berkeley. She was a longtime member of two of Fresno's earliest study clubs, the Wednesday Club and the Monday Club. A charter member of the Fresno Branch of the American Association of University Women, she also worked with the Los Feliz Guild, an auxiliary of Valley Children's Hospital. After her death in 1985, her estate was bequeathed to the Fresno Regional Foundation to be used for music projects and for street plantings within the city.

Minnie, who was married to Leopold Gundelfinger, was born in 1865. In 1894, she and Mrs. George Hoxie founded the Parlor Lecture Club. At the time of her death in 1909, her husband set up a fund in her memory, the income of which would be used "for assistance in maternity and confinement cases." Many years later, in 1981, the Fresno Regional Foundation designated that the Minnie R. Gundelfinger Fund would be used "in assistance of programs for unwed pregnant women, programs for unwed mothers, programs for battered women and programs for abandoned children." With other bequests from members of the Gundelfinger family, the fund provides help for many people in the Fresno community who might otherwise not receive the assistance they need.

Palmyre, Mrs. Henry Gundelfinger, was a gifted pianist. Her love for music benefited several generations of Fresnans because she was one of the founders of the Fresno Musical Club, a group that for many years brought the finest concert artists in the country to Fresno.

A community is truly rich when it has living within it people with the vision and generosity of the Gundelfinger women.

B efore there was a Clovis Rodeo, there was a Clovis Festival. And on that documented first festival day, April 1, 1916, six thousand people journeyed to Clovis from miles around on horseback, buggies, wagons, motor trucks, and the railroad. Excitement was in the air as the park filled with folks waiting for the picnic and barbecue. Over two thousand pounds of beef was cooked that day by chef Joe Sagniere.

All types of sporting events were held, as well as fat man and wheelbarrow races. The highlight of a parade of floats down Clovis Avenue was the Queen of the Festival, who presided over a floral chariot drawn by twenty school girls dressed in white. A good time was had by all.

By 1918, the event included cowboys from surrounding ranches including one named "Montana Kid." Within three years the event had become a full-blown rodeo with cowboys descending on Clovis not only from the local ranches, but the foothill areas as well.

With the addition of a horse show in the 1930s, the event grew bigger and better. The formation of the Clovis Horse Show Association led to the purchase of fifty-five acres of land where the event could be held each year. Memberships in the association were, in later years, passed down from father to son. In 1941, the parade was led by Hollywood movie star Victor McLaughlen, who owned the Balfe Ranch nearby.

For all those who have attended the Clovis Rodeo over the years and enjoyed the wonderful family fun that it provides, none has had more happy memories than John Weldon, who viewed his first Clovis Rodeo parade in the first decade of the 1900s. Weldon was grand marshal of the parade in 1983, continuing in the tradition of his father and his uncle, who had been grand marshals in earlier parades.

The Porter Tract, just north of the Fresno Normal School, the site of which is now Fresno City College, was developed between 1915 and 1923. The names of the streets in the tract, Cambridge, Harvard, Yale, Brown and Princeton, reflect the academic flavor of the neighborhood.

On one of these streets sits a residence that stands out from all the others. Its facade is of Neoclassical style. The four colossal Tuscan columns which support the triangular pediment over the front entrance give a timeless quality to the design. Painted white with green shutters, the large, stately residence gives dignity and beauty to its neighborhood.

Since it was built in 1919, it has been owned by only two families, each of which played a major role in the history of Fresno County.

The Shipp family arrived with the Nelsons, the Samples, and numerous flocks of sheep at Academy, in the foothills of Fresno County, in 1868. Young John Shipp, who would later build this home and marry Mary Maud Sample, was one year old.

Mr. and Mrs. Arthur Selland purchased the residence from the Shipps in 1945. Mr. Selland served on the Fresno City Board of Education for eleven years and was mayor of Fresno for five years. He was one of sixteen mayors that President John Kennedy chose to go on a goodwill tour of West Berlin under the leadership of the State Department.

Today, the Shipp-Selland Home is on the Local Register of Historic Resources.

The Beltless Firemen of 1888

The summer of 1888 was a difficult time for the men of the Fresno Volunteer Fire Department. The terrible heat seemed to fuel any fires that started, and the prevalence of wooden buildings and lack of enough manpower made matters worse. Fresno had experienced a number of fires and everyone realized that another hose company was desperately needed. Finally, a citizen's meeting was called to address the problem. Unfortunately, too many people were out of town attending a board of trade session, the object of which was to discuss methods of advertising Fresno in the East. So the problem had to wait. It also had been noted by concerned citizens that the volunteer fireman took far too long to attach the fire hoses to the hydrant. More practice was needed, they said—more men and more practice.

As if this was not enough to strain the tempers of those able volunteers who risked life and limb to fight Fresno's fires, another problem reared its ugly head. New uniforms had been ordered. When they arrived, the men were pleased with the new shirts, which were fine, and the trousers, which were quite comfortable and serviceable. But the belts, which were needed to hold up the trousers, had not been included. It seems that the leather belts were of inferior quality, so some well-meaning person canceled the order. The volunteers were not pleased with this turn of events. The matter was delegated to a committee formed to investigate the situation.

In the meantime, the poor firemen were left trying to figure out how they were going to fight fires and hook up hoses to hydrants with only one hand since the other hand was holding up their trousers. The summer of 1888 was not the happiest of times for the volunteers of the Fresno Fire Department.

The White King

Soon after the discovery of gold in the hills of California, a canny, long-haired man established a trading post on the Fresno River. This man, born in New York in 1817, had come west with his wife and daughter, neither of whom survived the journey.

When he reached Sutter's Fort, he volunteered for Fremont's California Battalion. He served for several months, was court-martialed and mustered out. He went to work for John Sutter and, while in his employ, helped James Marshall construct the mill where gold was discovered six months later. Like so many others he turned to gold mining, but he soon found that providing goods for the miners and the local Indians was a more lucrative business.

His establishment on the Fresno River flourished as did his ability to converse with the Indians. A perceptive man, he understood human nature and soon learned how to control the Indians through trickery. Concealing the real bullets in his hand, he loaded his gun with blanks in front of a group of Indians. He asked one of them to shoot him. He handed his gun to an Indian who pulled the trigger six times. Each time, he acted as though he caught the bullet. After the sixth shot, he showed the Indians the six bullets. From that time on they looked on him as their "white king." He took several Indian women as his concubines.

Even though tensions were building between the Indians and the white men, life went well for the "white king," James D. Savage, until he decided to take a chief of the Chawchila tribe to San Francisco. On the trip home, the chief drank too much and Savage slapped him. The chief called the tribal leaders together and declared war.

The Mariposa Indian War was a dark chapter in Fresno County history. It formally ended with the signing of the Camp Barbour Treaty on April 17, 1851. But, for the Indians, it ended their way of life. Forced onto reservations, their spirit was broken. And what of their "white king"? He died a year later, the victim of a shooting.

The Barton Vineyard

In 1879, Robert Barton purchased a large parcel of land, the boundaries of which would today be Belmont, McKinley, Cedar and Chestnut avenues. He paid $8,000 for the property. He planted the land in vineyards, which bore the choicest wine and raisin grapes, and spent $350,000 in improvements to the property, including the construction of a lovely mansion. In 1886, his vines produced 360,000 gallons of wine.

A year later, in 1887, his property was sold to an English company for $1 million. The company, Barton Estate Company Limited of London, sent Colonel H. A. Trevelyan to the Barton Vineyard to examine the finances of the business. Colonel Trevelyan was an astute businessman and was asked to stay on and oversee the operations. Under his guidance, the output of the vineyard continually increased. This, combined with other improvements that he made, made him a valuable manager.

Colonel Trevelyan had a noteworthy background. He was colonel of the Seventh Hussars in the Crimean campaign and was one of the Six Hundred at Balaclava, taking part in the Charge of the Light Brigade. His commemorative medal had three clasps—one for Balaclava, one for the Siege of Sebastopol and one for the Battle of Alma. His tour of duty in the Turkish Empire culminated in receiving a war medal from the Sultan of Turkey. When in Turkey, he was allowed to use the title of "Pasha."

In addition to Colonel Trevelyan, other department heads employed at Barton Vineyard were Englishmen from noted families. There was one exception, the wine maker, Charles Rossi. The Barton Vineyard was an agricultural showplace that Fresnans pointed to with pride.

Who's to Raisin Why?

Those inhabitants of the great Central Valley who pride themselves on being knowledgeable about matters of produce can answer the following question quite easily—What are the uses for the grapes that are grown in our local vineyards? The answer, of course, is that local grapes are grown to be enjoyed for eating right off the vine, for making wines and brandies, and for making raisins.

However, according to an article in the *Fresno Bee* on March 19, 1933, researchers at the University of California Fruit Products Laboratory had been experimenting with new uses for the noble grape for a number of years. One bold idea had to do with a syrup extracted from raisins. Noting how the American public enjoyed cola beverages, the researchers suggested that by adding raisin syrup to these drinks the consumer would have a product that would be more healthful. It also was noted that this would increase the price of a can of soda only from five cents to six cents. In 1920, the university folks had developed a carbonated Raisin Ale which was served at a large meeting of the members of Sun-Maid Raisin Growers. Consisting of muscat raisin syrup added to ginger ale, it made a brief hit, but then vanished into history.

Finding during their research that Thompson grapes were insipid in ice cream, they noted that, on the other hand, the Muscat raisin, which added flavor and color, made a delicious addition to ice cream. Raisin candy, raisin-rice pudding, raisin bread and raisin pie were uses that the researchers were sure would become popular with cooks everywhere. They also developed a Muscat raisin table syrup that could elevate the enjoyment of the simple pancake to new heights.

As one looks at the uses of the raisin from the perspective of the mid-1990s, it is interesting to note which of these ideas became part of the American diet and which did not. It might also be interesting for one to ponder what other uses might be discovered or rediscovered for our major local crop. Could there truly be a Raisin Cola in Fresno's future?

In the 1930s, racial and religious prejudice was rampant in Fresno. Certain ethnic groups could not buy property in designated neighborhoods or belong to select clubs.

In 1937, three local clergymen, Rabbi David L. Greenberg, Monsignor James Dowling, and Episcopal Dean James M. Malloch, began a radio program on KMJ called the "Radio Forum for Better Understanding" to combat prejudice. Their aim was to discuss religious beliefs and concepts to dispel myths and fears and to create a better understanding between peoples. They agreed never to argue or debate. This format for an ecumenical and interfaith program was revolutionary for the time. The chemistry among the three men led to lasting friendships and attracted a wide audience.

The three men had backgrounds in social work. One of the first projects that came out of the program was satellite medical clinics for migratory workers. An education program for the children of migrant workers followed.

The "Forum for Better Understanding" was broadcast on the West Coast and when the Second World War began it was carried on the Armed Forces Radio to Europe. After the war, the three clergymen could be heard discussing their beliefs on radio stations across America. The program lasted until the local advent of television in 1954.

Today, a statue by Clement Renzi called the *Brotherhood of Man* stands on the M Street side of Courthouse Park. It was placed there as a tribute to these three men who helped pioneer the worldwide ecumenical movement of the 1960s. The impact of their works and the example of their lives was felt not only in Fresno, but throughout the free world as well.

A Park & a Lake in the Tower District

In the late 1890s, W. A. Burnside brought his family to Fresno. He purchased twenty acres of property bounded by Blackstone, Patterson and Hedges avenues and Calaveras Street. Barns and houses were built on the northernmost part of the acreage. Dry Creek, which was crossed by a wooden bridge on Blackstone Avenue, cut a diagonal swath across the property. Buying and selling livestock was the family business.

In 1900, Burnside's daughter, Leota, married John Zapp. They moved to her father's ranch. John had been in the business of hauling sand and fill dirt to building contractors. Now, he used the sand from Dry Creek's banks to fill his orders, leaving holes along the creek bank. As the holes became larger and filled with creek water, people began to drive out to the site from Fresno so their children could play in the water of the shallow lakes that Zapp had created.

Sensing the recreational value of the lakes, Zapp dug another channel the full length of the property, creating another waterway. He planted Balm of Gilead trees on the banks. He built a dance pavilion near Calaveras Street with an arched bridge which crossed the Dry Creek Lagoon. Heated swimming pools, a bowling alley, a Ferris wheel, covered boardwalks, a small zoo and other attractions were added. Visitors rode the electric streetcar as far north as Belmont and then walked up Blackstone to the entrance of Zapp's Park.

In 1909, Mr. Burnside deeded the property to his daughter. Mrs. Zapp, an excellent horsewoman and horse trainer, always rode in local parades and put her horses through their paces doing the tricks she had taught them. In 1918, John Zapp died. Leota Zapp died six months later. The park continued for a year or so and then was leveled and the land was subdivided as Fresno grew northward.

Today, Zapp's Park is just a faint memory. But, the next time you cross Olive and Blackstone avenues, remember that at that site, John and Leota Zapp had created a place of beauty that gave pleasure to Fresnans in the early 1900s.

The
swimming
pool at
Zapp's Park c.
1912.
*Courtesy of
William L.
Eaton.*

When a property is listed in the National Register of Historic Places, it is included on the nation's official list of cultural resources and has been deemed worthy of preservation. Fresno County has a number of buildings and/or sites on this list.

A recent Fresno addition to this prestigious roster is a two-story brick structure just south of Tulare Street on Santa Fe Avenue. Built in 1926, it has served as one of the most important social institutions for the Basque community of Fresno. Located near the railroad station, it accommodated newly arrived immigrants by providing them with lodgings, helping them find employment and assisting them when they needed medical or legal aid. Many of the arrivals were sheepherders who used the building as a temporary home when they were not out on the range. When they retired, they found a comfortable permanent home there.

As the years went by, this colorful establishment became an important gathering place for all Fresnans. For many in this city, the dining room of the Santa Fe Hotel is a special place where not only is excellent food available in great abundance, but also where, for a little while, the visitor feels a sense of old-world timelessness. When the dinner gong rings, the sheep men come into the dining room to sit at the long center table, filled with bowls of steaming hot soup and decanters of red wine. The room fills with the sounds of the Basque language and laughter. The sense of friendship that develops as diners share the family-style dinner at the long table, or watch from side tables, is part of the Basque tradition of hospitality.

For the citizens of Fresno who have come to appreciate all that the Santa Fe Hotel means to this community, it is a comfort to know that it is now in the National Register and will continue to be a part of the life of this community for many years to come.

Vaudeville & Elegance

The era of vaudeville sparked the building of theaters designed for live, legitimate stage presentations. One of the more renowned managers of vaudeville, Alexander Pantages, together with the architect Marcus Priteca, built a series of theaters that, along with forty others that he operated, became known as the Pantages circuit.

In 1929, he built his sixteenth, and one of his finest theaters, in Fresno. The new structure was a blend of Italian Renaissance revival and Spanish Colonial revival elements, styles of European architecture that Pantages wanted to bring to Fresno. The beautiful exterior prepared theater-goers for the luxurious interior. After walking through the lobby with its ornamental plaster work and intricate ceiling design, the theater itself was entered. Row upon row of red leather and velvet seats filled the space, but the eye was drawn first to the stage which was framed by an ornate proscenium arch. It was on this stage that some of the finest vaudeville acts of the time gave their performances for enthusiastic audiences.

Today, the theater is being lovingly restored. Blessed with near-perfect acoustics, it is used for concerts and special performances. The original "announcer boxes," which told patrons who the next act would be, flank the stage. The "fly gallery" backstage contains a counterweight system that lowers and raises sets and curtains onto the stage. A huge control panel, using resistive dimmers that have to be operated by hand, regulates the house lights and some of the stage lighting. It is original to the theater and is like the panels that are used on the Broadway stage.

For the visitor of today, walking into the Warnors Theater is like stepping back in time to an era when attending the theater meant not only experiencing an excellent performance, but being surrounded by luxury and elegance. Located at the corner of Fulton and Tuolumne streets and listed in the National Register of Historic Places, the Warnors Theater is one of Fresno's special treasures.

A Creamery for Fresno

In 1895, a group of Danish immigrants decided they wanted to form a dairy cooperative similar to the ones they had known in Denmark. Led by Hans Graff, they formed the Danish Creamery Company, selling shares for one hundred dollars. There was no limitation on the number of shares one could buy, however, and soon control of the company rested in the hands of a few people.

On December 17, 1901, a meeting was held in Edgerly Hall to determine how to make the organization more democratic. The controlling stockholders agreed to sell their shares. The stock was then reissued on a one-man one-vote basis, each stockholder being allowed to buy only one fifty dollar share. The Danish Creamery Association that evolved from that meeting was now a true cooperative. The company began to grow and, by 1910, the plant moved from California and Fig avenues to its present site at E and Inyo streets.

A year later, Danish Creamery joined Challenge Dairy Products. Besides producing butter, the plant processed whole milk, made powdered milk and opened an evaporated milk plant in Chowchilla in 1941.

Today, Danish Creamery owns over 80 percent of Challenge Dairy Products and is the oldest and one of the largest dairy cooperatives in the United States.

However, growth has not changed the company's high standards of excellence and service. Just as the Fresno housewife of 1895 knew that the butter that was delivered to her door by horse and wagon was fresh, so does the shopper of today know that the package of Danish Creamery butter on the supermarket shelf was churned and wrapped only yesterday.

A Glorious Weed

An article in the *Fresno Morning Republican* on February 19, 1881, touted the appearance of a new kind of grass, brought to the Kingsburg area by Professor W. A. Sanders. Called *panicum spectable*, it was being extensively grown in Australia and New Zealand by a rather earnest botanist named Dr. S. M. Curl.

The knowledge that it could withstand flood, drought, and frost made this new grass exciting news, indeed, to the farmers who read this newspaper. But, of even greater moment was that it took only thirteen of Dr. Curl's seeds to produce, after four seasons' growth, a quarter of an acre of grass four feet high and so thick that a person could barely push his way through it.

One curious phenomenon of *panicum spectable* was that the root, initially, ran to an unknown depth. Professor Sanders dug down fifteen feet and found the tap roots little diminished in size, continuing their journey downward. With great excitement, the writer of the article stated that a forage grass superior to alfalfa had finally been found. Indeed, he gushed, this new grass did not cause animals to bloat; it was green even in the harshest winter frost; it yielded a tremendous amount of rich healthy seed; and, most important, all livestock, including hogs and goats, would eat it with an avidity that bordered on gluttony. What more perfect grass could a farmer ask for? It was all this, and inexpensive, too.

Luckily for the farming community *panicum spectable* did not catch on. If it had and the seeds of this grass had been sown in great abundance, it might be the Valley's only crop. It was for another generation to discover an aspect of this incredible grass that escaped Dr. Curl and Professor Sanders. It seems that *panicum spectable* does not send its tap roots down a mere fifteen feet, but sends them down at least forty feet, so that they are there to stay. The grass becomes impossible to control and its lush thickness threatens to choke out everything in its path. Today, this remarkable botanical find is called Johnson grass, a weed that sends terror into the hearts of farmers and garden enthusiasts alike.

Murder, Mischief & Johnson Grass

Professor W. A. Sanders, the man who introduced that scourge of the farmer's life, Johnson grass, to the Kingsburg area, had a checkered career. Born near Milwaukee, he attended the University of Wisconsin to study botany. He came to California to prospect for gold and stayed to teach in many schools throughout the state, including the school at Academy. He retired from teaching in 1882 and devoted his life to his agricultural experiments and to his wife and four children.

Sanders had a friend named William Wooten who owned a ranch several miles away. He often visited Wooten, usually staying overnight because the trip was an all-day journey. They had known one another for many years when a puzzling incident occurred. On February 1, 1897, the two men rode off in a buggy together. Wooten was never seen again.

Wooten had given Sanders a warehouse grain receipt for $1,400 from Kutner & Goldstein Company that was made out to Wooten and signed by him. When Sanders presented the receipt, he was charged with forgery. Many people felt that he had murdered Wooten; but, because, even after exhaustive searches, no one had been able to find a body, the only charge that could be brought against him was forgery.

Over the next three years, Sanders was brought to trial four times. The first trial resulted in a hung jury. The second trial brought a guilty verdict, which was appealed. The third trial ended in another indecisive jury; but, in the fourth trial he was found guilty and sentenced to fourteen years in prison.

Sanders' story of the fateful day was that, as a favor to Wooten, he had been trying to negotiate a sale of Wooten's ranch to two investors who gave Wooten $20,000 in gold coins and a promise to pay the balance by check later. The four men started out separately for Fresno, with Wooten in Sanders' buggy. Along the way, Wooten asked to get out of Sanders' buggy and left on his own. He was never seen again. Witnesses, including Wooten's farmhand, testified that they saw only Sanders that day.

During the trial, the prosecution argued that the investors did not exist. The mystery was never solved. Sanders spent nine years in San Quentin for a crime that was based entirely on circumstantial evidence. However, feelings against Sanders ran high in the Kingsburg/Reedley areas. The general consensus was that if he was not hanged for murder, he ought to be hanged for introducing Johnson grass to the San Joaquin Valley.

The Bullard Legacy

Today, as you drive through northwest Fresno with its lush landscaping and large residences, it is hard to imagine that this land was called the "hog wallows" a hundred years ago. It was called "hog wallows" because the area was covered with mounds about fifty feet in diameter which many people felt made it unfit for farming or, indeed, any other use.

In the late 1870s and early 1880s, this land, stretching from the northern boundaries of Fresno to the San Joaquin River, and bounded by Blackstone Avenue to the east and the Southern Pacific Railroad tracks to the west, was acquired section by section by an enterprising gentleman. It was developed into a 72,000-acre ranch where grain, mostly barley, was grown. The land had been acquired for about twenty-five cents an acre.

With the death of this gentleman in 1894, his son moved to Fresno to run his father's business. The son's interests went beyond farming. He became active in politics and served as a trustee for the school district northwest of Fresno. He also served his community as a member of the board of supervisors and the local draft board during World War I.

In 1912, a group headed by J. C. Forkner purchased the ranching operation for $1.2 million. At the same time, a right-of-way was granted to the Fresno Traction Company so it could build a streetcar line from Fresno to the San Joaquin River.

Land was also given for a school, which opened in 1916. Edgar J. Bullard and his father, Francis, were great believers in improving the educational standards in Fresno schools. It is appropriate that today two schools in Fresno bear the Bullard name, Bullard Project Talent and Bullard High School. Bullard Avenue, which transects the old Bullard properties, also is a reminder of this family's contributions to Fresno.

Parks, Boulevards & Cheney

One important element in the plan that Charles Henry Cheney drew for Fresno in 1918 was his design for boulevards, trees and parks. In his job as a planning consultant for many California cities he had the opportunity to study other cities thoroughly and felt Fresno compared to the best.

He called Kearney Boulevard one of the finest boulevards in the world and suggested that trees be planted along Fresno Street all the way to M Street, thus linking Kearney Boulevard with the Civic Center. He also discussed the potential of Van Ness Avenue and predicted that with careful planning Van Ness could become as fine a boulevard all the way north to the river. He envisioned a system of boulevards that would crisscross the city in every direction and form scenic roadways that would beautify the city. He suggested that some of these landscaped roadways should run next to existing canals, such as Dry Creek and Herndon. Such boulevards, he argued, would make Fresno world famous.

He also urged the city to acquire land along the south bank of the San Joaquin River as soon as possible. He felt that Fresno had the potential to grow quickly and advised the city to purchase at least 500 to 1,000 acres while the land was still inexpensive. Cheney stressed the importance of a park in this area where people could leave the stress of city life and relax in a setting of water and trees, where nature would be preserved in the special beauty of this natural setting. He also suggested expanding existing parks and creating new ones all over the city so that Fresnans could enjoy them easily.

Cheney's plan for a Fresno of tree-lined boulevards and canal-fronted roadways was a futuristic vision in 1918. As we read his plan from the perspective of the mid-1990s, we see in it the vision of one who saw tremendous potential and beauty in this city hewn from a hostile desert environment. Yet, with the development of the San Joaquin River Parkway, it seems that at least part of his vision will be realized.

Many people in Fresno feel a great regret for the historic buildings that have been torn down, the architectural gems that have been lost. And, although it is true that Fresno's track record in saving old buildings is not very good, if you take time to look around, it will become evident that there are some wonderful success stories.

Nestled among the new buildings in the Civic Center Square section of downtown Fresno is a structure of an older vintage. Built in 1921, this building was Fresno's first postal substation. After its period of usefulness was over, it was abandoned. During the 1970s, it became the subject of much debate. It was an eyesore and there were those who wanted to tear it down. Others felt it should be preserved because of the role it played in Fresno's history.

Fortunately, the developers of the Civic Center Square project saw that this building could be a centerpiece and could give a sense of history to an otherwise brand-new group of structures. They hired an architectural firm and an interior designer to restructure the interior so that it could house several businesses. They tackled the project with imagination and taste. What emerged was a structure that is unique in downtown Fresno. Set amid brick walks and colorful landscaping, the Galleria houses several popular restaurants, and a potpourri of other business enterprises. It bustles with activity and draws patrons from all over Fresno.

A real historic preservation success story, the Galleria stands as a tribute to the developers and merchants who were willing to make a commitment to downtown Fresno and to a part of Fresno's history.

On August 18, 1872, just a few months after the founding of Fresno, a post office was established. It was not easy to find because it was housed in a rather dark back corner of a store at Mariposa Street and Broadway. A clerk in the store, Russell H. Fleming, was made the town's first postmaster. It was he who helped the residents who came by each day to pick up their mail. At first called the Fresno City Post Office, in 1899 the word "city" was dropped from its name. Later the post office moved to other locations, renting space in various businesses, including a store at Fulton and Mariposa streets.

In 1888, a building was constructed at the southwest corner of Fresno and J streets (now Fulton Mall) by E. C. Winchell. Area merchants paid the rent to make it possible for the post office to move there. A few years later, again subsidized by local businessmen, the post office moved to Tulare and J streets, where it stayed until 1907. Finally, in March of 1908, the first United States Post Office building was constructed in Fresno. It stood at the northwest corner of Tulare Street and Van Ness Avenue.

In 1940, the post office moved to a much larger building on Tulare Street between M and N streets. This new structure housed not only the post office, but it also was the site of federal offices and courts. Its exterior walls were built of a type of concrete which bleached to a natural white. Two huge concrete eagles were placed over the two Tulare Street entrances. The building's doors were made of bronze. The lobby had a terrazzo floor with the walls of marble and terra cotta. The private post office boxes, which are still in use, were of cast bronze. A year after this building was completed, it was painted, because Fresnans did not like the natural concrete look, calling it "the Fresno warehouse."

In 1940, branch postal stations were established, so that the citizens of the community would be better served. As the city continued to grow the need for a larger central facility was apparent. In 1973, a new main post office was opened on E Street. It was projected that by 1990, the new building would serve about 500,000 people in the metropolitan area of Fresno. Over a hundred years after the little counter opened in a dark corner of a store, the new, large, airy facility continued Fresno's commitment to mail service to all the people of the Fresno area.

U ntil the year 1865, Fresno County did not have a newspaper. Its citizens depended on obtaining their news from such sources as the Mariposa *Gazette* and the Sacramento *California Weekly Republican*. Then Samuel J. Garrison, with the financial backing of Millerton hotel owner Ira McCray, moved from Visalia to Millerton to begin publishing the *Fresno Times*.

In Visalia, Garrison had been a partner in a publishing venture that had produced the *Equal Rights Expositor*, a newspaper that was so pro-Southern secessionist in its editorial viewpoint that in March of 1863, a mob had stormed the office and threw type out the windows.

When Garrison arrived in Millerton, with a press that had at one time been used by the *Tulare Post*, he set up shop in a wooden building directly across the street from the Oak Hotel. The first issue of the *Fresno Times* was published on January 28, 1865, two weeks later than had been anticipated. The editorial content reflected Garrison's strongly held conservative views.

In an ironic twist, several of the soldiers stationed at Fort Miller volunteered their time to help Garrison. The soldiers were part of the California Volunteers who had arrived with Union Colonel James Olney to help keep the peace between the pro-Southern secessionists and those who supported the Union. Boredom with life at Fort Miller might have had a great deal to do with their willingness to help pro-Southern Garrison.

After the tenth issue of the *Fresno Times* was published on April 5, 1865, McCray withdrew his financial support. Garrison packed up his press and headed back to Visalia and the *Fresno Times* faded into history.

The Fresno local election of 1955 ushered in a new age for the city. The progressive forces won a strong victory with the election of Ted Wills; Hattie May Hammat; J.D. Stephens, Jr., grandson of early-day mayor L.O. Stephens; Abe Segel; and J.O. Thorpe. Only one member of the city commission, James P. Owens, represented the opposition forces.

Within a year, this commission began a process that would result in a new charter to be submitted to the voters for approval in the 1957 election. Legal experts were employed to hammer out the details. The resulting document called for a full-time city administrator who would serve at the pleasure of an elected seven-member city council. The mayor would head the council, but would not have strong powers. He would have one vote and would preside over meetings. This charter proposal was approved by the voters on April 8, 1957.

During these years, Fresno experienced unprecedented growth. A new shopping center was built at the corner of Blackstone and Shields avenues. Called Manchester Center, it posed the first real competition to downtown businesses. The Downtown Association was very worried about this development.

A Redevelopment Agency was formed to designate blighted areas for urban development and rehabilitation. Federal urban renewal funds would be applied for this project. What resulted was local government using eminent domain to tear down slums and encourage private development to rebuild. The architectural firm of Gruen and Associates was hired to develop a plan which would transform the heart of the downtown business district.

In the next few years downtown Fresno would change in a way that few in the mid-1950s could imagine. The ultimate result of the Gruen plan would be the Fulton Mall. And, for many years to come, all of this change would be the subject of controversy.

In 1994 the voters of Fresno chose to return to the strong mayor type of government and in 1996 reelected seated Mayor Jim Patterson as the first strong mayor in many years.

The Old Administration Building

There is a building on the Fresno City College campus that many Fresnans regard with a sentimental attachment. From the time that it was built in 1915 until it was no longer used for classrooms in the late 1970s, it was the focal point of the Fresno Normal School campus, which became Fresno State Teachers College and then Fresno State College. When Fresno State moved to a new campus in northeast Fresno, it was then the center of the Fresno City College campus.

Designed by architect George McDougall in a Spanish Renaissance-style, the building features the extensive use of handmade hard-burned bricks and elegant stonework. A lavish use of Moorish geometric details and classic brick arches add to a feeling of graciousness. Two open courtyards within the structure provided a European feeling and proved to be a popular gathering place for students looking for a cool place to escape the hot Fresno sun. In late spring, College Day was held in the west court. Music and dance groups performed for this special event. Dances were held there in the summer in the wide hallways which encircled the court. The fish pond, which was in the center of the west court, was a popular spot for sorority pledges to fulfill their Hell Week requirements, such as fishing during lunch hour using a pole and a bobby pin.

Many Fresnans can say that at least three generations of their families attended class in this building. For a time the Training School, which was made up of grades one through eight and provided education students an opportunity to observe and teach on campus, was housed in the west wing. In the 1940s, a branch of the Fresno County Free Library also was located in this wing.

Today the hallways are stilled. The deserted structure stands lonely amid newer buildings. Only birds inhabit the courts which for years echoed with the sounds of joyful activity.

Although listed in the National Register of Historic Places, this architectural gem is in grave danger. Even though it has been the focus of intense preservation efforts in recent years, other interests want to see it torn down. If it is, the campus will gain a new parking lot and Fresno will have lost one of the finest examples of Spanish Renaissance architecture on a college campus anywhere in California.

Early Fresno photographer Roderick W. Riggs (1859-1940) created "rogues' galleries" of pioneer Fresnans by tearing photos and gluing them on heavy pieces of cardboard.
Fresno Historical Society Archives, R. W. Riggs Collection

R.W. Riggs, also known as John Rodd, B.G. (By God)
titled his portrait composites according to some shared trait.
This one he titled "Fresno Pioneer Merchants."
Fresno Historical Society Archives, R.W. Riggs Collection

"Our Fresno Girls", portrait composite on cardboard.
Fresno Historical Society Archives, R. W. Riggs Collection

Notes

LEGACY OF A SPANISH LIEUTENANT
  Wallace Smith, *Garden of the Sun*, pp. 33, 36.
  Charles W. Clough and William B. Secrest, Jr., *Fresno County - The Pioneer Years*, pg. 25.
EXPLORERS & TRAILBLAZERS
  Clough and Secrest, *Fresno County - The Pioneer Years*, pp. 27.
  Smith, *Garden of the Sun*, pg. 70.
THE OFFICERS & THE INDIAN TREATY
  Clough and Secrest, *Fresno County - The Pioneer Years*, pp. 14, 19, 51.
  Smith, *Garden of the Sun*, pg. 340.
THE COLONEL'S NEW CLOTHES
  Clough and Secrest, *Fresno County - The Pioneer Years*, pg. 77.
THE COLONEL AND THE TENPENNY NAIL
  Clough and Secrest, *Fresno County - The Pioneer Years*, pp. 84, 85.
  Wallace W. Elliot, *History of Fresno County, California*, p. 89.
A FAMOUS UNIVERSITY, A RAILROAD BOSS & A NEW TOWN
  Clough and Secrest, *Fresno County - The Pioneer Years*, pg. 121.
A GREEN BUSH & A NEW TOWN'S NAME
  Howard Miller, *Fresno Past & Present*, Vol. 27, No. 2, pp. 9-10.
  Interview with Richard Samuelian.
FROM MULESKINNER TO MERCHANT - THE BIG GAMBLE
  Clough and Secrest, *Fresno County - The Pioneer Years*, pg. 121.
WHISKEY, RAILROAD BOSSES AND THE ELECTION OF 1874
  Clough and Secrest, *Fresno County - The Pioneer Years*, pp. 121, 122.
  Elliot, *History of Fresno County, California*, pg. 121.
THE CITY MARSHAL & THE OUTLAW
  Clough and Secrest, *Fresno County - The Pioneer Years*, pp. 237, 238.
  Smith, *Garden of the Sun*, pg. 322.
FRESNO'S MOST BELOVED CITIZEN
  Schyler Rehart, *Fresno Past & Present*, Vol. 28, No. 1, pp. 1-5.
  Elliot, *History of Fresno County, California*, pg. 127.
MAYORS, PLOTS & CHAMBER POTS
  Ed Ainsworth, *Pot Luck*, pp. 13, 14, 86, 87.
THE BIRTH OF A GREAT NEWSPAPER
  Rehart, *Fresno Past & Present*, Vol. 28, No. 1, pg. 3.
THE MAYOR'S GIFT TO LOS ANGELES
  Ainsworth, *Pot Luck*, pp.118-123.
FRESNO'S OLDEST CONTINUOUS BUSINESS
  Charles. W. Clough, et. al., *Fresno County in the 20th Century*, pp. 203, 204.
THE TURKEYS & THE ARMY WORMS
  Clough and Secrest, *Fresno County - The Pioneer Years*, pg. 157.
DIRT MOVING MADE EASIER
  Maria Ortiz, *Fresno Past & Present*, Vol. 23, No. 4, pp. 1-8.
ONE MAN'S DREAM
  Rehart and Patterson, *M. Theo Kearney Prince of Fresno*, pp.42.
  Edwin Eaton, *Vintage Fresno*, pg. 12.
FRESNO'S LONGEST PRIVATE DRIVE
  Rehart and William K. Patterson, *M. Theo Kearney Prince of Fresno*, pp. 15-18.
MUSTANG ED & THE METHODIST EPISCOPAL CHURCH SOUTH
  Fresno Morning Republican. March 5, 1922, p. 8A. Fresno Historical Society Archives, Ben Walker Collection.
A PARK FOR FRESNO
  Clough, et. al., *Fresno County in the 20th Century*, pp.450.
INCORPORATION OF FRESNO
  Clough and Secrest, *Fresno County - The Pioneer Years*, pg. 141
  Ben Randall Walker, *Fresno: 1872-1885, A Municipality in the Making.*

Notes

A NEW CITY HALL
Clough, et. al., *Fresno County in the 20th Century,* pg.43.
Ainsworth, *Pot Luck,* pp. 106, 107.

THE BOY WITH THE LEAKING BOOT
Eaton, *Vintage Fresno,* pp. 117, 188.
Michael R. Waiczis and William B. Secrest, *A Portrait of Fresno 1885-1985,* pg. 11.
Sylvia Castro, "Leaking' fountain has new home," *The Fresno Bee,* August 28, 1997.

A MILL & A DITCH
Clough and Secrest, *Fresno County - The Pioneer Years,* pg. 315.
Eaton, *Vintage Fresno,* pp. 45, 46.

BERRY'S MONUMENT
Clough and Secrest, *Fresno County - The Pioneer Years,* pp. 130, 131.

THE JONES MILL
Clough and Secrest, *Fresno County - The Pioneer Years,* pg. 128.
Jones Family Papers, Fresno Historical Society Archives.

THE BUTCHER, THE BAKER & THE PRODUCE MAN
As told to the author by Eugenie Loverne Kinsley McKay.

BEER, FENCES & W. PARKER LYON
Ainsworth, *Pot Luck,* pp. 100-104.

THE ICE MAN COMETH
As told to the author by Eugenie Loverne Kinsley McKay and Catherine McKay Morison.

NEW CITY, NEW MAYOR & NEW LAWS
Walker, "Fresno 1872-1885 a Municipality in the Making"

FRESNO'S HORSE CAR LINES
Clough and Secrest, *Fresno County - The Pioneer Years,* pp. 319, 320.
Clough, et. al., *Fresno County in the 20th Century,* pg. 247, 248.

CHRISTMAS IN FRESNO IN 1903
The Grapevine, Vol. 8, Nos. 11,12, pg. 3.

WINTER AMID THE TULES
Smith, *Garden of the Sun,* pp. 1-6, 14.

WILBUR CHANDLER'S FIELD
Clough, et. al., *Fresno County in the 20th Century,* pg.265-268.

SOARING SPIRITS & BROKEN RECORDS
Clough, et. al., *Fresno County in the 20th Century,* pg.475, 476.

PHYSICIAN, BUSINESSMAN & BANK PRESIDENT
Clough and Secrest, *Fresno County - The Pioneer Years,* pp. 53, 70, 122, 317.
Eaton, *Vintage Fresno,* pg. 3.

THE CRUSADING EDITOR
Clough, et. al., *Fresno County in the 20th Century,* pg. 38-40, 46, 407, 408.

A SUBWAY FOR FRESNO STREET
Clough, et. al., *Fresno County in the 20th Century,* pg. 43.
Ainsworth, *Pot Luck,* pp.108-11.

PLUMBING & PREACHERS
Clough, et. al., *Fresno County in the 20th Century,* pg. 43.; Ainsworth, *Pot Luck,* pp.111-115

AN ELEPHANT NAMED NOSEY
The Fresno Bee, September 11, 1949.

FIREBUG ON THE LOOSE
Waiczis and Secrest, *A Portrait of Fresno 1885-1985,* pp.148, 149.

A SAD DEPARTURE
Clough, et. al., *Fresno County in the 20th Century,* pp.43, 44.

AN ACADEMY FOR THE FOOTHILLS
Clough and Secrest, *Fresno County - The Pioneer Years,* pp. 95-96.

THE RED BRICK CHURCH
Robby Antoyan and John Edward Powell, National Register Nomination, Holy Trinity Armenian Apostolic Church, October 15, 1985.

Notes

THE LONG TRAIL TO MILLERTON
  Baley Family Papers, Fresno Historical Society Archives.

MAHER'S SYMBOL FOR FRESNO
  Todd A. Shallat, *Water and the Rise of Public Ownerhip on the Fresno Plain, 1850- 1978*, pp. 43-46.
Fresno Historical Society Archives.
  Clough and Secrest, *Fresno County - The Pioneer Years*, pg. 321.

TELEPHONES, OPERATORS & A PARROT
  Clough and Secrest, *Fresno County - The Pioneer Years*, pp. 130, 321.
  Clough, et. al., *Fresno County in the 20th Century,* pg. 53.

THE MODERN DEXTER STABLES
  Fresno Historical Society, *Imperial Fresno,* pp.62-64.

FRESNO'S FOUNDER
  Harold J. Ledford, *Fresno Past & Present,* Vol. 28, No. 4, pp. 10-12.

THE CALL TO BATTLE
  Waiczis and Secrest, *A Portrait of Fresno 1885-1985,* pg. 89.

FIREWORKS & JUBILATION
  Waiczis and Secrest, *A Portrait of Fresno 1885-1985,* pg. 89.

TIMBER & THE TOLL HOUSE GRADE
  Claire Baird Zylka, Ken Greenberg, and Jessie Myers Thun, *Images of an Age, Clovis,* pp. 106, 107.

SAWMILLS, SWIFT & SHAVER
  Clough and Secrest, *Fresno County - The Pioneer Years*, pp. 202, 203, 206.

A FLUMING WE WILL GO
  Clough and Secrest, *Fresno County - The Pioneer Years*, pp. 206.

THE GATEWAY TO THE SIERRA
  Clough and Secrest, *Fresno County - The Pioneer Years*, pp. 304, 305.
  Fresno Past & Present, Vol. 30, No. 2, pp. 1, 2.

A COURTHOUSE FOR MILLERTON
  Clough and Secrest, *Fresno County - The Pioneer Years*, pg. 84, 90.
  Interview with State Park Ranger Jonathan M. Burgasser at the Millerton Courthouse.

THE FRESNO SANITARIUM
  American Association of University Women, *Heritage Fresno Women and Their Contributions,* pg. 53.

BIG DRY CREEK & ITS CHURCH
  Clough and Secrest, *Fresno County - The Pioneer Years*, pg. 94, 95.

TOPPLED HOPES
  The Fresno Bee, February 13, 1966.
  The Fresno Bee, March 8, 1966.
  The Fresno Bee, March 16, 1966.
  The Fresno Bee, April 8, 1966.

CRUSADERS & COURTHOUSES
  Clough and Secrest, *Fresno County - The Pioneer Years*, pg. 28-31.

THE CEMETARY AT ACADEMY
  Written during a visit to the cemetary.

A TUNEFUL TREASURE
  Sequoia Chapter, American Theatre Organ Society and San Joaquin Chapter, American Guild of
  Organists, *The Jewel of Fresno.*

FRESNO'S CIVIL WAR DOCTOR
  American Association of University Women, *Heritage Fresno Homes and People,* pg. 2.

A CATHEDRAL FOR SAINT JOHN
  Msgr. Culleton, Msgr. Singleton, et. al., *St. John the Baptist Parish 1882-1982.*

FRESNANS GO TO WAR
  Clough and Secrest, *Fresno County - The Pioneer Years*, pg. 287, 288.

COURTSHIP, CARTS & HORSES
  As told to the author by Eugenie Loverne Kinsley McKay.

Notes

FRESNO'S FIRST HIGH SCHOOL
Clough and Secrest, *Fresno County - The Pioneer Years*, pg.301, 317, 318.

FRESNO'S FAVORITE NATIVE SON
Interview with Karen Moore Reynolds, head librarian, Gillis Branch Library.
Aram Saroyan, *William Saroyan*, pp. xvii, xviii.

CHENEY'S VISION FOR FRESNO
Charles Henry Cheney, *Progress of a City Plan for Fresno*, pg. 39.

WAREHOUSE ROW
Jack Weyant, National Register Nomination, Warehouse Row.
Interview with Art Dyson.

THE LEGEND OF MURRIETA
Clough and Secrest, *Fresno County - The Pioneer Years*, pp. 223-226.

A JOYOUS FUNERAL
Marcelle B. Weigandt, *Fulton G. Berry*, pp. 1-4.

THE PHYSICIANS BUILDING
John Edward Powell, The Physicians Building, National Register Nomination, May 18, 1978.

THE TEN-MINUTE MAYOR
Schyler Rehart, "Fresno's Turbulent Youth, 1885-1901, Part II: Joe Spin's City Hall," *Fresno Past &
Present*, Vol. 27, No. 1, pp. 5-11.
Clough, et. al., *Fresno County in the 20th Century*, pg. 38.

THE "FATHER OF FRESNO"
Clough and Secrest, *Fresno County - The Pioneer Years*, pg. 310.
Eaton, *Vintage Fresno*, pg. 34.
Benjamin Bencomo, "Thomas E. Hughes: The Father of Fresno," *Fresno Past & Present*,
Vol. 18, No. 1, pp. 1-6, Vol. 18, No. 2, pp. 1-6.

SEROPIANS, RAISINS & BOUREG
Clough and Secrest, *Fresno County - The Pioneer Years*, pg. 156.
Clough, et. al., *Fresno County in the 20th Century*, pg. 6.

PROHIBITION& PARCELS OF LAND
Clough and Secrest, *Fresno County-The Pioneer Years*, pg. 144

A NAME IS A NAME?
Ibid, pg. 283, 285, 286
"Railroad Men Name Sanger for Fellow Worker," *Fresno Past & Present*, Vol. 30, no. 1, pg. 5

FRESNO'S CASTLE
David Lazarus, Kindler Home, National Register Nomination, October 29, 1982.

A BRICK CHURCH ON U STREET
"Carter Memorial African Methodist Episcopal Church," *100 Year Souvenir Book, Fresno Past &
Present*, Vol. 24, No. 1, pp. 1-7.

A SIGN FOR VAN NESS
Doug Hansen, "Sketchbook" *The Fresno Bee*, Nov. 1, 1991

KMJ—FRESNO'S FIRST RADIO STATION
Bob Long, tape of radio segments covering KMJ Radio's 70 year history.

FRESNO'S FINEST FIGHTER
Clough, et. al., *Fresno County in the 20th Century*, pp. 464. 465.
The Fresno Bee, February 26, 1933.

PAEAN TO A DECADE
Wright, Earl, Jr., *The Fresno Bee*, October 3, 1991.

BANTA'S BICYCLE MAIL
Charles Baley, "The Bicycle Express," *Fresno Past & Present*, Vol. 32, No. 3, pp. 5-9.

THE NATION'S CHRISTMAS TREE
Sanger District Chamber of Commerce, Brochure, *66th Annual Trek To The General Grant Tree.*

A MEMORIAL FOR GENERAL GRANT
Lizzie Gamlin McGee, Speech to the Naturalist Camp Fire Progran in the Kings Canyon
National Park, September, 1951.

Notes

FRESNO'S LONGEST STREET
  Interview with Ken Hohmann.
  Interview with Roger Taylor.
THE JERSEY LILY
  Eaton, *Vintage Fresno,* pp. 87, 88.
PRESERVATIONIST PHIPPS
  Interview with Esther Phipps.
BISHOP KIP
  L. A. Winchell Papers, Ms. 3, Chapter 22, pp. 14-17.
A HOUSE OF LEARNING
  Ron Byrd, *Fresno City College Library Building.*
STEAMBOATS ON THE SAN JOAQUIN
  L. A. Winchell Papers, *Steamboat Freighting on the San Joaquin.*
THE BLOCKHOUSE AT FORT MILLER
  Clough and Secrest, *Fresno County - The Pioneer Years,* pp. 69-79.
A GREAT HUMANITARIAN
  American Association of University Women, *Heritage Fresno Homes and People,* pg. 36.
RIGHT OUT OF HOLLYWOOD
  David Bice James, *Reminisceces of Early Days in the "Southern Mines,"* Ms. 3, pg. 11.
  Clough and Secrest, *Fresno County - The Pioneer Years,* pp. 219, 221.
OLD FIG GARDEN
  J. C. Forkner and Wylie Giffen, Garden Home Tract advertisements.
KUTNER & GOLDSTEIN
  Clough and Secrest, *Fresno County - The Pioneer Years,* pp. 124, 314
  Fresno Weekly Expositor, pg. 5c3.
  Fresno Evening Expositor, pg. 3c2.
  The Fresno Bee, Louis Kutner obituary.
MR. BASEBALL
  The Fresno Bee, John M. Euless obituary.
  American Association of University Women, *Heritage Fresno Homes and People,* pg. 76.
A HEROIC DEED
  American Association of University Women, *Heritage Fresno Women and Their Contributions,* pg. 26.
THE TOWER THEATRE
  John Edward Powell, National Register Nomination, Tower Theatre.
TOWER THEATRE—BEHIND THE SCENES
  John Edward Powell, National Register Nomination, Tower Theatre.
THE EWING HOME
  American Association of University Women, *Heritage Fresno Homes and People,* pg. 11.
100 YEARS OF GOOD BOOKS
  Mary Ann Parker, *History of the Fresno County Free Library 1910-1970,* pp. 6, 7.
CARNEGIE'S LIBRARY
  Clough, et. al., *Fresno County in the 20th Century,* pp.24, 25.
  Eaton, *Vintage Fresno,* pp. 109, 110.
PACIFIC SOUTHWEST BUILDING
  Eaton, *Vintage Fresno,* pp. 62-64.
A ONE-SIDED DUEL
  Clough and Secrest, *Fresno County - The Pioneer Years,* pp. 250, 251.
POSTMAN WEIR'S WHISTLE
  Fresno Morning Republican, November 18, 1927.
THE PIONEER WOMEN OF FRESNO
  Clough and Secrest, *Fresno County - The Pioneer Years,* pg. 122.
FRESNO'S WAR HERO
  Waiczis and Secrest, *A Portrait of Fresno 1885-1985,* pp.146, 147.
  The Fresno Bee, November 30, 1940.
  The Fresno Bee, September 15, 1951.

Catherine Morison Rehart

Notes

COURTHOUSE PARK
  Clough and Secrest, *Fresno County - The Pioneer Years*, pp. 123, 126.
A TOWN FIT TO LIVE IN
  The Fresno Bee, July 23, 1948.
GORDON G. DUNN
  The Fresno Bee, February 2, 1949.
A NEW MAYOR FOR FRESNO
  The Fresno Bee, February 9, 1949.
"NO FUN DUNN"
  Clough, et. al., *Fresno County in the 20th Century,* pp. 63, 64.
  The Fresno Bee, January 27, 1950.
FRESNO COMES OF AGE
  Clough, et. al., *Fresno County in the 20th Century,* pp. 63-67.
  The Fresno Bee, April 23, 1952.
FRESNO COUNTY'S FIRST RECORDED MARRIAGE
  American Association of University Women, *Heritage Fresno Women and Their Contributions,* pg.15.
FRESNO'S SCOTS BELL
  American Association of University Women, *Heritage Fresno Women and Their Contributions,* pg. 87.
A SQUIRREL NAMED JIMMIE
  The Fresno Bee, March 24, 1940.
NEW YEARS EVE - 1883
  Fresno Morning Republican, January 1, 1884.
PERMELIA E. BALEY
  Winchell, Ernestine, "Fresno Memories," *Fresno Morning Republican,* November 29, 1925.
  Fresno Morning Republican, December 9, 1906.
A LYON'S RETURN
  The Fresno Bee, September 19, 1947.
THE LADIES OF THE CLUB
  Parlor Lecture Club, Leisure Hour Club and Query Club program books. Fresno Historical Society
  Archives.
  Eaton, *Vintage Fresno,* pg. 53.
LEWIS SWIFT EATON
  The Fresno Bee, May 7, 1990, pg. 1A.
  The Fresno Bee, September 26, 1992, pg.1A.
STAGES & STEVENSES
  Eaton, *Vintage Fresno,* pg. 64.
  As told to the author by Eugenie Loverne Kinsley McKay.
FRESNO'S FIRST BUSINESSES
  Clough and Secrest, *Fresno County - The Pioneer Years*, pp. 123-130.
MR. CEARLEY & HIS STORE
  Fresno Historical Society, *Imperial Fresno,* pp. 69, 70.
MR. TAYLOR & MR. WHEELER
  Sanford Nax, "Taylor Wheeler Builders Accomplishments Recalled," *The Fresno Bee,* April 1, 1989,
  pg.C1.
  The Fresno Bee, Wheeler Obituary, August 7, 1991.
THE UNDOMED COURTHOUSE
  Fresno Past & Present, Vol. 25, No. 3, pp. 6, 7.
THE SUN MAID GIRL
  Dave Larsen, *Los Angeles Times,* interview with Lorraine Collett Petersen.
FRESNO, FIRES & FIRE TRUCKS
  Clough and Secrest, *Fresno County - The Pioneer Years*, pp. 139-141.
NATURAL DISASTERS IN EARLY FRESNO
  Clough and Secrest, *Fresno County - The Pioneer Years*, pg. 139.

Notes

THE COLONY SYSTEM - THE DREAM THAT BECAME A REALITY
Clough and Secrest, *Fresno County - The Pioneer Years*, pp. 133, 134.

CALIFORNIA'S FIRST RAISIN BARON
Rehart and Patterson, *M. Theo Kearney Prince of Fresno*, pg. 6.

PRANKSTER & COLORFUL CITIZEN
Eaton, *Vintage Fresno*, pp. 48-50.
Clough, et. al., *Fresno County in the 20th Century*, pg. 216.
Fresno Historical Society, *Imperial Fresno*, pp. 98-100.

STRIKE UP THE BAND
Fresno Morning Republican, November 25, 1919.

THE MOTTO IS "SERVICE"
History of Gottschalk's, pp. 1-4.

FRESNO'S FIRST THEATER
Clough and Secrest, *Fresno County - The Pioneer Years*, pg. 327.
Eaton, *Vintage Fresno*, pp. 83-88.

FRESNO'S FIRST WOMAN OF AGRICULTURE
American Association of University Women, *Heritage Fresno Women and Their Contributions*,
pp. 90, 91.
Clough and Secrest, *Fresno County - The Pioneer Years*, pp. 159, 341, 342.
Eaton, *Vintage Fresno*, pp. 23-25.

INVITATION TO A HANGING
Clough and Secrest, *Fresno County - The Pioneer Years*, pp. 235, 241, 242.

WATER TANKS & WELLS
Shallat, *Water and the Rise of Public Ownerhip on the Fresno Plain, 1850-1978*, pp. 43-46. Fresno
Historical Society Archives.
Clough and Secrest, *Fresno County - The Pioneer Years*, pg. 130.
Eaton, *Vintage Fresno*, pg. 77.

FRESNO'S SHOWPLACE
Clough, et. al., *Fresno County in the 20th Century*, pg.216.
Eaton, *Vintage Fresno*, pp. 51-53.
Clough and Secrest, *Fresno County - The Pioneer Years*, pg. 310.

AN ASSASSINATION ATTEMPT
Clough, et. al., *Fresno County in the 20th Century*, pp. 54-58.

TAKE ME OUT TO THE BALLGAME
Clough, et. al., *Fresno County in the 20th Century*, pp. 459-463.

JIM WHITE'S BRIDGE
Elliot, *History of Fresno County, California*, pg. 201.
Clough and Secrest, *Fresno County - The Pioneer Years*, pg. 257.

THE LAND BOOM OF 1887
Clough and Secrest, *Fresno County - The Pioneer Years*, pg. 307.

PIONEER BANK PRESIDENT
Stephen R. Smith, *Fresno Past & Present*, Vol. 24, No. 2, pp. 1-5.

CHRISTMAS TREE LANE
Mrs. H. D. Bartlett, *Fresno's Christmas Tree Lane*.

CANDELIGHT CHRISTMAS
Penny Raven. Background material on Candelight Christmas. Huntington Boulevard
Homeowners Association.

THE FIG & ITS WASP
Clough and Secrest, *Fresno County - The Pioneer Years*, pp. 339, 340.
Wanda Podgorski Russell, "George C. Roeding - The Man and His Trees," *Fresno Past & Present*, Vol.
26. No. 2, pp. 1, 2.

LIFE UNDERGROUND IN FRESNO
Lorraine Faulks Forestiere, Fresno Underground Gardens, National Register Nomination. March
28, 1977.

Notes

A LEGACY OF MUSIC
  Clough, et. al., *Fresno County in the 20th Century,* pp. 373, 386.
  Fresno Musical Club 1905-1980. Copyright and Editor, Ruth Winton, pp. 3-23.
  Gladys Peters, "The Fresno Musical Club," *Fresno Past & Present*, Vol. 27, No. 3, pp. 16-19.
THE GOLDEN RULE
  Interview with Bud Warner.
AN OIL BARON'S MANSION
  Ephraim K. Smith and John Edward Powell. The Brix Mansion. National Register Nomination.
  March 7, 1983.
  John Edward Powell, "Edward T. Foulkes," *Fresno Past & Present,* Vol. 25, N0. 1. pp. 2-5.
THE ORIGINAL FIG GARDENS
  Interview with Buddy Arkelian.
  Eaton, *Vintage Fresno,* pg. 37.
HOG WALLOWS & FIGS
  Eaton, *Vintage Fresno,* pp. 36-40.
SPEAKEASIES & SUDS
  Patrick Supple. Fresno Brewery. National Register Nomination. March 15, 1983.
  Clough, et. al., *Fresno County in the 20th Century,* pp. 208.
MORGAN'S DESIGN FOR FRESNO
  Interview with John Edward Powell.
  Valerie D. Comegys, Y. W. C. A. Residence Hall, National Register Nomination. February 9, 1978.
BAMBOO POLES & SOARING HEIGHTS
  Clough, et. al., *Fresno County in the 20th Century,* pp. 319, 476.
  Joe Gergen, "How High Could Warmerdam Have Vaulted?" *The Sporting News,* pg. 6.
  Statistical information, Provided by Sports Information Office. California State University,
  Fresno.
SISTERS OF THE HOLY CROSS
  About Saint Agnes 1929-1979: 50 Years of Progress. Information provided by the Public Relations
  Office, St. Agnes Medical Center.
A PENTHOUSE IN THE SKY
  James Oakes, Maubridge Building, National Register Nomination, August 14, 1980.
POLLASKY, THE SMOOTH-TALKING PROMOTER
  Eaton, *Vintage Fresno,* pp. 32, 33.
FRESNO COUNTY SEPARATES
  Charles W. Clough, *Madera,* pp. 13-15.
THE JAIL AND ITS BUILDER
  Clough and Secrest, *Fresno County - The Pioneer Years*, pp. 90, 222.
REEDLEY'S GRAND OPERA HOUSE
  Patricia Berthold, Reedley Opera House, National Register Nomination, April 15, 1983.
A PRINTING PRESS & PRESERVATION
  John Edward Powell, The Republican Printery, National Register Nomination,
  September 18, 1978.
FRESNO'S LARGEST ENGLISH COTTAGE
  Valerie Comegys, Einstein Home, National Register Nomination, August 31, 1977.
OMAR KHAYYAM'S
  Interview with Dr. Arthur Margosian.
  George Mardikian. *Song of America.*
FRESNO'S MISSION-STYLE DEPOT
  Diane Seeger, Santa Fe Depot, National Register Nomination, May 28, 1976.
THE GREY BRICK HOUSE
  John Edward Powell, The Rehorn Home, National Register Nomination, November 1, 1980.
FRESNO'S SOHO DISTRICT
  Powell, Tower Theatre, National Register Nomination, April 3, 1992.
THE TEMPLE BAR
  Eaton, *Vintage Fresno,* pp. 70-73.

Notes

AN EGGS-ACTING CONTEST
  Chamber of Commerce newsletter, Spring, 1927.

KINGSBURG'S SWEDISH COFFEE POT
  Pauline Mathes, *Bit of Sweden in the Desert*, pp. 21, 27, 28, 31.

THE TOWER DISTRICT PHARMACY
  Interview with Charles Alstrom.

THE TWIN SISTERS
  American Association of University Women, *Heritage Fresno Homes and People*, pg. 35.

THE WORLD'S SMALLEST PARISH
  Interview with Alan Mar, Jr.
  John DeGano, *Insight*, October 26, 1977, pg. 6.

FRESNO'S CHINESE ASSOCIATIONS
  Interview with Lillie Lew.
  William E. Patnaude, Historic Resources Inventory, Bing Tong Kong Association Building, City of Fresno.
  William E. Patnaude, Historic Resources Inventory, Bow On Tong Association Building, City of Fresno.

FRESNO'S CHINESE SCHOOL OF CONFUCIUS
  Clough, et. al., *Fresno County in the 20th Century*, pg. 5.
  Interview with Lillie Lew.
  Chinese Papers Collection. Fresno Historical Society Archives.

THE MOSGROVE HOME
  American Association of University Women, *Heritage Fresno Homes and People*, pg. 49.

THE PRESCOTT MANSION
  Eaton, *Vintage Fresno*, pp. 105-108.

FRESNO'S LEGAL NEWSPAPER
  Interview with Norman A. Webster and Gordon M. Webster.

THE COCKTAIL NAPKIN POLICY
  Interviews with Ray Appleton and B. Franklin Knapp.
  The Insurance Journal. January 26, 1956.

A HAPPY PRESERVATION STORY
  Karen Weitzie, Study of 13 Potential National Register Structures in Freeway 180 GAP Project for CalTrans District 6, 1991.

CUTTING A RUG
  The Fresno Bee, August 24, 1939.

FRESNO'S SHOPKEEPER & ENTREPRENEUR
  Clough and Secrest, *Fresno County - The Pioneer Years*, pp. 80, 87, 91, 92, 121, 128-130, 149.

MINATURE GOLF INDOORS
  The Fresno Bee, August 24, 1930.
  The Fresno Bee, October 1, 1930.

A SACRED RIGHT
  Fresno Morning Republican, October 12, 1911.
  Fresno Morning Republican, October 14, 1911.

A FAIR BEGINNING
  Dave Terrill and Lorena Molen, Fresno District Fair Public Relations Office, articles on the 100-year history of the Fresno District Fair, June 18, 1984.

THE THOMPSON TAPESTRY
  American Association of University Women, *Heritage Fresno Homes and People*, pp. 54, 55.

CANTUA MAN
  William Rintoul, "Fresno County's Petrified People," *Fresno County - The Pioneer Years*, pg. 271.

JUSTICE IN THE 1880S
  Paul Vandor, *History of Fresno County, California, with Brief Biographical Sketches*, pp. 674-678.

VARTANIAN'S BLOCK
  American Association of University Women, *Heritage Fresno Homes and People*, pp. 38, 39.

THE PARKERS' STEAMBOAT RIDE
  L. A. Winchell Papers, *Steamboat Freighting on the San Joaquin*.

Notes

AUTUMN IN FRESNO
  L. A. Winchell Papers, *Eisen/Winchell Letters.*
THE HOTEL FRESNO
  Clough, et. al., *Fresno County in the 20th Century,* pp. 50, 216.
THE WATCHMAKER & HIS CLOCK
  Interview with Iver Eriksen.
FRESNO'S ELECTRIC HOUSE
  Grant and Ann Schreiber, The Blum House, Historic Resources Inventory, City of Fresno.
YOSEMITE'S FRIEND
  American Association of University Women, *Heritage Fresno Homes and People,* pg. 74.
THE LEGACY OF EMMA MILLER
  Interview with Mary Helen McKay.
  American Association of University Women, *Heritage Fresno Women and Their Contrbutions,* pg. 75.
A BAKERY FOR THE VALLEY
  The Fresno Bee, October 26, 1992.
FRESNO'S BANK OF ITALY
  Robert L. Triplett, Jr., Bank of Italy, National Register   Nomination, October 24, 1981.
THE EXPOSITOR
  Clough and Secrest, *Fresno County - The Pioneer Years*, pg. 316.
  Benjamin Bencomo, "J. W. Ferguson and the Fresno Expositor," *Fresno Past & Present,* Vol. 19, No. 2, p. 1-5.
THE OTHER PRESCOTT MANSION
  American Association of University Women, *Heritage Fresno Homes and People,* pg. 8.
CHARMING NELLIE BOYD
  American Association of University Women, *Heritage Fresno Women and Their Contrbutions,* pg. 14.
THE COLLINS HOME
  American Association of University Women, *Heritage Fresno Homes and People,* pg. 4.
THE SWIFT HOME
  American Association of University Women, *Heritage Fresno Homes and People,* pp. 20, 21.
LEE'S THEATER
  The Fresno Bee, October 8, 1987, pg. F6.
HATTIE MAY HAMMAT
  Clough, et. al., *Fresno County in the 20th Century,* pp. 66, 68, 69.
  American Association of University Women, *Heritage Fresno Women and Their Contrbutions,* pp. 51, 52. Author's memories.
A LADY NAMED JANE
  Clough and Secrest, *Fresno County - The Pioneer Years*, pg. 88.
  American Association of University Women, *Heritage Fresno Women and Their Contrbutions,* pg. 25.
REPORTER PAR EXCELLENCE
  American Association of University Women, *Heritage Fresno Women and Their Contrbutions,* pp. 17, 18.
FRESNO'S FIRST ARTIST
  American Association of University Women, *Heritage Fresno Women and Their Contrbutions,* pg. 38.
AN ACTRESS NAMED BERRY
  American Association of University Women, *Heritage Fresno Women and Their Contrbutions,* pg. 11.
SARAH McCARDLE
  American Association of University Women, *Heritage Fresno Women and Their Contrbutions,* pg. 70.
  The Fresno Bee, December 21, 1945.
MR. WISHON'S BUILDING
  Clough, et. al., *Fresno County in the 20th Century,* pp. 152, 248, 249.
  Informational tour of building courtesy of the Public Relations Office of the U. S. International Trade Center.

Notes

FRESNO'S ARMLESS AVIATOR
  Clough, et. al., *Fresno County in the 20th Century,* pp. 268, 269.
  Fresno Morning Republican, January 11, 1924.

THE WISHON HOME
  American Association of University Women, *Heritage Fresno Homes and People,* pg. 62.

THE SUN-MAID GIRL
  Dave Larsen, *Los Angeles Times;* interview with Lorraine Collett Petersen.

THE GAMES YOKUTS PLAY
  Clough and Secrest, *Fresno County - The Pioneer Years,* pg. 16.

THE CHILDREN'S LIBRARIAN
  American Association of University Women, *Heritage Fresno Women and Their Contrbutions,*
  pp. 39, 40.

A PARK FOR MR. KEARNEY
  French Strother, "A Unique Estate in Central California," *Country Life in America,* pp. 408-410.

THE "PROSPERITY SPECIAL"
  Fresno Morning Republican, September 22, 1931.

FRESNO, THE "ELECTRIC CITY"
  Fresno Morning Republican, April 3, 1930.

THE RAILROAD & THE OVERRIPE EGGS
  Golden Bear, June, 1933, pg. 4. Reprinted in *Fresno Morning Republican,* 1883.

THE WRONG CHRISTOPHER
  Joe Smith, "Tales of the San Joaquin," *The Fresno Bee.*

FRESNO'S FIRST TEACHER
  American Association of University Women, *Heritage Fresno Women and Their Contributions,* pp. 59.

MALVINA & "DOC"
  Donna M. Hill, *And Then There Were Ten Thousand,* reprinted in Clough and Secrest, *Fresno County
  The Pioneer Years,* pp. 48, 49.

A PLETHORA OF LAWS
  The Fresno Bee, February 6, 1938.

THE RAT PATROL
  The Fresno Bee, January 17, 1938.

WILLIAM H. HENDERSON
  Fresno Morning Republican, January 18, 1931.
  Interview with Don Kleim.

STREET NAMES
  John Walter Caughey, *California,* pp. 49, 50.
  Clough and Secrest, *Fresno County - The Pioneer Years,* pg. 25.

THE MUNGER/PORTEOUS HOME
  Interview with BrigGen. Edward E. Munger.
  American Association of University Women, *Heritage Fresno Homes and People,* pg. 47.

LA PALOMA GUILD
  Author's memories

A NEW DEPOT FOR FRESNO
  "Fifty Years Ago," *The Fresno Bee,* May 22, 1938.

A SLAVE NAMED EMMA
  The Fresno Bee, May 13, 1940.

THE GUNDLEFINGER WOMEN
  American Association of University Women, *Heritage Fresno Women and Their Contrbutions,*
  pp. 45, 46.

CLOVIS RODEO
  Clovis Rodeo Program, 1989.

THE SHIPP-SELLAND HOME
  Prudence Zalewski, The Shipp-Selland Residence, Historic Resources Inventory Form,
  May 10, 1990.

Notes

THE BELTLESS FIREMEN OF 1888
"Fifty Years Ago," *The Fresno Bee,* July 17, 1938.
"Fifty Years Ago," *The Fresno Bee,* August 28, 1938.

THE WHITE KING
Clough and Secrest, *Fresno County - The Pioneer Years,* pp. 14-21.

THE BARTON VINEYARD
Fresno Historical Society, *Imperial Fresno,* pp. 24-27.

WHO'S TO RAISIN WHY?
The Fresno Bee, March 19, 1933.

THE BROTHERHOOD OF MAN
Interview with the late Rabbi David L. Greenberg.

A PARK & A LAKE IN THE TOWER DISTRICT
Clough, et. al., *Fresno County in the 20th Century,* pp. 455, 456.
The Fresno Guide, April 21, 1971, pg. 5.

BASQUE FOOD & FELLOWSHIP
Wanda M. Lespade, Santa Fe Hotel, National Register Nomination. March, 1989.

VAUDEVILLE & ELEGANCE
Interview and tour of Warnor's Theater with Rose Caglia.
Rose M. Caglia, Alexander Pantages Theater, National Register Nomination, September 10, 1977.

A CREAMERY FOR FRESNO
Danish Creamery Public Relations office. *The History of Danish Creamery.*

A GLORIOUS WEED
Elliot, *History of Fresno County, California,* pp. 33, 36, 121, 122.
Clough and Secrest, *Fresno County - The Pioneer Years,* pg. 156.
Fresno Morning Republican, February 19, 1881.

MURDER, MISCHIEF & JOHNSON GRASS
Judy Riley, "Where Is William Wooten," *Fresno Past & Present,* Vol. 33, No. 4, pp. 1-9.

THE BULLARD LEGACY
Bullard Family Papers. Fresno Historical Society Archives.

PARKS, BOULEVARDS & CHENEY
Charles Henry Cheney, *Progress of a City Plan for Fresno.* June 1, 1918.

THE GALLERIA
William E. Patnaude, Historic Resources Inventory, City of Fresno.

FRESNO POSTAL SERVICE
Clough and Secrest, *Fresno County - The Pioneer Years,* pp. 121, 122.
Eaton, *Vintage Fresno,* pp. 54, 55.

THE OLD ADMINISTRATION BUILDING
Ephraim K. Smith, The Old Administration Building, National Register Nomination, May 1, 1974.

Bibliography

About Saint Agnes 1929-1979: 50 Years of Progress. Information provided by the Public Relations Office. St. Agnes Medical Center.

Ainsworth, Ed. *Pot Luck.* George Palmer Putnam, Inc., Hollywood, 1940.

Antoyan, Robby and John Edward Powell. Holy Trinity Armenian Apostolic Church. "Summary of Statement for Historical and Architectural Significance." National Register Nomination. October 15, 1985. Fresno Historical Society Archives.

American Association of University Women. *Heritage Fresno Homes and People.* Pioneer Publishing Company, Fresno, 1975.

American Association of University Women. *Heritage Fresno Women and Their Contributions.* Pioneer Publishing Company, Fresno, 1987.

Baley, Charles."The Bicycle Express." *Fresno Past & Present.* Quarterly Journal. Fresno Historical Society. Vol. 32, No. 3.

Baley Family Papers. Fresno Historical Society Archives.

Bartlett, Mrs. H. D. *Fresno's Christmas Tree Lane.* Fresno Historical Society Archives.

Bencomo, Benjamin. "J. W. Ferguson and the Fresno Expositor," *Fresno Past & Present.* Quarterly Journal. Fresno Historical Society. Vol. 19, No. 2.

Bencomo, Benjamin. "Thomas E. Hughes: The Father of Fresno." *Fresno Past & Present.* Quarterly Journal. Fresno Historical Society. Vol. 18, No. 1. Vol. 18, No. 2.

Bergthold, Patricia. Reedley Opera House. "Summary of Statement for Historical and Architectural Significance." National Register Nomination. April 15, 1983. Fresno Historical Society Archives.

"Bob Duncan." Biographical information provided by the Sports Information Office. California State University at Fresno.

Broeske, John. KMJ Radio. News Release. Information gathered from California Highway Patrol Offices in Bakersfield, Fresno, Ft. Tejon, and San Bernardino; CalTrans Offices in Fresno, Bakersfield, and San Bernardino; and the Fresno County Library Reference desk, June 22, 1993.

Bryd, Ron. *Fresno City College Library Building.* Informational flier.

Bullard Family Papers. Fresno Historical Society Archives.

Caglia, Rose M. Alexander Pantages Theater. "Summary of Statement for Historical and Architectural Significance." National Register Nomination. September 10, 1977. Fresno Historical Society Archives.

"Carter Memorial African Methodist Episcopal Church." *100 Year Souvenir Book. Fresno Past & Present.* Quarterly Journal. Fresno Historical Society. Vol. 24, No. 1.

Caughey, John Walter. *California.* Prentice-Hall, Inc., New Jersey, 1940.

Chamber of Commerce newsletter. Spring, 1927. Fresno Historical Society Archives.

Cheney, Charles Henry. *Progress of a City Plan for Fresno.* June 1, 1918. Reprinted by Fresno-Clovis area Planning Commission. Files of John Edward Powell.

Chinese Papers Collection. Fresno Historical Society Archives.

Clough, Charles W. and William B. Secrest, Jr. *Fresno County - The Pioneer Years.* Panorama West Books, Fresno, 1984.

Clough, Charles W., et. al. *Fresno County in The 20th Century, from 1900 to the 1980s.* Panorama West Books, Fresno, 1986.

Clough, Charles W. *Madera.* Panorama West Books, Fresno, 1983.

Clovis Rodeo Program. 1989.

Comegys, Valerie D. Y. W. C. A. Residence Hall. "Summary of Statement for Historical and Architectural Significance." National Register Nomination. February 9, 1978. Fresno Historical Society Archives.

Comegys, Valerie D. Einstein Home. "Summary of Statement for Historical and Architectural Significance." National Register Nomination. August 31, 1977. Fresno Historical Society Archives.

Danish Creamery Public Relations office. *The History of Danish Creamery.*

DeGano, John. *Insight.* Journalism Department publication. California State University at Fresno. October 26, 1977.

Drago, Jim. Editor. *Going Places.* California Department of Transportation. May/June, 1991.

Eaton, Edwin M. *Vintage Fresno.* The Huntington Press, Fresno, 1965.

Elliot, Wallace W. & Co. *History of Fresno County, California.* Wallace W. Elliot & Co, San Francisco, 1882.

English, June. *Ash Tree Echo.* Vol. 4.

Forestiere, Lorraine Faulks. Fresno Underground Gardens. "Summary of Statement for Historical and Architectural Significance." National Register Nomination. March 28, 1977. Fresno Historical Society Archives.

Forkner, J. C. and Wylie Giffen. Garden Home Tract advertisements. Courtesy of John Edward Powell.

Fresno County Centennial Committee. *Fresno County Centennial Almanac.* Artcraft Printers, Fresno, 1956.

Fresno Historical Society. *Imperial Fresno.* Facsimile reproduction. Pioneer Publishing Company, Fresno, 1979.

Fresno Musical Club 1905-1980. Copyright and Editor Ruth Winton.

Fresno Past & Present. Fresno Historical Society. Quarterly Journal. Vol. 25, No. 3.

Golden Bear. June, 1933. Reprinted in *Fresno Morning Republican.* 1883. Fresno Historical Society Archives.

Goodman, Stephen Kent. "Fresno's Forgotten Ragtime Composers." *West Coast Rag.* Vol. 3, No. 3. February, 1991.

Hamlin, Kent. *Fresno Daily Legal Report.* April 5, 1984.

Hayden, Max. *Fresno Past & Present.* Quarterly Journal. Fresno Historical Society. Vol. 32, No. 1.

Hill, Donna M. *And Then There Were Ten Thousand.* Reprinted in Clough and Secrest. *Fresno County - The Pioneer Years.*

History of Gottschalk's. 75th Anniversary Edition. September 20, 1974. Provided by Gottschalks.

James, David Bice. *Reminisceces of Early Days in the "Southern Mines,"* edited , with annotations, by L. A. Winchell. Ms. 3. Fresno Historical Society Archives.

Jenkins, Kevin. "An Ancestry of Print." *Fresno Past & Present.* Quarterly Journal. Fresno Historical Society. Vol. 25, No. 3.

Jones Family Papers. Fresno Historical Society Archives.

Kiester, Edwin, Jr. "A Christmas That Never Was," *Modern Maturity.* Vol. 34. No.6. December 1991-January, 1992.

Bibliography

Larsen, Dave. *Los Angeles Times.* Interview with Lorraine Collett Petersen. Information provided by Sun-Maid Raisins Office of Public Relations.

Lazarus, David. Kindler Home. "Summary of Statement for Historical and Architectural Significance." National Register Nomination. October 29, 1982. Fresno Historical Society Archives.

Ledford, Harold J. *Fresno Past & Present.* Fresno Historical Society. Quarterly Journal. Vol. 28, No. 4.

Lespade, Wanda M. Santa Fe Hotel. "Summary of Statement for Historical and Architectural Significance." National Register Nomination. March, 1989. Fresno Historical Society Archives.

Long, Bob. Tape of radio segments covering KMJ Radio's 70 year history. Provided by KMJ.

McGee, Lizzie Gamlin. "Speech to the Naturalist Camp Fire Program in the Kings Canyon National Park." September, 1951. *Fresno Past & Present.* Quarterly Journal. Vol. 15, No. 4.

Mardikian, George. *Song of America.* McGraw Hill, New York, 1956.

Mathes, Pauline. *Bit of Sweden in the Deser.,* Pioneer Publishing Company. Fresno, 1991.

Miller, Howard. "From Green Bush Spring Flows the Story of a City Called Fresno." *Fresno Past & Present.* Quarterly Journal. Fresno Historical Society. Vol. 27, No. 2.

Nax, Sanford. "Taylor Wheeler Builders Accomplishments Recalled." *The Fresno Bee.* April 1, 1989. Courtesy of John Edward Powell.

Oakes, James. Maubridge Building. "Summary of Statement for Historical and Architectural Significance." National Register Nomination. August 14, 1980.. Fresno Historical Society Archives.

Ortiz, Maria. "James Porteous, Fresno's Forgotten Inventor." *Fresno Past & Present.* Fresno Historical Society.Quarterly Journal. Vol. 23, No. 4.

Parker, Mary Ann. *History of the Fresno County Free Library 1910-1970.* Thesis. Master of Arts Degree. History Department. California State University at Fresno, August, 1977.

Parlor Lecture Club, Leisure Hour Club and Query Club program books. Fresno Historical Society Archives.

Patnaude, William E. Historic Resources Inventory. Post Office. City of Fresno.

Patnaude, William E. Historic Resources Inventory. Bing Tong Kong Association Building. City of Fresno.

Patnaude, William E. Historic Resources Inventory. Bow On Tong Association Building. City of Fresno.

Peters, Gladys. "The Fresno Musical Club." *Fresno Past & Present.* Quarterly Journal. Fresno Historical Society. Vol. 27, No. 3.

Powell, John Edward. "Edward T. Foulkes." *Fresno Past & Present.* Quarterly Journal. Fresno Historical Society.Vol. 25, No. 1. pp. 2-5.

Powell, John Edward. The Fresno Bee Building. "Summary of Statement for Historical and Architectural Significance." National Register Nomination. March 29, 1982. Fresno Historical Society Archives.

Powell, John Edward. The Physicians Building. "Summary of Statement for Historical and Architectural Significance." National Register Nomination. May 18, 1978. Fresno Historical Society Archives.

Powell, John Edward. The Rehorn Home. "Summary of Statement for Historical and Architectural Significance." National Register Nomination. November 1, 1980. Fresno Historical Society Archives.

Powell, John Edward. The Republican Printery. "Summary of Statement for Historical and Architectural Significance." National Register Nomination. September 18, 1978. Fresno Historical Society Archives.

Powell, John Edward. Tower Theatre."Summary of Statement for Historical and Architectural Significance." National Register Nomination. April 3, 1992. Fresno Historical Society Archives.

Raven, Penny. Background material on Candlelight Christmas. Huntington Boulevard Homeowners Association.

Rehart, Schyler. "Dr. Chester Rowell-Crusading Newspaperman, State Political Leader and Mayor of Fresno." *Fresno Past & Present.* Fresno Historical Society. Quarterly Journal. Vol. 28, No. 1.

Rehart, Schyler. "Fresno's Turbulent Youth, 1885-1901, Part II: Joe Spin's City Hall." *Fresno Past & Present.* Quarterly Journal.   Fresno Historical Society. Vol. 27, No. 1.

Rehart, Schyler and William K. Patterson. *M. Theo Kearney Prince of Fresno.* Fresno Historical Society, Fresno, 1988.

Riley, Judy. "Where Is William Wooten." *Fresno Past & Present.* Quarterly Journal. Fresno Historical Society. Vol. 33, No. 4.

Rintoul, William. "Fresno County's Petrified People." *Fresno County - The Pioneer Years.* pg. 271.

Russell, Wanda Podgorski. "George C. Roeding - The Man and His Tree." *Fresno Past & Present.* Quarterly Journal. Fresno Historical Society. Vol. 26. No. 2

Sanger District Chamber of Commerce. Brochure. *66th Annual Trek To The General Grant Tree.* Sanger, 1991.

Saroyan, Aram. *William Saroyan.* Harcourt Brace Jovanovich, New York, 1983.

Schreiber, Grant and Ann. The Blum House. Historic Resources Inventory. City of Fresno.

Seeger, Diane. Santa Fe Depot. "Summary of Statement for Historical and Architectural Significance." National Register Nomination. May 28, 1976. Fresno Historical Society Archives.

Sequoia Chapter, American Theatre Organ Society and San Joaquin Chapter, American Guild of Organists. *The Jewel of Fresno.* October 20, 1989.

Shallat, Todd A. *Water and the Rise of Public Ownerhip on the Fresno Plain, 1850-1978.* City of Fresno Public Works Department, October, 1978.

Shipp Family Papers. Fresno Historical Society Archives.

Singleton, Msgr. Francis X., Msgr. Culleton, et. al. *St. John the Baptist Parish 1882-1982.*

Skei, Carolyn. "Saga of CSUF Mascots, The Bittersweet Life of a Battlin' Bulldog." *Contact.* Vol. 3, No. 2. Winter, 1983. Article provided by the Public Information Office. California State University, Fresno.

Smith, Dr. Ephraim K. The Old Administration Building. "Summary of Statement for Historical and Architectural Significance." National Register Nomination. May 1, 1974. Fresno Historical Society Archives.

Smith, Dr. Ephraim K. and John Edward Powell. The Brix Mansion. "Summary of Statement for Historical and Architectural Significance." National Register Nomination. March 7, 1983. Fresno Historical Society Archives.

Smith, Joe. "Tales of the San Joaquin." *The Fresno Bee.* Fresno Historical Society Archives.

Smith, Stephen R. "Oscar J. Woodward, Frontier Entrepreneur." *Fresno Past & Present.* Quarterly Journal. Fresno Historical Society. Vol. 24, No. 2.

Bibliography

Smith, Wallace. *Garden of the Sun.* 8th edition. California History Books, Fresno, 1960.

Steinberg, Jim. "'Fresno' saga of 'greed, lust' takes to the streets." *The Fresno Bee.* July 16, 1986.

Strother, French. "A Unique Estate in Central California." *Country Life in America.* February, 1907. Fresno Historical Society Archives.

Supple, Patrick. Fresno Brewery. "Summary of Statement for Historical and Architectural Significance." National Register Nomination. March 15, 1983. Fresno Historical Society Archives.

Terrill, Dave and Lorena Molen. Fresno District Fair Public Relations Office. Articles on the 100-year history of the Fresno District Fair. June 18, 1984.

The Ansel Adams Gallery. Yosemite. Biographical information.

The Insurance Journal. January 26, 1956.

Triplett, Robert L., Jr. Bank of Italy. "Summary of Statement for Historical and Architectural Significance." National Register Nomination. October 24, 1981.Fresno Historical Society Archives.

Tweed, William. Gamlin Cabin. "Summary of Statement for Historical and Architectural Significance." National Register Nomination. March 9, 1976. Fresno Historical Society Archives.

Tweed, William. Shorty Lovelace Historic District. "Summary of Statement for Historical and Architectural Significance." National Register Nomination. August 29, 1977. Fresno Historical Society Archives.

U. S. International Trade Center. Public Relations Office. Informational tour of historic San Joaquin Light and Power Company building.

Vandor, Paul. *History of Fresno County, California, with Brief Biographical Sketches.* Vol. I. Los Angeles: Historic Records Company, 1919.

Villager. 30th Anniversary of Fig Garden Village Edition. Fig Garden Village 30th Anniversary Commorative Poster. Provided by Greg Newman.

Waiczis, Michael R. and William B. Secrest, Jr. *A Portrait of Fresno 1885-1985.* Val Print, Fresno, 1985.

Walker, Ben Collection. Fresno Historical Society Archives.

Wash, Robert. Pioneer Families Dinner Speech. Fresno City Centennial. November 14, 1985.

Weigandt, Marcelle B. *Fulton G. Berry.* 1965. Fresno Historical Society Archives.

Weitzie, Karen. Study of 13 Potential National Register Structures in Freeway 180 GAP Project for CalTrans District 6. 1991.

Weitzie, Karen and John Edward Powell. "Short Historical Notes Descriptive of The Industrial Bank of Fresno." October, 18, 1992.

Weyant, Jack. Warehouse Row. "Summary of Statement for Historical and Architectural Significance." National Register Nomination. June, 1977. Fresno Historical Society Archives.

Winchell, L. A. Papers. Fresno Historical Society Archives.

Winchell, L. A. Papers. *Eisen/Winchell Letters.Fresno Historical Society Archives*

Wright, Earl, Jr. *The Fresno Bee.* Column. October 3, 1991.

Zalewski, Prudence. The Shipp-Selland Residence. Historic Resources Inventory Form. City of Fresno. May 10, 1990.

Bibliography

Zylka, Claire Baird; Ken Greenberg; and Jessie Myers Thun. *Image of An Age Clovis.* Pacific Printing Press, Fresno, 1984.

Fresno Weekly Expositor, October 11, 1882.

Fresno Evening Expositor, October 9, 1889.

Fresno Morning Republican, February 19, 1881.

Fresno Morning Republican, January 1, 1884.

Fresno Morning Republican, Permelia E.Baley obituary. December 9, 1906.

Fresno Morning Republican, April 19, 1906.

Fresno Morning Republican, October 12, 1911.

Fresno Morning Republican, October 14, 1911.

Fresno Morning Republican, May 25, 1912.

Fresno Morning Republican, May 26, 1912.

Fresno Morning Republican, May 27, 1912.

Fresno Morning Republican, September 17, 1917.

Fresno Morning Republican, May 15, 1919.

Fresno Morning Republican, November 25, 1919

Fresno Morning Republican, July 7, 1921.

Fresno Morning Republican, January 11, 1924.

Fresno Morning Republican, November 29, 1924.

Fresno Morning Republican, Mary Donleavy obituary. June 8, 1927.

Fresno Morning Republican, November 18, 1927.

Fresno Morning Republican, July 7, 1928.

Fresno Morning Republican, April 3, 1930.

Fresno Morning Republican, January 18, 1931.

Fresno Morning Republican, June 20, 1931.

Fresno Morning Republican, September 7, 1931.

Fresno Morning Republican, September 22, 1931.

The Fresno Bee, March 26, 1926.

The Fresno Bee, June 15, 1926.

The Fresno Bee, July 21, 1927.

The Fresno Bee, August 24, 1930.

The Fresno Bee, October 1, 1930.

The Fresno Bee, February 26, 1933.

The Fresno Bee, March 19, 1933.

The Fresno Bee, October 27, 1935.

The Fresno Bee, October 22, 1936.

The Fresno Bee, January 17, 1938.

The Fresno Bee, February 6, 1938.

The Fresno Bee, May 22, 1938.

The Fresno Bee, June 16, 1938.

Bibliography

The Fresno Bee, July 3, 1938.

The Fresno Bee, July 17, 1938.

The Fresno Bee, August 28, 1938.

The Fresno Bee, September 11, 1938.

The Fresno Bee, July 10, 1939.

The Fresno Bee, August 24, 1939.

The Fresno Bee, March 24, 1940.

The Fresno Bee, May 13, 1940.

The Fresno Bee, September 1, 1940.

The Fresno Bee, October 2, 1940.

The Fresno Bee, November 30, 1940.

The Fresno Bee, April 29, 1942.

The Fresno Bee, September 1, 1943. Louis Kutner obituary.

The Fresno Bee, March 29, 1944.

The Fresno Bee, December 21, 1945. McCardle Obituary.

The Fresno Bee, July 7, 1947.

The Fresno Bee, September 19, 1947.

The Fresno Bee, October 8, 1987.

The Fresno Bee, July 23, 1948.

The Fresno Bee, September 11, 1949.

The Fresno Bee, February 2, 1949.

The Fresno Bee, February 9, 1949.

The Fresno Bee, January 27, 1950.

The Fresno Bee, September 15, 1951.

The Fresno Bee, April 23, 1952.

The Fresno Bee, February 13, 1966.

The Fresno Bee, March 8, 1966.

The Fresno Bee, March 16, 1966.

The Fresno Bee, April 8, 1966.

The Fresno Bee, John M. Euless obituary. May 6, 1969.

The Fresno Bee, June 22, 1969.

The Fresno Bee, October 13, 1974.

The Fresno Bee, August 21, 1977.

The Fresno Bee, April 1, 1989, pg.C1.

The Fresno Bee, May 7, 1990, pg. 1A.

The Fresno Bee, Dennis Wheeler Obituary, August 7, 1991. Courtesy of John Edward Powell.

The Fresno Bee, September 26, 1992, pg.1A.

The Fresno Guide, April 21, 1971.

The Grapevine, newsletter, Fresno Historical Society. December, 1985 - January, 1986.

Index

Index

Index

About the Author

Cathy Rehart's mother's family arrived in Fresno Station in 1873, the year after the town was founded. She was born in the Sample Sanitarium on Fulton Street, is a third generation graduate of Fresno High School and a second generation graduate of Fresno State College with a BA in English and history. She is the mother of three grown children.

During the years her children were in school, her involvement in their activities resulted in service on several PTA boards, the Fresno High School Site Council and the Cub Scouts. Later she served as first Vice-Chairwoman for the Historic Preservation Commission for the City of Fresno; as a member of the Board of Directors of the Fresno City and County Historical Society; as chair of the Preservation Committee of the FCCHS; and a President of the La Paloma Guild, the FCCH's auxiliary.

From 1986 to 1994, she held the position of Education/Information Director for the FCCHS.

Her work as a freelance writer includes writing the KMJ Radio scripts for "The Valley's Legends and Legacies" —from which this book is derived—and other writing projects on local history.

Presently, she is employed at Petunia's Place, a children's bookstore.